Sunset

BEST HOME PLANS

Energy-Efficient Homes

Sunlight passing through the glass roof overhead warms the tile floor of
this contemporary home's living room. Other energy-saving features
include a wood stove and 2 by 6 framing that allows for R-19 insulation.
See plans H-947-1A and -1B on page 83.

Sunset Publishing Corporation ■ Menlo Park, California

Photographers: **Mark Englund/ HomeStyles:** 4, 5; **Philip Harvey:** 10 top, back cover; **Stephen Marley:** 11 top left and right; **Russ Widstrand:** 10 bottom; **Tom Wyatt:** 11 bottom.

Cover: Pictured is plan B-91010 on page 223. Cover design by Naganuma Design & Direction. Photography by Mark Englund/ HomeStyles.

Editor, Sunset Books: Elizabeth L. Hogan

First printing September 1993

 printed on recycled paper

A Dream Come True

Planning and building a house is one of life's most creative and rewarding challenges. Whether you're seriously considering building a new home or you're just dreaming about it, this book offers a wealth of inspiration and information to help you get started.

On the following pages, you'll learn how to plan and manage a home-building project—and how to ensure its success. Then you'll discover more than 200 proven home plans, designed for families just like yours by architects and professional designers. Peruse the pages and study the floor plans; you're sure to find a home that's just right for you. When you're ready to order blueprints, you can simply call or mail in your order, and you'll receive the plans within days.

Enjoy the adventure!

Compact passive-solar home features well-insulated walls and ceilings, an air-lock entry, a solar-collecting room, and other energy-conserving amenities. See plans H-975-1 and -1A on page 93.

Contents

Energy Savers

Smart use of the sun together with energy-efficient construction can take a huge bite out of the cost of heating and cooling a home at the same time that they conserve precious energy resources and reduce pollution. In this book, you'll find a wealth of proven, energy-efficient home plans created by some of America's foremost architects and designers. These plans feature sun-catching, passive-solar design, high-efficiency glazing, thermal walls, and much more.

You'll discover a wide variety of home styles, from traditional classics to striking contemporaries, and from country charmers to affordable starters.

The two keys to success in building are capable project management and good design. The next few pages will walk you through some of the most important aspects of project management: you'll find an overview of the building process, directions for selecting the right plan and getting the most from it, and methods for successfully working with a builder and other professionals.

The balance of the book presents professionally designed stock plans. Once you find a plan that will work for you—perhaps with a few modifications made later to personalize it for your family—you can order construction blueprints for a fraction of the cost of a custom design, a savings of many thousands of dollars (see pages 12–15 for information on how to order).

Formal on the outside, contemporary and angular on the inside, this French-style home offers 12-foot ceilings in the kitchen, living room, and dining area. Each of those rooms makes extensive use of glass. See plan E-2004 on page 130.

Luxurious single-level home is built around a central living room with a large fireplace and a 13-foot ceiling. The master suite is isolated from the other bedrooms for more privacy. See plan E-2208 on page 143.

Traditional two-story home offers efficient use of space with open-plan family living downstairs and three bedrooms plus a bonus room on the second floor. Exterior cedar-shake accents and formal millwork give the façade plenty of style. See plan NW-406-A on page 74.

Floor-to-ceiling windows rounding the corner of this distinctive home's formal living room fill the space with warmth and light. Entertaining spaces are on the main floor, bedrooms are upstairs. See plan CDG-2019 on page 199.

The Art of Building

As you embark on your home-building project, think of it as a trip—clearly not a vacation but rather an interesting, adventurous, at times difficult expedition. Meticulous planning will make your journey not only far more enjoyable but also much more successful. By careful planning, you can avoid—or at least minimize—some of the pitfalls along the way.

Start with realistic expectations of the road ahead. To do this, you'll want to gain an understanding of the basic house-building process, settle on a design that will work for you and your family, and make sure your project is actually doable. By taking those initial steps, you can gain a clear idea of how much time, money, and energy you'll need to invest to make your dream come true.

The Building Process

Your role in planning and managing a house-building project can be divided into two parts: prebuilding preparation and construction management.

■ **Prebuilding preparation.** This is where you should focus most of your attention. In the hands of a qualified contractor whose expertise you can rely on, the actual building process should go fairly smoothly. But during most of the prebuilding stage, you're generally on your own. Your job will be to launch the project and develop a talented team that can help you bring your new home to fruition.

When you work with stock plans, the prebuilding process usually goes as follows:

First, you research the general area where you want to live, selecting one or more possible home sites (unless you already own a suitable lot). Then you choose a basic house design, with the idea that it may require some modification. Finally, you analyze the site, the design, and your budget to determine if the project is actually attainable.

If you decide that it is, you purchase the land and order blueprints. If you want to modify them, you consult an architect, designer, or contractor. Once the plans are finalized, you request bids from contractors and arrange any necessary construction financing.

After selecting a builder and signing a contract, you (or your contractor) then file the plans with the building department. When the plans are approved, often several weeks—or even months—later, you're ready to begin construction.

■ **Construction management.** Unless you intend to act as your own contractor, your role during the building process is mostly one of quality control and time management. Even so, it's important to know the sequence of events and something about construction methods so you can discuss progress with your builder and prepare for any important decisions you may need to make along the way.

Decision-making is critical. Once construction begins, the builder must usually plunge ahead, keeping his carpenters and subcontractors progressing steadily. If you haven't made a key decision—which model bathtub or sink to install, for example—it can bring construction to a frustrating and expensive halt.

Usually, you'll make such decisions before the onset of building, but, inevitably, some issue or another will arise during construction. Being knowledgeable about the building process will help you anticipate and circumvent potential logjams.

Selecting a House Plan

Searching for the right plan can be a fun, interactive family experience—one of the most exciting parts of a house-building project. Gather the family around as you peruse the home plans in this book. Study the size, location, and configuration of each room; traffic patterns both inside the house and to the outdoors; exterior style; and how you'll use the available space. Discuss the pros and cons of the various plans.

Browse through pictures of homes in magazines to stimulate ideas. Clip the photos you like so you can think about your favorite options. When you visit the homes of friends, note special features that appeal to you. Also, look carefully at the homes in your neighborhood, noting their style and how they fit the site.

Mark those plans that most closely suit your ideals. Then, to narrow down your choices, critique each plan, using the following information as a guide.

■ **Overall size and budget.** How large a house do you want? Will the house you're considering fit your family's requirements? Look at the overall square footage and room sizes. If you have a hard time visualizing room sizes, measure some of the rooms in your present home and compare.

It's often better for the house to be a little too big than a little too small, but remember that every extra square foot will cost more money to build and maintain.

■ **Number and type of rooms.** Beyond thinking about the number of bedrooms and baths you want, consider your family's life-style and how you use space. Do you want both a family room and a living room? Do you need a formal dining space? Will you require some extra rooms, or "swing spaces," that can serve multiple purposes, such as a home office–guest room combination?

■ **Room placement and traffic patterns.** What are your preferences for locations of formal living areas, master bedroom, and children's rooms? Do you prefer a kitchen that's open to family areas or one that's private and out of the way? How much do you use exterior spaces and how should they relate to the interior?

Once you make those determinations, look carefully at the floor plan of the house you're considering to see if it meets your needs and if the traffic flow will be convenient for your family.

■ **Architectural style.** Have you always wanted to live in a Victorian farmhouse? Now is your chance to create a house that matches your idea of "home" (taking into account, of course, styles in your neighborhood). But don't let your preference for one particular architectural style dictate your home's floor plan. If the floor plan doesn't work for your family, keep looking.

■ **Site considerations.** Most people choose a site before selecting a plan—or at least they've zeroed in on the basic type of land where they'll situate their house. It sounds elementary, but choose a house that will fit the site. This is particularly important with energy-efficient homes, since most are designed for a very specific orientation to the sun.

When figuring the "footprint" of a house, you must know about any restrictions that will affect your home's height or proximity to the property lines. Ask your local building department about any restrictions that will affect what you can build on the site (see "Working with City Hall," at right).

When you visit potential sites, note trees, rock outcroppings, slopes, views, winds, sun, neighboring homes, and other factors. All will impact on how your house works on a particular site.

Once you've narrowed down the choice of sites, consult an architect or building designer (see page 8) to help you evaluate how some potential houses will work on the sites you have in mind.

Is Your Project Doable?

Before you purchase land, make sure your project is doable. Although it's too early at this stage to pinpoint costs, making a few phone calls will help you determine whether your project is realistic. You'll be able to learn if you can afford to build the house, how long it will take, and what obstacles may stand in your way.

To get a ballpark estimate of cost, multiply a house's total square footage (of livable space) by the local average cost per square foot for new construction. (To obtain local averages, call a contractor, an architect, a realtor, or the local chapter of the National Association of Home Builders.) Some contractors may even be willing to give you a preliminary bid. Once you know approximate costs, speak to your lender to explore financing.

It's a good idea to discuss your project with several contractors (see page 8). They may be aware of problems in your area that could limit your options—bedrock that makes digging basements difficult, for example. These conversations are actually the first step in developing a list of contractors from which you'll choose the one who will build your home.

Working with City Hall

For any building project, even a minor one, it's essential to be familiar with building codes and other restrictions that can affect your project.

■ **Building codes,** generally implemented by the city or county building department, set the standards for safe, lasting construction. Codes specify minimum construction techniques and materials for foundations, framing, electrical wiring, plumbing, insulation, and all other aspects of a building. Although codes are adopted and enforced locally, most regional codes conform to the standards set by the national Uniform Building Code, Standard Building Code, or Basic Building Code. In some cases, local codes set more restrictive standards than national ones.

■ **Building permits** are required for home-building projects nearly everywhere. If you work with a contractor, the builder's firm should handle all necessary permits.

More than one permit may be needed; for example, one will cover the foundation, another the electrical wiring, and still another the heating equipment installation. Each will probably involve a fee and require inspections by building officials before work can proceed. (Inspections benefit *you,* as they ensure that the job is being done satisfactorily.) Permit fees are generally a percentage (1 to 1.5 percent) of the project's estimated value, often calculated on square footage.

It's important to file for the necessary permits. Failure to do so can result in fines or legal action against you. You can even be forced to undo the work performed. At the very least, your negligence may come back to haunt you later when you're ready to sell your house.

■ **Zoning ordinances,** particular to your community, restrict setbacks (how near to property lines you may build), your house's allowable height, lot coverage factors (how much of your property you can cover with structures), and other factors that impact design and building. If your plans don't conform to zoning ordinances, you can try to obtain a variance, an exception to the rules. But this legal work can be expensive and time-consuming. Even if you prove that your project won't negatively affect your neighbors, the building department can still refuse to grant the variance.

■ **Deeds and covenants** attach to the lot. Deeds set out property lines and easements; covenants may establish architectural standards in a neighborhood. Since both can seriously impact your project, make sure you have complete information on any deeds or covenants before you turn over a spadeful of soil.

Recruiting Your Home Team

A home-building project will interject you and your family into the building business, an area that may be unfamiliar territory. Among the people you'll be working with are architects, designers, landscapers, contractors, and subcontractors.

Design Help

A qualified architect or designer can help you modify and personalize your home plan, taking into account your family's needs. In fact, you may want to consider consulting such a professional while you're selecting a plan to ensure that the house is properly oriented to the sun.

Design professionals are capable of handling any or all aspects of the design process. For example, they can review your house plans, suggest options, and then provide rough sketches of the options on tracing paper. Many architects will even secure needed permits and negotiate with contractors or subcontractors, as well as oversee the quality of the work.

Of course, you don't necessarily need an architect or designer to implement minor changes in a plan; although most contractors aren't trained in design, some can help you with modifications.

An open-ended, hourly-fee arrangement that you work out with your architect or designer allows for flexibility, but it often turns out to be more costly than working on a flat-fee basis. On a flat fee, you agree to pay a specific amount of money for a certain amount of work.

To find architects and designers, contact such trade associations as the American Institute of Architects (AIA), American Institute of Building Designers (AIBD), American Society of Landscape Architects (ASLA), and American Society of Interior Designers (ASID). Although many professionals choose not to belong to trade associations, those who do have met the standards of their respective associations. For phone numbers of local branches, check the Yellow Pages.

■ **Architects** are licensed by the state and have degrees. They're trained in all facets of building design and construction. Although some can handle interior design and structural engineering, others hire specialists for those tasks.

■ **Building designers** are generally unlicensed but may be accredited by the American Institute of Building Designers. Their backgrounds are varied: some may be unlicensed architects in apprenticeship; others are interior designers or contractors with design skills.

■ **Draftspersons** offer an economical route to making simple changes on your drawings. Like building designers, these people may be unlicensed architect apprentices, engineers, or members of related trades. Most are accomplished at drawing up plans.

■ **Interior designers,** as their job title suggests, design interiors. They work with you to choose room finishes, furnishings, appliances, and decorative elements. Part of their expertise is in arranging furnishings to create a workable space plan. Some interior designers are employed by architectural firms; others work independently. Financial arrangements vary, depending on the designer's preference.

Related professionals are kitchen and bathroom designers, who concentrate on fixtures, cabinetry, appliances, materials, and space planning for the kitchen and bath.

■ **Landscape architects, designers, and contractors** design outdoor areas. Landscape architects are state-licensed to practice landscape design. A landscape designer usually has a landscape architect's education and training but does not have a state license. Licensed landscape contractors specialize in garden construction, though some also have design skills and experience.

■ **Soils specialists and structural engineers** may be needed for projects where unstable soils or uncommon wind loads or seismic forces must be taken into account. Any

structural changes to a house require the expertise of a structural engineer to verify that the house won't fall down.

Services of these specialists can be expensive, but they're imperative in certain conditions to ensure a safe, sturdy structure. Your building department will probably let you know if their services are required.

General Contractors

To build your house, hire a licensed general contractor. Most states require a contractor to be licensed and insured for worker's compensation in order to contract a building project and hire other subcontractors. State licensing ensures that contractors have met minimum training standards and have a specified level of experience. Licensing does not guarantee, however, that they're good at what they do.

When contractors hire subcontractors, they're responsible for overseeing the quality of work and materials of the subcontractors and for paying them.

■ **Finding a contractor.** How do you find a good contractor? Start by getting referrals from people you know who have built or remodeled their home. Nothing beats a personal recommendation. The best contractors are usually busily moving from one satisfied client to another prospect, advertised only by word of mouth.

You can also ask local real estate brokers and lenders or even your building inspector for names of qualified builders. Experienced lumber dealers are another good source of names.

In the Yellow Pages, look under "Contractors–Building, General"; or call the local chapter of the National Association of Home Builders.

■ **Choosing a contractor.** Once you have a list of names of prospective builders, call several of them. On the telephone, ask first whether they handle your type of job and can work within your schedule. If they can, arrange a meeting with each one and ask them to be prepared with references of former clients and photos of previous jobs. Better still, meet them at one of their current work sites so you can get a glimpse of the quality of their work and how organized and thorough they are.

Take your plan to the meeting and discuss it enough to request a rough estimate (some builders will comply, while others will be reluctant to offer a ballpark estimate, preferring to give you a hard bid based on complete drawings). Don't hesitate to probe for advice or suggestions that might make building your house less expensive.

Be especially aware of each contractor's personality and how well you communicate. Good chemistry between you and your builder is a key ingredient for success.

Narrow down the candidates to three or four. Ask each for a firm bid, based on the exact same set of plans and specifications. For the bids to be accurate, your plans need to be complete and the specifications as precise as possible, calling out particular appliances, fixtures, floorings, roofing material, and so forth. (Some of these are specified in a stock-plan set; others are not.)

Call the contractors' references and ask about the quality of their work, their relationship with their clients, their promptness, and their readiness to follow up on problems. Visit former clients to check the contractor's work firsthand.

Be sure your final candidates are licensed, bonded, and insured for worker's compensation, public liability, and property damage. Also, try to determine how financially solvent they are (you can call their bank and credit references). Avoid contractors who are operating hand-to-mouth.

Don't automatically hire the contractor with the lowest bid if you don't think you'll get along well or if you have any doubts about the quality of the person's work. Instead, look for both the most reasonable bid and the contractor with the best credentials, references, terms, and compatibility with your family.

A word about bonds: You can request a performance bond that guarantees that your job will be finished by your contractor. If the job isn't completed, the bonding company will cover the cost of hiring another contractor to finish it. Bonds cost from 2 to 6 percent of the value of the project.

Your Building Contract

A building contract (see below) binds and protects both you and your contractor. It isn't just a legal document. It's also a list of the expectations of both parties. The best way to minimize the possibility of misunderstandings and costly changes later on is to write down every possible detail. Whether the contract is a standard form or one composed by you, have an attorney look it over before both you and the contractor sign it.

The contract should clearly specify all the work that needs to be done, including particular materials and work descriptions, the time schedule, and method of payment. It should be keyed to the working drawings.

A Sample Building Contract

Project and participants. Give a general description of the project, its address, and the names and addresses of both you and the builder.

Construction materials. Identify all construction materials by brand name, quality markings (species, grades, etc.), and model numbers where applicable. Avoid the clause "or equal," which allows the builder to substitute other materials for your choices. For materials you can't specify now, set down a budget figure.

Time schedule. Include both start and completion dates and specify that work will be "continuous." Although a contractor cannot be responsible for delays caused by strikes and material shortages, your builder should assume responsibility for completing the project within a reasonable period of time.

Work to be performed. State all work you expect the contractor to perform, from initial grading to finished painting.

Method and schedule of payment. Specify how and when payments are to be made. Typical agreements specify installment payments as particular phases of work are completed. Final payment is withheld until the job receives its final inspection and is cleared of all liens.

Waiver of liens. Protect yourself with a waiver of liens signed by the general contractor, the subcontractors, and all major suppliers. That way, subcontractors who are not paid for materials or services cannot place a lien on your property.

Personalizing Stock Plans

The beauty of buying stock plans for your new home is that they offer tested, well-conceived design at an affordable price. And stock plans dramatically reduce the time it takes to design a house, since the plans are ready when you are.

Because they were not created specifically for your family, stock plans may not reflect your personal taste. But it's not difficult to make revisions in stock plans that will turn your home into an expression of your family's personality. You'll surely want to add personal touches and choose your own finishes.

Ideally, the modifications you implement will be fairly minor. The more extensive the changes, the more expensive the plans. Major changes take valuable design time, and those that affect a house's structure may require a structural engineer's approval.

If you anticipate wholesale changes, such as moving a number of bearing walls or changing the roofline significantly, you may be better off selecting another plan. On the other hand, reconfiguring or changing the sizes of some rooms can probably be handled fairly easily.

Some structural changes may even be necessary to comply with local codes. Your area may have specific requirements for snow loads, energy codes, seismic or wind resistance, and so forth. Those types of modifications are likely to require the services of an architect or structural engineer.

Plan Modifications

Before you pencil in any changes, live with your plans for a while. Study them carefully—at your building site, if possible. Try to picture the finished house: how rooms will interrelate, where the sun will enter and at what angle, what the view will be from each window. Think about traffic patterns, access to rooms, room sizes, window and door locations, natural light, and kitchen and bathroom layouts.

Typical changes might involve adding windows or skylights to bring in natural light or capture a view. Or you may want to widen a hallway or doorway for roomier access, extend a room, eliminate doors, or change window and door sizes. Perhaps you'd like to shorten a room, stealing the gained space for a large closet. Look closely at the kitchen; it's not difficult to reconfigure the layout if it makes the space more convenient for you.

Above all, take your time—this is your home and it should reflect your taste and needs. Make your changes now, during the planning stage. Once construction begins, it will take crowbars, hammers, saws, new materials, and, most significantly, time to alter the plans. Because changes are not part of your building contract, you can count on them being expensive extras once construction begins.

Specifying Finishes

One way to personalize a house without changing its structure is to substitute your favorite finishes for those specified on the plan.

Would you prefer a stuccoed exterior rather than the wood siding shown on the plan? In most cases, this is a relatively easy change. Do you like the look of a wood shingle roof rather than the composition shingles shown on the plan? This, too, is easy. Perhaps you would like to change the windows from sliders to casements, or upgrade to high-efficiency glazing. No problem. Many of those kinds of changes can be worked out with your contractor.

Inside, you may want hardwood where vinyl flooring is shown. In fact, you can—and should—choose types, colors, and styles of floorings, wall coverings, tile, plumbing fixtures, door hardware, cabinetry, appliances, lighting fixtures, and other interior details, for it's these materials that will personalize your home. For help in making selections, consult an architect or interior designer (see page 8).

Each material you select should be spelled out clearly and precisely in your building contract.

Finishing touches can transform a house built from stock plans into an expression of your family's taste and style. Clockwise, from far left: Colorful tilework and custom cabinetry enliven a bathroom (Design: Osburn Design); highly organized closet system maximizes storage space (Architect: David Jeremiah Hurley); low-level deck expands living space to outdoor areas (Landscape architects: The Runa Group, Inc.); built-ins convert the corner of a guest room into a home office (Design: Lynn Williams of The French Connection); French country cabinetry lends style and old-world charm to a kitchen (Design: Garry Bishop/Showcase Kitchens).

What the Plans Include

Complete construction blueprints are available for every house shown in this book. Clear and concise, these detailed blueprints are designed by licensed architects or members of the American Institute of Building Designers (AIBD). Each plan is designed to meet standards set down by nationally recognized building codes (the Uniform Building Code, Standard Building Code, or Basic Building Code) at the time and for the area where they were drawn.

Remember, however, that every state, county, and municipality has its own codes, zoning requirements, ordinances, and building regulations. Modifications may be necessary to comply with such local requirements as snow loads, energy codes, seismic zones, and flood areas.

Although blueprint sets vary depending on the size and complexity of the house and on the individual designer's style, each set may include the elements described below and shown at right.

■ **Exterior elevations** show the front, rear, and sides of the house, including exterior materials, details, and measurements.

■ **Foundation plans** include drawings for a full, partial, or daylight basement, crawlspace, pole, pier, or slab foundation. All necessary notations and dimensions are included. (Foundation options will vary for each plan. If the plan you choose doesn't have the type of foundation you desire, a generic conversion diagram is available.)

■ **Detailed floor plans** show the placement of interior walls and the dimensions of rooms, doors, windows, stairways, and similar elements for each level of the house.

■ **Cross sections** show details of the house as though it were cut in slices from the roof to the foundation. The cross sections give the home's construction, insulation, flooring, and roofing details.

■ **Interior elevations** show the specific details of cabinets (kitchen, bathroom, and utility room), fireplaces, built-in units, and other special interior features.

■ **Roof details** give the layout of rafters, dormers, gables, and other roof elements, including clerestory windows and skylights. These details may be shown on the elevation sheet or on a separate diagram.

■ **Schematic electrical layouts** show the suggested locations for switches, fixtures, and outlets. These details may be shown on the floor plan or on a separate diagram.

■ **General specifications** provide instructions and information regarding excavation and grading, masonry and concrete work, carpentry and woodwork, thermal and moisture protection, drywall, tile, flooring, glazing, and caulking and sealants.

Other Helpful Building Aids

In addition to the construction information on every set of plans, you can buy the following guides.

■ **Reproducible blueprints** are helpful if you'll be making changes to the stock plan you've chosen. These blueprints are original line drawings produced on erasable, reproducible paper for the purpose of modification. When alterations are complete, working copies can be made.

■ **Itemized materials list** details the quantity, type, and size of materials needed to build your home. (This list is extremely helpful in obtaining an accurate construction bid. It's not intended for use to order materials.)

■ **Mirror-reverse plans** are useful if you want to build your home in the reverse of the plan that's shown. Because the lettering and dimensions read backwards, be sure to buy at least one regular-reading set of blueprints.

■ **Description of materials** gives the type and quality of materials suggested for the home. This form may be required for obtaining FHA or VA financing.

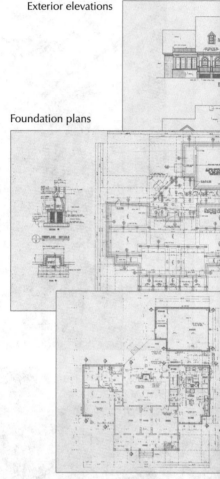

Exterior elevations

Foundation plans

Detailed floor plans

■ **How-to diagrams** for plumbing, wiring, solar heating, framing and foundation conversions show how to plumb, wire, install a solar heating system, convert plans with 2 by 4 exterior walls to 2 by 6 construction (or vice versa), and adapt a plan for a basement, crawlspace, or slab foundation. These diagrams are not specific to any one plan.

NOTE: Due to regional variations, local availability of materials, local codes, methods of installation, and individual preferences, detailed heating, plumbing, and electrical specifications are not included on plans. The duct work, venting, and other details will vary, depending on the heating and cooling system you use and the type of energy that operates it. These details and specifications are easily obtained from your builder or local supplier.

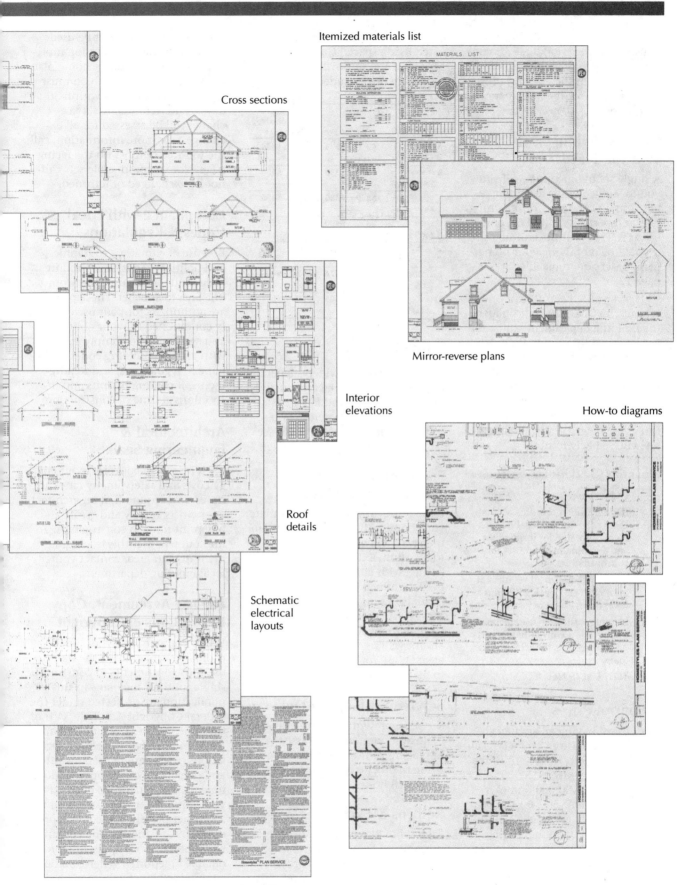

Cross sections

Itemized materials list

Mirror-reverse plans

Interior
elevations

How-to diagrams

Roof
details

Schematic
electrical
layouts

General specifications

Before You Order

Once you've chosen the one or two house plans that work best for you, you're ready to order blueprints. Before filling in the form on the facing page, note the information that follows.

How Many Blueprints Will You Need?

A single set of blueprints will allow you to study a home design in detail. You'll need more for obtaining bids and permits, as well as some to use as reference at the building site. If you'll be modifying your home plan, order a reproducible set (see page 12).

Figure you'll need at least one set each for yourself, your builder, the building department, and your lender. In addition, some subcontractors—foundation, plumber, electrician, and HVAC—may also need at least partial sets. If they do, ask them to return the sets when they're finished. The chart below can help you calculate how many sets you're likely to need.

Blueprint Checklist

____Owner's set(s)

____Builder usually requires at least three sets: one for legal documentation, one for inspections, and a minimum of one set for subcontractors.

____Building department requires at least one set. Check with your local department before ordering.

____Lending institution usually needs one set for a conventional mortgage, three sets for FHA or VA loans.

____TOTAL SETS NEEDED

Blueprint Prices

The cost of having an architect design a new custom home typically runs from 5 to 15 percent of the building cost, or from $5,000 to $15,000 for a $100,000 home. A single set of blueprints for the plans in this book ranges from $250 to $535, depending on the house's size. Working with these drawings, you can save enough on design fees to add a deck, a swimming pool, or a luxurious kitchen.

Pricing is based on "total finished living space." Garages, porches, decks, and unfinished basements are not included.

Price Code (Size)	1 Set	4 Sets	7 Sets	Reproducible Set
A (under 1,500 sq. ft.)	$250	$295	$325	$425
B (1,500-1,999 sq. ft.)	$285	$330	$360	$460
C (2,000-2,499 sq. ft.)	$320	$365	$395	$495
D (2,500-2,999 sq. ft.)	$355	$400	$430	$530
E (3,000-3,499 sq. ft.)	$390	$435	$465	$565
F (3,500-3,999 sq. ft.)	$425	$470	$500	$600
G (4,000 sq. ft. and up)	$460	$505	$535	$635

Building Costs

Building costs vary widely, depending on a number of factors, including local material and labor costs and the finishing materials you select. For help estimating costs, see "Is Your Project Doable?" on page 7.

Foundation Options & Exterior Construction

Depending on your site and climate, your home will be built with a slab, pier, pole, crawlspace, or basement foundation. Exterior walls will be framed with either 2 by 4s or 2 by 6s, determined by structural and insulation standards in your area. Most contractors can easily adapt a home to meet the foundation and/or wall requirements for your area. Or ask for a conversion how-to diagram (see page 12).

Service & Blueprint Delivery

Service representatives are available to answer questions and assist you in placing your order. Every effort is made to process and ship orders within 48 hours.

Returns & Exchanges

Each set of blueprints is specially printed and shipped to you in response to your specific order; consequently, requests for refunds cannot be honored. However, if the prints you order cannot be used, you may exchange them for another plan from any Sunset home plan book. For an exchange, you must return all sets of plans within 30 days. A nonrefundable service charge will be assessed for all exchanges; for more information, call the toll-free number on the facing page. Note: Reproducible sets cannot be exchanged or returned.

Compliance with Local Codes & Regulations

Because of climatic, geographic, and political variations, building codes and regulations vary from one area to another. These plans are authorized for your use expressly conditioned on your obligation and agreement to comply strictly with all local building codes, ordinances, regulations, and requirements, including permits and inspections at time of construction.

Architectural & Engineering Seals

With increased concern about energy costs and safety, many cities and states now require that an architect or engineer review and "seal" a blueprint prior to construction. To find out whether this is a requirement in your area, contact your local building department.

License Agreement, Copy Restrictions & Copyright

When you purchase your blueprints, you are granted the right to use those documents to construct a single unit. All the plans in this publication are protected under the Federal Copyright Act, Title XVII of the United States Code and Chapter 37 of the Code of Federal Regulations. Each designer retains title and ownership of the original documents. The blueprints licensed to you cannot be used by or resold to any other person, copied, or reproduced by any means. The copying restrictions do not apply to reproducible blueprints. When you buy a reproducible set, you may modify and reproduce it for your own use.

Blueprint Order Form

Complete this order form in just three easy steps. Then mail in your order or, for faster service, call toll-free.

1. Blueprints & Accessories

BLUEPRINT CHART

Price Code	1 Set	4 Sets	7 Sets	Reproducible Set*
A	$250	$295	$325	$425
B	$285	$330	$360	$460
C	$320	$365	$395	$495
D	$355	$400	$430	$530
E	$390	$435	$465	$565
F	$425	$470	$500	$600
G	$460	$505	$535	$635

Prices subject to change

*A reproducible set is produced on erasable paper for the purpose of modification. It is only available for plans with prefixes AG, AGH, AH, AHP, APS, AX, B, C, CAR, CPS, DD, DW, E, EOF, FB, GL, GML, GSA, H, HFL, J, K, KLF, LMB, LRD, M, NW, OH, PH, PI, PM, S, SDG, THD, UDG, V.

Mirror-Reverse Sets: $40 surcharge. From the total number of sets you ordered above, choose the number you want to be reversed. *Note: All writing on mirror-reverse plans is backwards. Order at least one regular-reading set.*

Itemized Materials List: One set $40; each additional set $10. Details the quantity, type, and size of materials needed to build your home.

Description of Materials: Sold in a set of two for $40 (for use in obtaining FHA or VA financing).

Typical How-To Diagrams: One set $12.50; two sets $23; three sets $30; four sets $35. General guides on plumbing, wiring, and solar heating, plus information on how to convert from one foundation or exterior framing to another. *Note: These diagrams are not specific to any one plan.*

2. Sales Tax & Shipping

Determine your subtotal and add appropriate local state sales tax, plus shipping and handling (see chart below).

SHIPPING & HANDLING

	1–3 Sets	4–6 Sets/ Reproducible Set	7 or More Sets
U.S. Regular (4–6 working days)	$12.50	$15.00	$17.50
U.S. Express (2 working days)	$25.00	$27.50	$30.00
Canada Regular (2–3 weeks)	$12.50	$15.00	$17.50
Canada Express (4–6 working days)	$25.00	$30.00	$35.00
Overseas/Airmail (7–10 working days)	$50.00	$60.00	$70.00

3. Customer Information

Choose the method of payment you prefer. Include check, money order, or credit card information, complete name and address portion, and mail to:

Sunset/HomeStyles Plan Service
P.O. Box 50670
Minneapolis, MN 55405

FOR FASTER SERVICE CALL 1-800-547-5570

SS08

COMPLETE THIS FORM

Plan Number _____ **Price Code** _____

Foundation _____
(Review your plan carefully for foundation options—basement, pole, pier, crawlspace, or slab. Many plans offer several options; others offer only one.)

Number of Sets: $_____
(See chart at left)
- ☐ One Set
- ☐ Four Sets
- ☐ Seven Sets
- ☐ One Reproducible Set

Additional Sets _____ $_____
($35 each)

Mirror-Reverse Sets _____ $_____
($40 surcharge)

Itemized Materials List $_____
Only available for plans with prefixes AH, AHP, APS*, AX, B*, C, CAR, CDG*, CPS, DD*, DW, E, FB, GSA, H, HFL, I, J, K, LMB*, LRD, N, NW*, P, PH, R, S, SD*, THD, U, UDG, VL.*Not available on all plans. Please call before ordering.

Description of Materials $_____
Only available for plans with prefixes AHP, C, DW, H, HFL, J, K, KY, LMB, N, P, PH, VL.

Typical How-To Diagrams $_____
- ☐ Plumbing ☐ Wiring ☐ Solar Heating ☐ Foundation & Framing Conversion

SUBTOTAL $_____

SALES TAX $_____

SHIPPING & HANDLING $_____

GRAND TOTAL $_____

☐ Check/money order enclosed (in U.S. funds)
☐ VISA ☐ MasterCard ☐ AmEx ☐ Discover

Credit Card # _____ **Exp. Date** _____

Signature _____

Name _____

Address _____

City _____ **State** ____ **Country** _____

Zip _____ **Daytime Phone** (____) _____

☐ Please check if you are a contractor.

Mail form to: Sunset/HomeStyles Plan Service
P.O. Box 50670
Minneapolis, MN 55405

Or Fax to: (612) 338-1626

FOR FASTER SERVICE CALL 1-800-547-5570

SS08

15

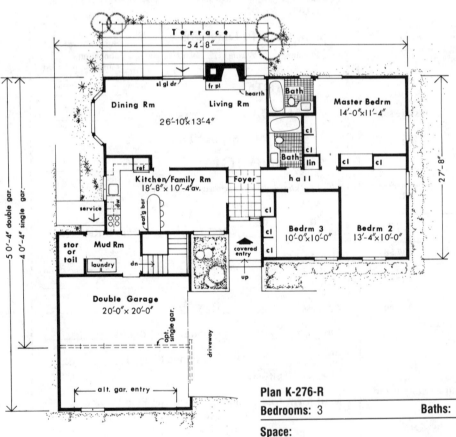

Compact, Economical to Build

- This economically-structured L-shaped ranch puts a great many desirable features into a mere 1,193 sq. ft. of living space. A wood-burning fireplace highlights the living area. Sliding glass doors open to the backyard terrace.
- The kitchen/family room features an eating bar.
- Covered entry welcomes you to the central foyer for easy channeling to any part of the house.
- Located in a wing of their own are three bedrooms and two baths.
- For a narrow lot, the garage door could face the front.

Plan K-276-R

Bedrooms: 3	Baths: 2

Space:	
Total living area:	1,193 sq. ft.
Basement:	1,193 sq. ft.
Garage, mud room, etc.:	551 sq. ft.

Exterior Wall Framing:	2x4 or 2x6

Foundation options:
Standard basement.
Crawlspace.
Slab.
(Foundation & framing conversion diagram available — see order form)

Blueprint Price Code: A

Plan K-276-R

PRICES AND DETAILS ON PAGES 12-15

Sunny Chalet

- This captivating home is designed to maximize indoor and outdoor living. It features expansive windows, an open main floor and a large deck.
- A lower-level entry leads up a staircase to the spacious living room, which features a high cathedral ceiling with a balcony overhead, an energy-efficient fireplace and sliding glass doors to a sizable deck.
- The adjacent dining room boasts a bay window and easy access to the kitchen, which offers ample counter space and a sunny skylight. A half-bath is nearby.
- The lower floor features two spacious bedrooms that share a full bath, complete with a whirlpool tub.
- A quiet den could serve as a third bedroom or a guest room.

Plan K-532-L

Bedrooms: 2+	Baths: 1½
Living Area:	
Main floor	492 sq. ft.
Lower floor	488 sq. ft.
Total Living Area:	**980 sq. ft.**
Exterior Wall Framing:	2x4 or 2x6
Foundation Options:	
Crawlspace	
BLUEPRINT PRICE CODE:	**A**

VIEW INTO LIVING ROOM
AND DINING ROOM

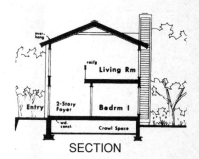

SECTION

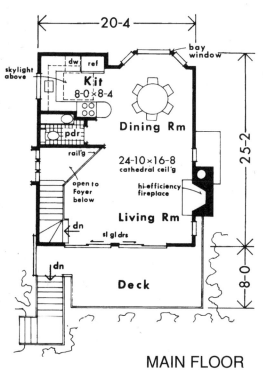

MAIN FLOOR

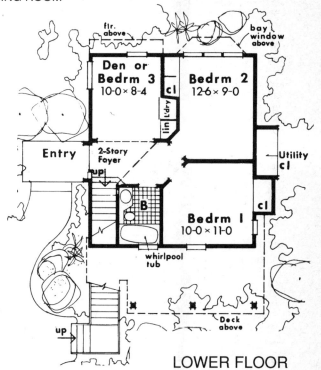

LOWER FLOOR

Make It a Double!

- This compact design can be built as a single-family home or as a duplex. The second unit may be added later.
- The main floor's open layout is designed for informal family living. The living and dining areas share a cozy fireplace and views of the backyard.
- The efficient, U-shaped kitchen nicely services the dining room, which opens to a patio through sliding glass doors.
- Laundry facilities are located in the convenient powder room off the entry.
- A large clerestory window brightens the open stairway, which leads from the two-story entry to the upper floor. A railed overlook offers views of the living room and the entry below.
- The upper floor hosts three bedrooms and a full bath. A balcony railing at the top of the stairs overlooks the vaulted entry below.

Plan SD-8231	
Bedrooms: 3	**Baths:** 1½
Living Area:	
Upper floor	536 sq. ft.
Main floor	448 sq. ft.
Total Living Area:	**984 sq. ft.**
Garage	203 sq. ft.
Exterior Wall Framing:	2x4 or 2x6
Foundation Options:	
Crawlspace	
BLUEPRINT PRICE CODE:	**A**

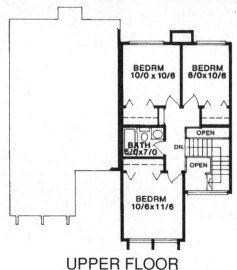

UPPER FLOOR

MAIN FLOOR

TO ORDER THIS BLUEPRINT, CALL TOLL-FREE 1-800-547-5570

Plan SD-8231

PRICES AND DETAILS ON PAGES 12-15

Living With Sunpower

Angled wood siding accentuates the architectural geometry of this flexible leisure home. The house is designed to exploit sun power and conserve energy. Focal point of the plan is an outsized living lounge that has pitched ceiling and overall dimensions of 18'-8" by 26'-0". Note the glass wall that leads to the spacious sun deck. A roomy kitchen is accessible from another sun deck and serves two eating bars as well as the dining room. The three bedrooms are well isolated from noise and traffic. Adjacent to the kitchen is the utility-storage room that can accommodate laundry facilities.

As an option, two solar collectors can be installed on the roof, either over the living lounge, or on the opposite roof, depending on the southern exposure. Solar equipment may be installed now or in the future.

Total living area: 1,077 sq. ft.

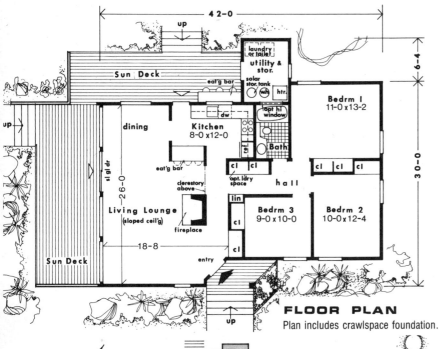

FLOOR PLAN

Plan includes crawlspace foundation.

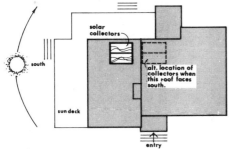

ORIENTATION FEASIBILITY

mirror plan also possible
home may be built without solar system

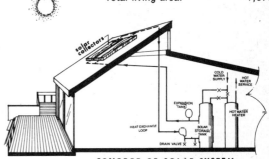

**CONCEPT OF SOLAR SYSTEM
FOR DOMESTIC HOT WATER**

Blueprint Price Code A

Plan K-166-T

Dynamite Detailing

- Fine detailing, both inside and out, drenches this diminutive two-bedroom home in style, function and charm.
- The multi-gabled roofline combined with the recessed, double-door entry makes a strong statement on the outside.
- The reception hall is brightened by a clerestory window in its sloped ceiling. The huge living and dining area is expanded by a cathedral ceiling and complemented by a bay window, a built-in china niche, skylights and a fireplace. A sliding glass door opens to a terrace for easy outdoor entertaining.
- A pass-through links the living/dining area to the eat-in kitchen, which is given added dimension by a bumped-out window and an angled wall.
- The main hall leads to a full bath and a den or second bedroom. The blueprints include details for completely framing in the second bedroom, or creating an opening to the living room that can be closed off by folding doors.
- The roomy master suite includes a private terrace, a large walk-in closet and a full bath.

Plan K-677-R

Bedrooms: 1-2	Baths: 2
Living Area:	
Main floor	1,094 sq. ft.
Total Living Area:	**1,094 sq. ft.**
Standard basement	1,045 sq. ft.
Garage	400 sq. ft.
Exterior Wall Framing:	2x4 or 2x6

Foundation Options:
Standard basement
Slab
(Typical foundation & framing conversion diagram available—see order form.)

BLUEPRINT PRICE CODE: **A**

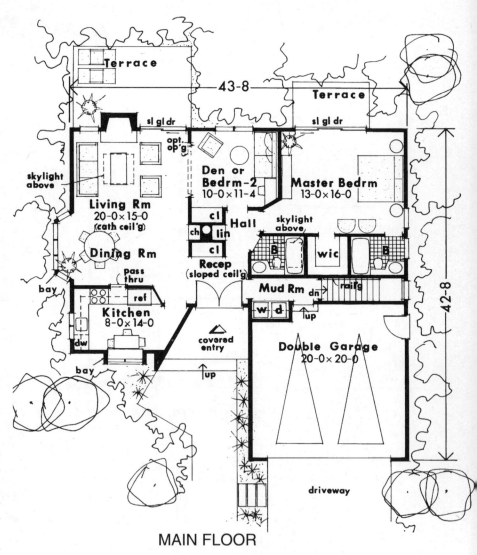

MAIN FLOOR

TO ORDER THIS BLUEPRINT,
CALL TOLL-FREE 1-800-547-5570

Plan K-677-R

PRICES AND DETAILS
ON PAGES 12-15

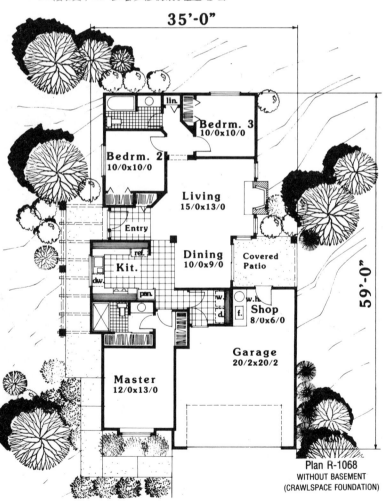

35'-0"

59'-0"

Bedrm. 3
10/0x10/0

Bedrm. 2
10/0x10/0

lin.

Living
15/0x13/0

Entry

ref.

Dining
10/0x9/0

Covered
Patio

Kit.

dw

pan.

w
d

w.h.

Shop
8/0x6/0

Garage
20/2x20/2

Master
12/0x13/0

Plan R-1068
WITHOUT BASEMENT
(CRAWLSPACE FOUNDATION)

Charming And Comfortable

This comfortable three-bedroom home shows off its good looks in a functional plan with less than 1,200 sq. ft. Its charming exterior is highlighted with some interesting detailing, making this home a unique and pleasant addition to almost any neighborhood.

To lend privacy to the master bedroom, it has been isolated from the other bedrooms at opposite ends of the house. The master bedroom also features two double closets, one of which is located within the master bath opposite the vanity, making that space an ideal dressing area. At the other end of the home, a graceful archway defines the division between the living area and bedroom wing.

Notice how the fireplace, accented by a pair of picturesque windows, acts as a focal point within the cozy living room. Adjoining the living room, the informal dining room is visually expanded through a sliding glass door to the covered patio beyond.

Looking into the U-shaped kitchen, we find a functional layout with all the standard amenities, plus the added convenience of a built-in pantry. This design features 2x6 exterior walls for energy efficiency.

Total living area: 1,185 sq. ft.
(Not counting garage)

TO ORDER THIS BLUEPRINT,
CALL TOLL-FREE 1-800-547-5570

Blueprint Price Code A
Plan R-1068

PRICES AND DETAILS
ON PAGES 12-15   **21**

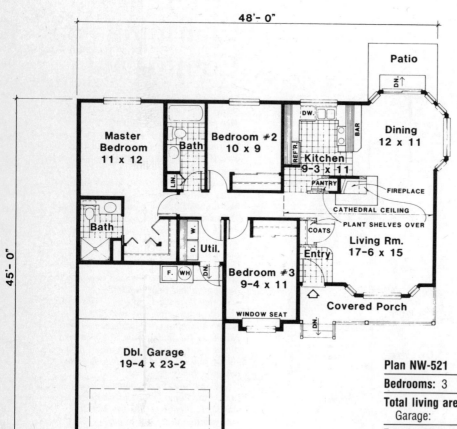

48'- 0"

45'- 0"

Patio

DN.

Master Bedroom
11 x 12

Bath

Bedroom #2
10 x 9

DW.

BAR

Dining
12 x 11

REF'R.

Kitchen
9-3 x 11

PANTRY

FIREPLACE

Bath

LIN.

CATHEDRAL CEILING

PLANT SHELVES OVER

D. W.

Util.

F. WH

DN.

COATS

Living Rm.
17-6 x 15

Bedroom #3
9-4 x 11

Entry

WINDOW SEAT

DN.

Covered Porch

Dbl. Garage
19-4 x 23-2

Classic One-Story Farmhouse

- This classic farmhouse design features a shady and inviting front porch.
- Inside, vaulted ceilings in the living and dining rooms make the home seem larger than it really is.
- An abundance of windows brightens up the living room and dining area.
- The functional kitchen includes a pantry and plenty of cabinet space.
- The master bedroom boasts a mirrored dressing area, private bath and abundant closet space.
- Bedroom 3 includes a cozy window seat.

Plan NW-521	
Bedrooms: 3	Baths: 2
Total living area:	1,187 sq. ft.
Garage:	448 sq. ft.
Exterior Wall Framing:	2x6

Foundation options:
   Crawlspace only.
(Foundation & framing conversion diagram available — see order form.)

Blueprint Price Code:	A

Comfortable Ranch Design

- This affordable ranch design offers numerous amenities and is ideally structured for comfortable living, both indoors and out.
- A tiled reception hall leads into the spacious living and dining rooms, featuring a handsome brick fireplace, a high sloped ceiling and two sets of sliding glass doors to the rear terrace.
- The adjacent family room, designed for privacy, showcases a large boxed-out window with a built-in seat. The kitchen features an efficient U-shaped counter, an eating bar and a walk-in pantry.
- The master suite boasts a private terrace and a master bath with a whirlpool tub.
- Two additional bedrooms share a second full bath.
- The garage has two separate storage areas—one accessible from the interior and the other from the backyard.

Plan K-518-A	
Bedrooms: 3	**Baths:** 2
Living Area:	
Main floor	1,276 sq. ft.
Total Living Area:	**1,276 sq. ft.**
Standard basement	1,247 sq. ft.
Garage and storage	579 sq. ft.
Exterior Wall Framing:	2x4 or 2x6
Foundation Options:	
Standard basement	
Slab	
BLUEPRINT PRICE CODE:	**A**

VIEW INTO LIVING ROOM AND DINING ROOM

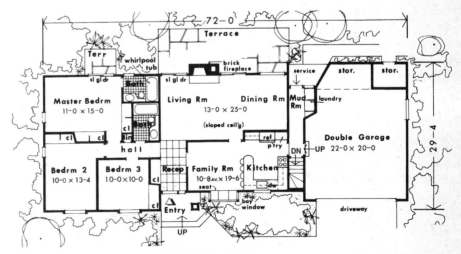

MAIN FLOOR

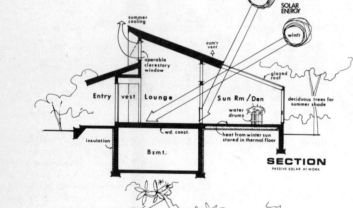

summer
cooling

sum'r

SOLAR
ENERGY

sum'r
vent

wint'r

operable
clerestory
window

glazed
roof

Entry | vest | Lounge

Sun Rm / Den

deciduous trees for
summer shade

water
drums

wd. const.

insulation

heat from winter sun
stored in thermal floor

Bsmt.

SECTION
PASSIVE SOLAR AT WORK

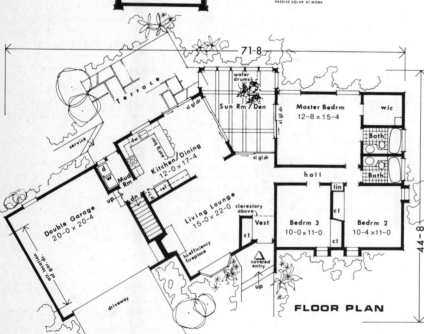

71-8

44-8

FLOOR PLAN

Terrace

service

sl gl dr

water
drums

Sun Rm / Den

Master Bedrm
12-8 x 15-4

wic

Bath

Bath

sl gl dr

dw

Mud
Rm

d
w

ref

Kitchen / Dining
12-0 x 17-4

dn

hall

lin

Double Garage
20-0 x 20-4

alt. location
for sl gl dr

Living Lounge
15-0 x 22-0

clerestory
above

Bedrm 3
10-0 x 11-0

cl

cl

Bedrm 2
10-4 x 11-0

cl

Vest

hi-efficiency
fireplace

cl

covered
entry

up

driveway

Dramatic Angles

Dramatically angled to maximize the benefits of passive solar technology, this compact one-story home can be adapted to many sites and orientations. South-facing rooms, including sun room/den, absorb and store heat energy in thermal floors for night time radiation. Heavy insulation in exterior walls and ceilings, plus double glazing in windows, keep heat loss to a minimum. During the summer, heat is expelled through an operable clerestory window and through an automatic vent in the sun room.

Inside, entrance vestibule overlooks a breathtaking view of the sun room and the outdoors beyond; kitchen/dining area opens to a large rear terrace. Three bedrooms are isolated for total privacy. Living area, excluding sun room, is 1,223 sq. ft.; garage, mud room, etc. 504 sq. ft.; partial basement, 1,030 sq. ft.

Living Area:	1,223 sq. ft.
Garage and Mud Room:	504 sq. ft.
Basement (Opt.):	1,030 sq. ft.

(Alternate slab-on-grade foundation plan included.)

Blueprint Price Code A
Plan K-505-R

PRICES AND DETAILS
ON PAGES 12-15

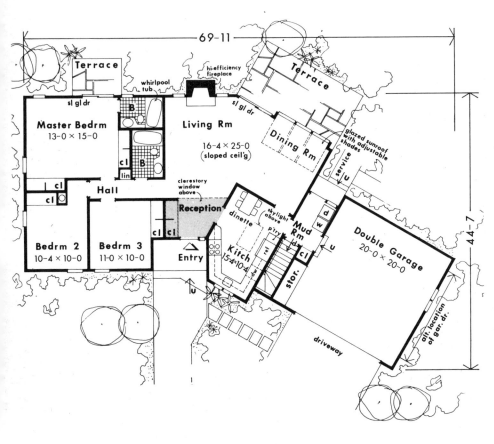

Angled Design Captures the Sun

Finished in traditional clapboard siding and rustic roof shingles, this single-story passive solar design is deliberately angled at its core to capture optimum sunlight and to accommodate regular as well as irregular sites.

The living room is highlighted by a dramatic sloped ceiling and a wood-burning fireplace. The adjacent dining room is accentuated by the glazed ceiling and wall that flood the area with sunshine and solar warmth. The glazed ceiling panels have adjustable screens for summer shading. The U-shaped kitchen features a dinette area, crowned with a large skylight above.

Three bedrooms are isolated in a wing of their own. The master bedroom has a terrace and a private bath, equipped with a whirlpool tub. For best benefits, it is recommended that the rear of house faces south, or nearly south. Total living area is 1,237 sq. ft.; garage, mud room, etc., 525 sq. ft.; optional basement is 1,264 sq. ft.

Total living area: (Not counting basement or garage)	1,237 sq. ft.
Garage, mud room:	525 sq. ft.
Basement (optional):	1,264 sq. ft.

Blueprint Price Code A

Plan K-523-C

Unexpected Amenities

- This good-looking design has a casual exterior but an interior filled with amenities you'd expect to find in a much larger and more elegant home.
- Open living areas are created with the use of vaulted ceilings and a minimum number of walls.
- The living room, dining room and kitchen merge in a comfortable setting that overlooks a fireplace and a huge side patio through a pair of sliding glass doors.
- One bedroom and bath, plus an oversized utility room with washer and dryer, extra freezer and storage space for recreational equipment complete the main level.
- Located on the upper level, a spacious master suite with a walk-in closet, private bath and a loft area that overlooks the living room.

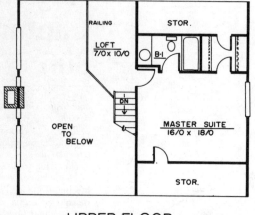

UPPER FLOOR

Plan I-1249-A

Bedrooms: 2	Baths: 2
Living Area:	
Upper floor	297 sq. ft.
Main floor	952 sq. ft.
Total Living Area:	**1,249 sq. ft.**
Standard basement	952 sq. ft.
Exterior Wall Framing:	**2x6**

Foundation Options:
Standard basement
Crawlspace
(Typical foundation & framing conversion diagram available—see order form.)

BLUEPRINT PRICE CODE: A

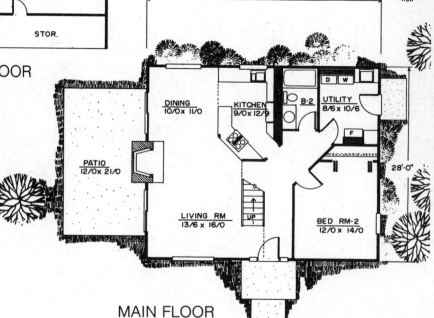

MAIN FLOOR

Plan I-1249-A

PRICES AND DETAILS ON PAGES 12-15

Simple, Stylish and Affordable

- This affordable three-bedroom, single-story home is perfect for the young family or for retirees.
- Vaulted ceilings in the living room and dining room create drama and volume. The big fireplace and rear windows bring in light and warmth.
- The efficient design of the kitchen includes a corner sink framed by windows and a breakfast bar open to the dining room.
- The adjoining screen porch could serve as expansion space.
- A main-floor laundry closet is conveniently located in the bedroom wing. The large master bedroom features a vaulted ceiling, a walk-in closet and a private bath. The two secondary bedrooms show off lovely window seats and share a second bath.

Plan B-91016

Bedrooms: 3	Baths: 2
Living Area:	
Main floor	1,263 sq. ft.
Total Living Area:	**1,263 sq. ft.**
Standard basement	1,263 sq. ft.
Garage	441 sq. ft.
Screen porch	126 sq. ft.
Exterior Wall Framing:	2x6
Foundation Options:	

Standard basement
(Typical foundation & framing conversion diagram available—see order form.)

BLUEPRINT PRICE CODE:	A

Floor Plan

53'—4"

46'—0"

Kitchen
10x10

Living
12x16
vaulted

MBr
13x14—8
vaulted

Screen Porch

Dining
10—4x9—6
vaulted

wood storage

W   D

DN

L

Br 3
10x10—4
seat

Br 2
11—4x10—4
seat

Garage
21—4x20—8

MAIN FLOOR

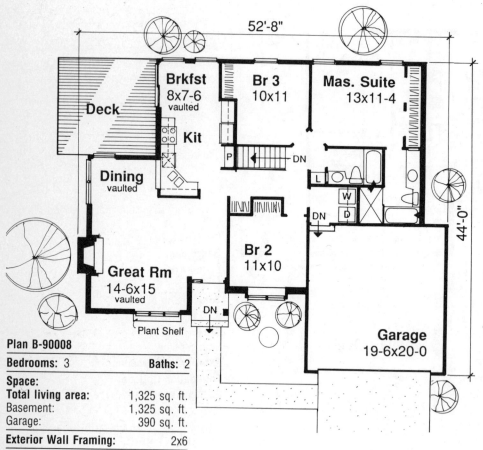

52'-8"

Deck

Brkfst
8x7-6
vaulted

Br 3
10x11

Mas. Suite
13x11-4

Kit

Dining
vaulted

P

DN

44'-0"

DN

W

D

L

Br 2
11x10

DN

Great Rm
14-6x15
vaulted

Plant Shelf

DN

Garage
19-6x20-0

Plan B-90008

Bedrooms: 3	Baths: 2

Space:	
Total living area:	1,325 sq. ft.
Basement:	1,325 sq. ft.
Garage:	390 sq. ft.

Exterior Wall Framing:	2x6

Foundation options:
Standard basement.
(Foundation & framing conversion
diagram available — see order form.)

Blueprint Price Code:	A

Window Wonderland

- The focal point of this open, efficient plan is a dramatic window in the Great Room with square transom windows plus half round glass above and plant shelf below.
- The resulting window-wall dramatizes the exterior and the interior as well.
- The Great Room also features an attractive fireplace and vaulted ceiling, and flows into the dining room.
- The vaulted kitchen incorporates a breakfast room with sliders to a deck. The kitchen also has a handy pass-thru to the dining room.
- The three bedrooms include a master suite with private bath which offers a separate tub and shower.

Plan B-90008

PRICES AND DETAILS
ON PAGES 12-15

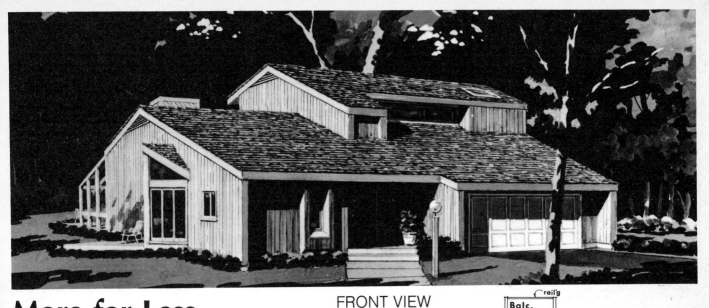

FRONT VIEW

More for Less

- Big in function but small in footage, this two-story passive solar plan puts every inch of space to efficient use, and is designed in such a way that it can be built as a free-standing unit or as part of a multiple unit complex.
- The plan flows visually from its entry, through its high-ceilinged Great Room, to a brilliant south-facing sun room.
- The master bedroom includes a deluxe private bath and two roomy closets.
- Upstairs, two more bedrooms share a second bath, and one bedroom offers a private balcony.

Plan K-507-S

Bedrooms: 3	Baths: 2½
Space:	
Upper floor	397 sq. ft.
Main floor	942 sq. ft.
Total Living Area	**1,339 sq. ft.**
Basement	915 sq. ft.
Garage	400 sq. ft.
Exterior Wall Framing	2x4/2x6

Foundation options:

Standard Basement

Slab

(Foundation & framing conversion diagram available—see order form.)

Blueprint Price Code   **A**

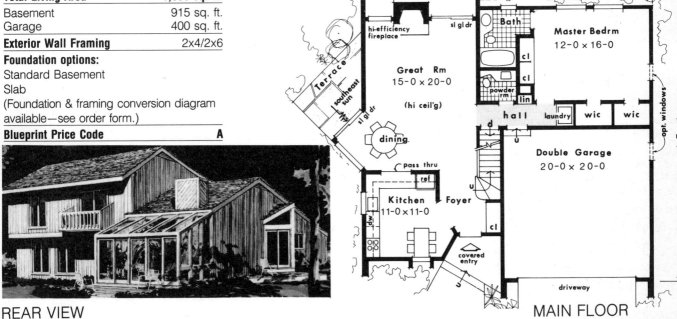

REAR VIEW

UPPER FLOOR

Bedrm 2
11-0 x 12-0

Bedrm 3
11-0 x 11-0

Balc.

MAIN FLOOR

43-6

45-4

Terrace

Sun Rm

water drums

hi-efficiency fireplace

Great Rm
15-0 x 20-0
(hi ceil'g)

dining

Kitchen
11-0 x 11-0

pass thru

ref

Foyer

covered entry

driveway

Bath

Master Bedrm
12-0 x 16-0

powder rm

hall

laundry

wic

wic

Double Garage
20-0 x 20-0

High-Profile Contemporary

- This design does away with wasted space, putting the emphasis on quality rather than on size.
- The angled floor plan minimizes hall space and creates smooth traffic flow while adding architectural appeal. The roof framing is square, however, to allow for economical construction.
- The spectacular living and dining rooms share a cathedral ceiling and a fireplace. Geared to take advantage of green spaces, both rooms have lots of glass overlooking an angled rear terrace.
- The dining room includes a glass-filled alcove and sliding patio doors topped by transom windows. Tall windows frame the living room fireplace and trace the slope of the ceiling.
- A pass-through joins the dining room to the combination kitchen and family room, which features a snack bar and a clerestory window.
- The sleeping wing provides the option of a den or a third bedroom. The second bedroom offers a sloped ceiling. The super master suite boasts a skylighted dressing area and a luxurious bath.

Plan K-688-D

Bedrooms: 2-3	Baths: 2½
Living Area:	
Main floor	1,340 sq. ft.
Total Living Area:	**1,340 sq. ft.**
Standard basement	1,235 sq. ft.
Garage	484 sq. ft.
Exterior Wall Framing:	2x4 or 2x6
Foundation Options:	
Standard basement	
Slab	
(Typical foundation & framing conversion diagram available—see order form.)	
BLUEPRINT PRICE CODE:	A

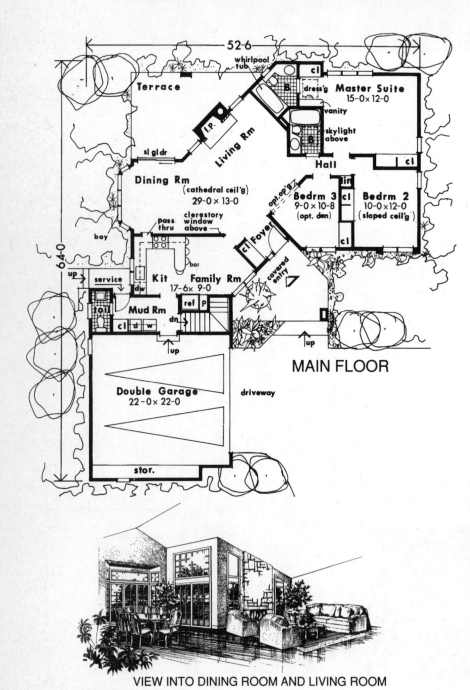

MAIN FLOOR

VIEW INTO DINING ROOM AND LIVING ROOM

TO ORDER THIS BLUEPRINT,
CALL TOLL-FREE 1-800-547-5570

Plan K-688-D

PRICES AND DETAILS
ON PAGES 12-15

Massive, Windowed Great Room

- This attractive, open design can function as a cabin, mountain retreat or permanent residence.
- The kitchen and Great Room merge to form a large family activity area; an open balcony loft above offers an elevated view of the massive front window wall.
- A third sleeping room upstairs could be split into two smaller bedrooms.
- The main level of the home is entered via a split-landing deck off the Great Room.

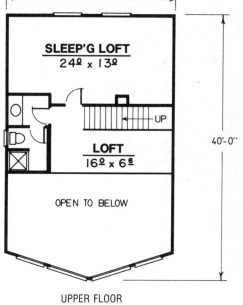

26'-0''

SLEEP'G LOFT
24º x 13º

40'-0''

LOFT
16º x 6º

OPEN TO BELOW

UPPER FLOOR

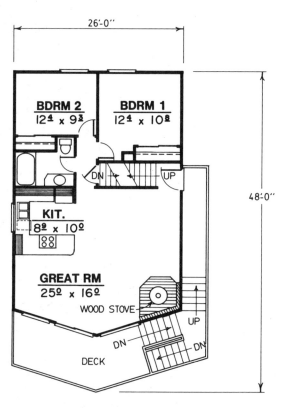

26'-0''

BDRM 2
12⁴ x 9³

BDRM 1
12⁴ x 10⁸

DN   UP

KIT.
8º x 10º

48'-0''

GREAT RM
25º x 16º

WOOD STOVE

UP

DN   DN

DECK

MAIN FLOOR

Plan I-1354-B

Bedrooms: 2-3	Baths: 2
Space:	
Upper floor:	366 sq. ft.
Main floor:	988 sq. ft.
Total living area:	1,354 sq. ft.
Garage and basement:	1,000 sq. ft.
Exterior Wall Framing:	2x6

Foundation options:
Standard basement.
(Foundation & framing conversion diagram available — see order form.)

Blueprint Price Code: A

Cozy and Energy-Efficient

Planned for year-round comfort and energy efficiency, this passive solar design boasts a highly livable floor plan. Vertical wood siding and deep overhang give the exterior a natural appeal. Inside, the open plan is carefully designed to provide ample natural light with a minimum heat loss; windows and sliding doors are double-paned; heavy insulation is specified. In summer, operable clerestory windows aid in air circulation, cooling the house by convection.

The high-ceilinged reception hall neatly channels traffic. To the right is the family room/kitchen, equipped with an eating bar. Straight ahead are the living and dining rooms, dramatically accented by a sloped ceiling, a wood-burning fireplace and a light-filled sunroom. Sliding glass doors lead to a rear terrace.

Isolated on the left side are the quiet sleeping quarters, with three bedrooms. Master bedroom has a private terrace, a walk-in closet and a personal bath that features a whirlpool tub.

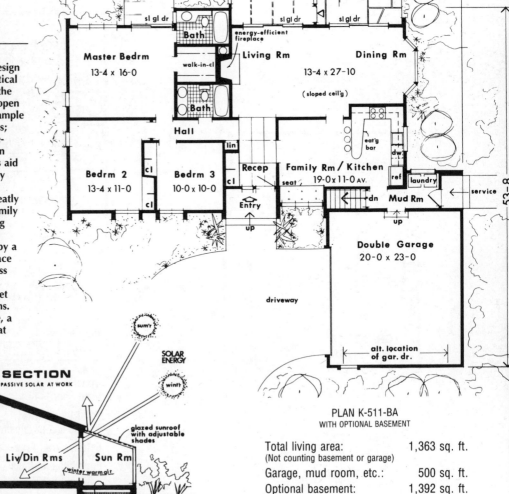

PLAN K-511-BA
WITH OPTIONAL BASEMENT

Total living area:	1,363 sq. ft.
(Not counting basement or garage)	
Garage, mud room, etc.:	500 sq. ft.
Optional basement:	1,392 sq. ft.

SECTION
PASSIVE SOLAR AT WORK

Blueprint Price Code A
Plan K-511-BA

PRICES AND DETAILS ON PAGES 12-15

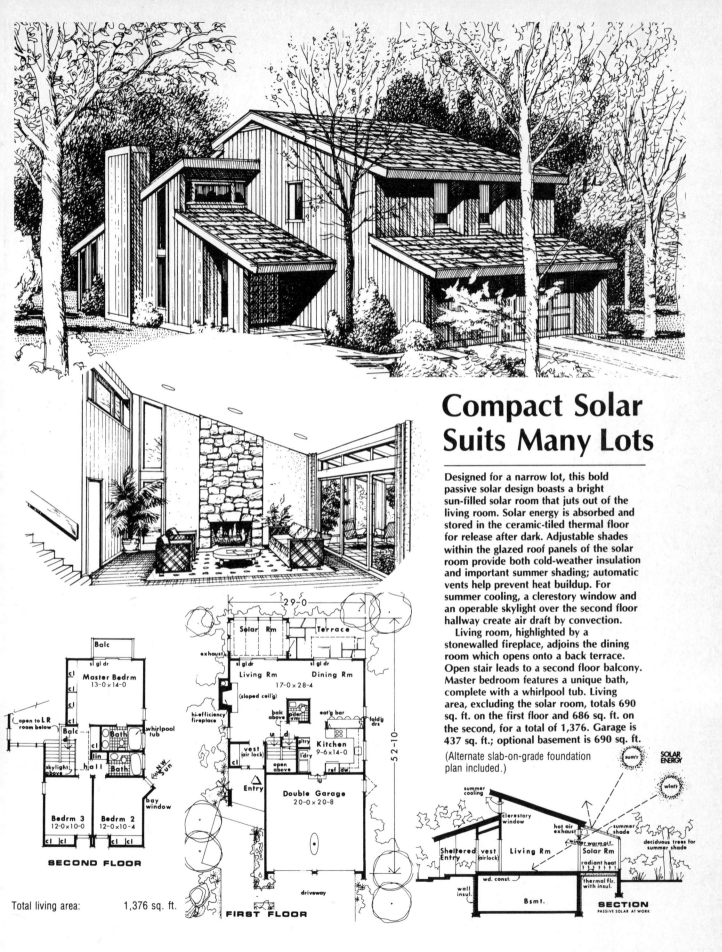

Compact Solar Suits Many Lots

Designed for a narrow lot, this bold passive solar design boasts a bright sun-filled solar room that juts out of the living room. Solar energy is absorbed and stored in the ceramic-tiled thermal floor for release after dark. Adjustable shades within the glazed roof panels of the solar room provide both cold-weather insulation and important summer shading; automatic vents help prevent heat buildup. For summer cooling, a clerestory window and an operable skylight over the second floor hallway create air draft by convection.

Living room, highlighted by a stonewalled fireplace, adjoins the dining room which opens onto a back terrace. Open stair leads to a second floor balcony. Master bedroom features a unique bath, complete with a whirlpool tub. Living area, excluding the solar room, totals 690 sq. ft. on the first floor and 686 sq. ft. on the second, for a total of 1,376. Garage is 437 sq. ft.; optional basement is 690 sq. ft.

(Alternate slab-on-grade foundation plan included.)

Total living area: 1,376 sq. ft.

Blueprint Price Code A
Plan K-521-C

PRICES AND DETAILS ON PAGES 12-15

MASTER BEDROOM
13' × 11'4''

BEDROOM 3
12'8'' × 10'4''

BEDROOM 2
11'8'' × 12'

UPPER FLOOR

Stylish Two-Story

- This two-story home boasts contemporary and traditional elements.
- The open main floor offers a large front living room and attached dining room.
- A sunny breakfast dinette with sliders joins a functional kitchen with plenty of counter space.
- A family room bordered by the dinette and garage may be added later. The blueprints do not show the family room.
- Three nice-sized bedrooms occupy the upper level.

Plan GL-1382

Bedrooms: 3	Baths: 2 ½
Space:	
Upper floor	710 sq. ft.
Main floor	672 sq. ft.
Total Living Area	**1,382 sq. ft.**
Basement	672 sq. ft.
Garage	420 sq. ft.
Exterior Wall Framing	2x6
Foundation options:	
Standard Basement	
(Foundation & framing conversion diagram available—see order form.)	
Blueprint Price Code	**A**

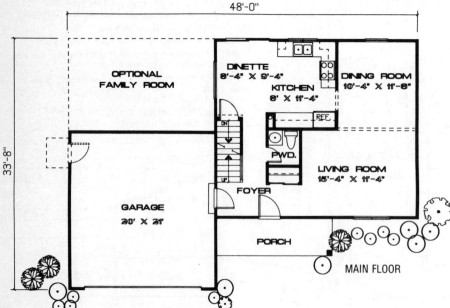

48'-0"

33'-8"

OPTIONAL FAMILY ROOM

DINETTE
8'-4'' × 9'-4''

KITCHEN
8' × 11'-4''

DINING ROOM
10'-4'' × 11'-8''

REF.

DN

PWD.

LIVING ROOM
15'-4'' × 11'-4''

GARAGE
20' × 21'

FOYER

PORCH

MAIN FLOOR

Plan GL-1382

**PRICES AND DETAILS
ON PAGES 12-15**

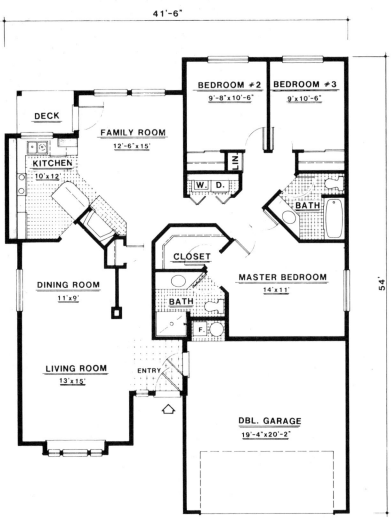

DECK

FAMILY ROOM
12'-6"x15'

BEDROOM #2
9'-8"x10'-6"

BEDROOM #3
9'x10'-6"

KITCHEN
10'x12'

LIN.

W.D.

BATH

DINING ROOM
11'x9'

CLOSET

MASTER BEDROOM
14'x11'

BATH

F.

LIVING ROOM
13'x15'

ENTRY

DBL. GARAGE
19'-4"x20'-2"

41'-6"

54'

Angles Add Interior Excitement

- Eye-catching exterior leads into exciting interior.
- You'll find cathedral ceilings throughout the living and dining area.
- Angular kitchen includes eating bar, plenty of cabinet and counter space.
- Master suite includes angled double-door entry, private bath and large walk-in closet.
- Family room and kitchen join together to make large casual family area.
- Main bathroom continues the angled motif, and the washer and dryer are conveniently located in the bedroom hallway.

Plan NW-864

Bedrooms: 3	Baths: 2
Total living area:	1,449 sq. ft.
Garage:	390 sq. ft.
Exterior Wall Framing:	2x6

Foundation options:
   Crawlspace only.
(Foundation & framing conversion diagram available — see order form.)

Blueprint Price Code:	A

Traditional Retreat

- This traditional vacation retreat maximizes space by offering an open, flowing floor plan.
- The spacious living room's luxurious features include a cathedral ceiling, fireplace and wet bar; its openness is extended by an exciting adjoining covered deck.
- Sweeping diagonally from the living room is the formal dining room with both front-facing and roof windows.
- The merging kitchen is separated from the living areas by a counter bar.
- The first floor bedroom features a unique triangular window seat, a dressing area and a full bath.
- The second floor is devoted entirely to a private master suite, complete with a lovely window seat, walk-in closet and attached bath.

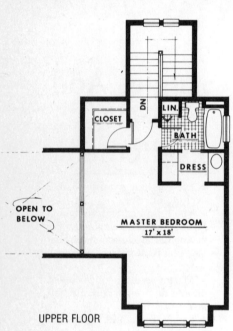

UPPER FLOOR

Plan NW-334

Bedrooms: 2	Baths: 2
Space:	
Upper floor:	438 sq. ft.
Main floor:	1,015 sq. ft.
Total living area:	1,453 sq. ft.
Carport:	336 sq. ft.
Exterior Wall Framing:	2x6

Foundation options:
Crawlspace.
(Foundation & framing conversion diagram available — see order form.)

Blueprint Price Code: A

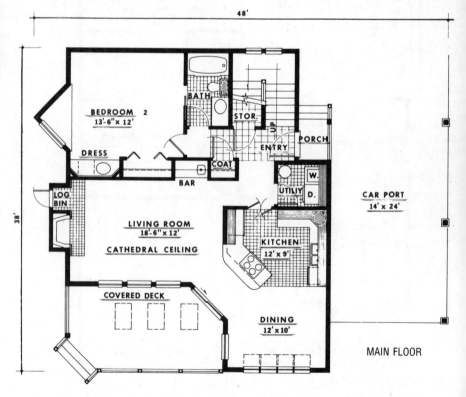

MAIN FLOOR

TO ORDER THIS BLUEPRINT,
CALL TOLL-FREE 1-800-547-5570

Plan NW-334

PRICES AND DETAILS
ON PAGES 12-15

Economical and Functional

- Economically structured and architecturally refined, this four-bedroom ranch home offers lots of light-filled spaces.
- The entry area is brightened by optional skylights. Guests proceed into the large living and dining rooms, which are further expanded by a sloped ceiling. Other features include a bay window, a brick fireplace and sliders to a rear terrace.
- A cozy family room, dinette and kitchen boast a peninsula serving bar and a nearby half-bath and laundry area.
- The master suite offers a private bath with whirlpool tub and sliding glass doors to a secluded terrace.
- The three remaining bedrooms share a full bath with a dual-sink vanity.

Plan K-659-U

Bedrooms: 4	Baths: 2½

Living Area:	
Main floor	1,580 sq. ft.

Total Living Area:	**1,580 sq. ft.**

Standard basement	1,512 sq. ft.
Garage and storage	439 sq. ft.

Exterior Wall Framing:	2x4 or 2x6

Foundation Options:

Standard basement

Slab

(Typical foundation & framing conversion diagram available—see order form.)

BLUEPRINT PRICE CODE:	B

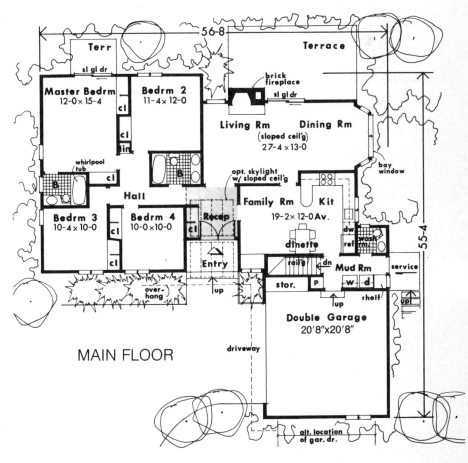

MAIN FLOOR

Private Decks Abound

- With two bedrooms opening to their own private deck, and another deck extending the full length of the living room, the scenic views can be fully enjoyed, both inside and out.
- The sunken living room features a fireplace, a dramatic 19-foot ceiling with skylights, and three sliding glass doors opening to the deck.
- The efficient kitchen overlooks the front yard and the rear view over the breakfast bar and dining room with opening to the living room.

Plan CAR-81007

Bedrooms: 3	Baths: 1½
Space:	
Upper floor:	560 sq. ft.
Main floor:	911 sq. ft.
Total living area:	1,471 sq. ft.
Basement:	911 sq. ft.
Exterior Wall Framing:	2x6

Foundation options:
Standard basement.
(Foundation & framing conversion diagram available — see order form.)

Blueprint Price Code:	A

MAIN FLOOR

UPPER FLOOR

TO ORDER THIS BLUEPRINT, CALL TOLL-FREE 1-800-547-5570   Plan CAR-81007   *PRICES AND DETAILS ON PAGES 12-15*

Compact, Cozy, Inviting

- Liberal-sized living room is centrally located and features corner fireplace and sloped ceilings.
- Separate two-car garage is included with plan.
- Two-bedroom loft overlooks living room and entryway below.
- Full-width porches, both front and rear, invite guests and family alike for leisure time rest and relaxation.

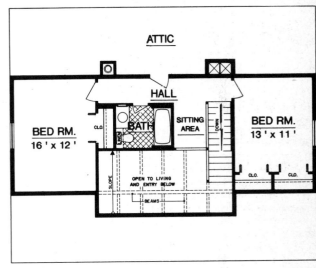

UPPER FLOOR

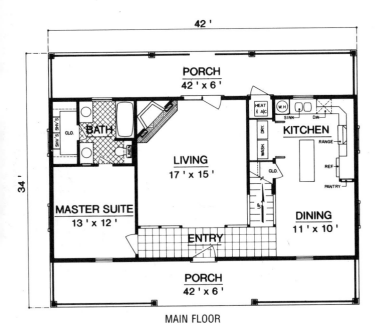

MAIN FLOOR

Plan E-1421

Bedrooms: 3	Baths: 2

Space:

Upper floor:	561 sq. ft.
Main floor:	924 sq. ft.

Total living area:	**1,485 sq. ft.**
Basement:	approx. 924 sq. ft.
Porches:	504 sq. ft.

Exterior Wall Framing:	2x6

Foundation options:
Standard basement.
Crawlspace.
Slab.
(Foundation & framing conversion diagram available — see order form.)

Blueprint Price Code:	A

Unique Indoor/Outdoor Living

- Indoor/outdoor living is at its best in this uniquely designed contemporary home.
- An expansive deck skirts the home's main entry and the adjoining living areas. Off the angled entry are an open stairway and a spacious, vaulted Great Room with a dramatic corner fireplace.
- The fireplace also can be seen from the vaulted dining room, which accesses the deck through sliding glass doors.
- The adjoining kitchen provides a windowed sink and plenty of counter space. In the basement version of the plan, the storage closet becomes the stairway down.
- Two bedrooms and a full bath are located at the end of the hall, conveniently close to the laundry room.
- The front-facing bedroom has sliding glass doors that lead to a private deck.
- A large vaulted loft area, a skylighted sitting or reading area and another bath occupy the upper floor.
- Plans for an optional garage are included with the blueprints.

Plans P-539-3A & -3D

Bedrooms: 2+	Baths: 2
Living Area:	
Upper floor	390 sq. ft.
Main floor	1,095 sq. ft.
Total Living Area:	**1,485 sq. ft.**
Daylight basement	1,065 sq. ft.
Optional garage	459 sq. ft.
Exterior Wall Framing:	2x6
Foundation Options:	**Plan #**
Daylight basement	P-539-3D
Crawlspace	P-539-3A
BLUEPRINT PRICE CODE:	**A**

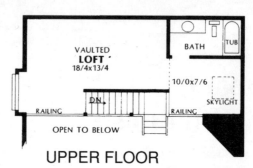

UPPER FLOOR

BASEMENT STAIRWAY LOCATION

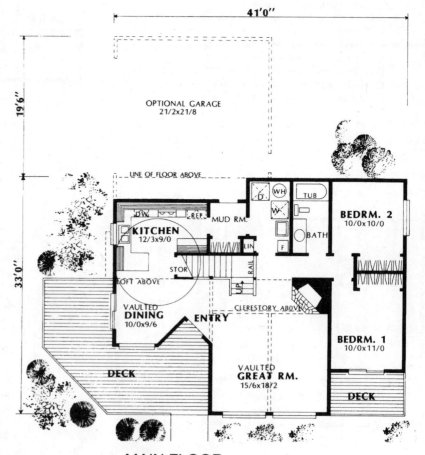

MAIN FLOOR

TO ORDER THIS BLUEPRINT,
CALL TOLL-FREE 1-800-547-5570

Plans P-539-3A & -3D

PRICES AND DETAILS
ON PAGES 12-15

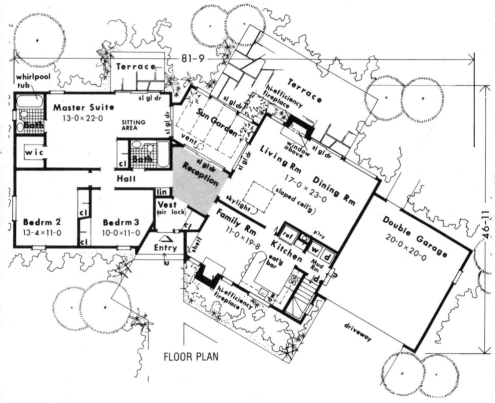

FLOOR PLAN

Master Suite 13-0×22-0
SITTING AREA
whirlpool tub
Bath
w i c
Bath
cl
Hall
lin
Bedrm 2 13-4×11-0
Bedrm 3 10-0×11-0
cl
Vest (air lock)
Entry
Terrace
sl gl dr
Sun Garden
vent
Reception
skylight
Family Rm 11-0×19-8
Kitchen
eat's bar
ref
p'try
w d
Mud Rm
hi-efficiency fireplace
Terrace
hi-efficiency fireplace
sl gl dr
sl gl dr
window above
Living Rm   Dining Rm
17-0 × 23-0
(sloped ceil'g)
Double Garage 20-0×20-0
driveway
81-9
46-11

SECTION
PASSIVE SOLAR AT WORK

SOLAR ENERGY
sum'r
wint'r
summer vent
deciduous trees for summer shade
summer shade to reflect sun
winter warmth
Terrace
Sun Garden
Recep
Vest air lock
Sheltered Entry
thermal flr. with insul. to store energy
wd. const.
Bsmt.
wall insulation

Passive Solar with Many Orientation Options

This angled passive solar design is planned to suit almost any plot and many orientation alternatives. Exterior siding of vertical natural wood and a high front chimney give the house an interesting appearance.

Inside, the central focus is the light-filled south-facing sun garden that greets occupants and visitors as they enter the reception hall. The large combination living room and dining room are highlighted by a dramatic sloped ceiling and a high-efficiency wood-burning fireplace. Glass around and above the fireplace contributes more light and provides a panoramic view of the rear landscaping. Sharing a second fireplace is the informal area that includes the family room and U-shaped kitchen.

Three bedrooms are located in the left wing of the house. The large master suite has a cheerful sitting area which borders on the sun garden. Living area, excluding the sun garden, is 1,574 sq. ft.; optional basement is 1,522 sq. ft.; garage is 400 sq. ft.

Total living area: 1,574 sq. ft.
(Not counting basement or garage)

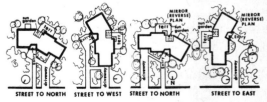

STREET TO NORTH   STREET TO WEST   STREET TO NORTH   STREET TO EAST
MIRROR (REVERSE) PLAN   MIRROR (REVERSE) PLAN

IMAGINE THE ORIENTATION POSSIBILITIES

Blueprint Price Code B

Plan K-526-C

Angled
Solar Design

- This passive solar design with a six-sided core is angled to capture as much sunlight as possible.
- Finished in natural vertical cedar planks and stone veneer, this contemporary three-bedroom requires minimum maintenance.
- Double doors at the entry open into the spacious living and dining areas.
- The formal area features a domed ceiling with skylights, a free-standing fireplace and three sets of sliding glass doors. The central sliders lead to a glass-enclosed sun room.
- The bright U-shaped kitchen is an extension of the den; sliding glass doors lead to one of two large backyard terraces.
- The master bedroom, in a quiet sleeping wing, boasts ample closets, a private terrace and a luxurious bath, complete with a whirlpool tub.

Plan K-534-L

Bedrooms: 3	Baths: 2
Living Area:	
Main floor	1,647 sq. ft.
Total Living Area:	**1,647 sq. ft.**
Standard basement	1,505 sq. ft.
Garage	400 sq. ft.
Exterior Wall Framing:	2x4 or 2x6

Foundation Options:
Standard basement
Slab
(Typical foundation & framing conversion diagram available—see order form.)

BLUEPRINT PRICE CODE:	**B**

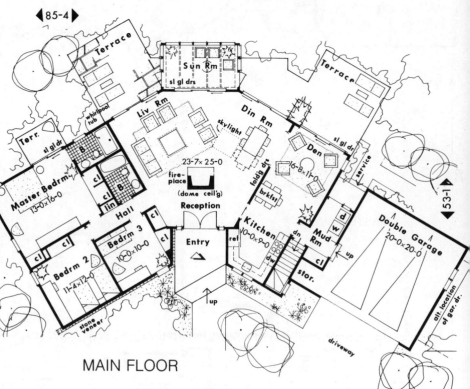

VIEW OF LIVING ROOM
LOOKING INTO
DINING ROOM

MAIN FLOOR

TO ORDER THIS BLUEPRINT,
CALL TOLL-FREE 1-800-547-5570

Plan K-534-L

PRICES AND DETAILS
ON PAGES 12-15

Private Courtyard Protects Entry

AREAS

Living	1497 sq. ft.
Porch	24 sq. ft.
Garage & Storage	528 sq. ft.
Total	2049 sq. ft.

Exterior walls are 2x6 construction.
Specify crawlspace or slab foundation.

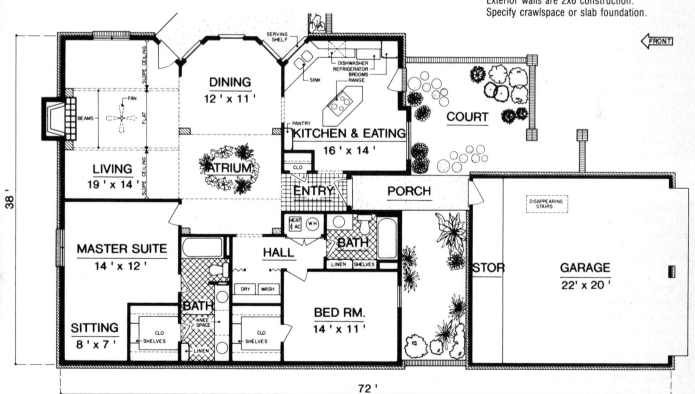

TO ORDER THIS BLUEPRINT,
CALL TOLL-FREE 1-800-547-5570

Blueprint Price Code A
Plan E-1418

PRICES AND DETAILS
ON PAGES 12-15
43

Bold, Sweeping Architecture

- The immediate architectural appeal of this contemporary three-bedroom design is characterized by the interplay of sloping rooflines and a dominating stone chimney.
- Inside, the open airy plan is cleverly organized in three natural zones: active, private and service.
- A sloped ceiling and wood-burning fireplace grace the formal living and dining rooms.
- The kitchen, dinette and family room area, ideal for casual living and informal meals, faces the rear and opens onto a back-yard terrace.
- A second fireplace in the family room generates much warmth.
- Three bedrooms and two full baths are sequestered in a private zone.
- Master suite features many amenities, including a personal bath and an optional loft, situated over the bathrooms and served by a spiral stairway.
- The loft, which is an added bonus, can double as a hobby corner, study spot or just a cozy private den. Basement is optional.

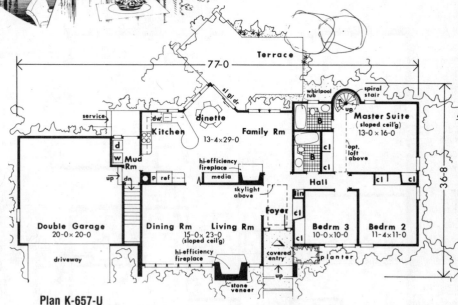

Plan K-657-U

Bedrooms: 3	Baths: 2

Space:

Total living area:	1,506 sq. ft.
Basement:	1,552 sq. ft.
Garage:	400 sq. ft.
Mud room, etc.:	90 sq. ft.

Exterior Wall Framing: 2x4 or 2x6

Foundation options:
Standard basement.
Slab.
(Foundation & framing conversion diagram available — see order form)

Blueprint Price Code: B

Luxury in a Small Package

- The elegant exterior of this design sets the tone for the luxurious spaces within.
- The foyer opens to the centrally located living room, which features a cathedral ceiling, a two-way fireplace and sliding glass doors that open to a lovely rear terrace.
- The unusual kitchen design includes an angled snack bar that lies between the bayed nook and the formal dining room. Patio doors open to another terrace.
- The master suite is a dream come true, with its romantic fireplace, built-in desk and tray ceiling. The private bath includes a whirlpool tub.
- Another full bath serves the remaining two bedrooms, one of which boasts a cathedral ceiling and a tall arched window.

Plan AHP-9300

Bedrooms: 3	Baths: 2
Living Area:	
Main floor	1,513 sq. ft.
Total Living Area:	**1,513 sq. ft.**
Standard basement	1,360 sq. ft.
Garage	400 sq. ft.
Exterior Wall Framing:	2x4 or 2x6

Foundation Options:
Standard basement
Crawlspace
Slab
(Typical foundation & framing conversion diagram available—see order form.)

BLUEPRINT PRICE CODE:	B

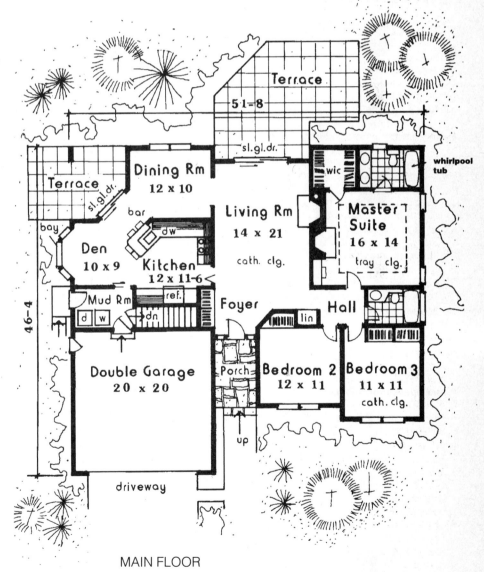

MAIN FLOOR

REAR VIEW

For Vacation or Year-Round Casual Living

- More than 500 square feet of deck area across the rear sets the theme of casual outdoor living for this compact plan.
- The living/dining/kitchen combination is included in one huge, 15' x 39' Great Room, which is several steps down from the entry level for an even more dramatic effect.
- Two large downstairs bedrooms share a bath. Upstairs, a hideaway bedroom includes a private bath, a walk-in closet and a romantic private deck.
- A utility room is conveniently placed in the garage entry area.
- The optional basement features a large recreation room with a fireplace and sliders to a patio underneath the rear deck.
- A fourth bedroom and a third bath in the basement would be ideal for guests.
- At the front of the basement is a large area that could be used for a hobby room or a children's play area.

Plans H-877-1 & -1A

Bedrooms: 3-4	Baths: 2-3
Living Area:	
Upper floor	320 sq. ft.
Main floor	1,200 sq. ft.
Daylight basement	1,200 sq. ft.
Total Living Area:	**1,520/2,720 sq. ft.**
Garage	155 sq. ft.
Exterior Wall Framing:	2x6
Foundation Options:	
Daylight basement	
Crawlspace	
(Typical foundation & framing conversion diagram available—see order form.)	
BLUEPRINT PRICE CODE:	**B/D**

UPPER FLOOR

BASEMENT STAIRWAY LOCATION

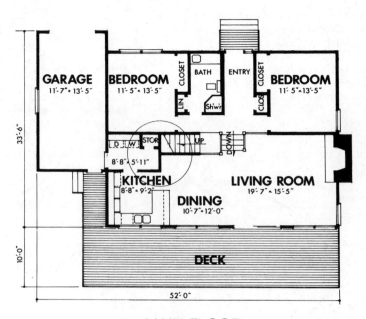

MAIN FLOOR

*TO ORDER THIS BLUEPRINT,
CALL TOLL-FREE 1-800-547-5570*

Plan H-877-1 & -1A

*PRICES AND DETAILS
ON PAGES 12-15*

Energy-Saving Sun Room

- This unique angled design offers spectacular rear views.
- From the high-ceilinged reception area is a view of the large inviting atmosphere created by the living room and the dining room. More high ceilings, a stone fireplace and a rear wall of glass that overlooks the terrace are attractions in this huge setting.
- The adjoining family room features an entertainment wall and a pair of sliders that access the attached energy-saving sun room.
- The comfortable kitchen has a handy snack counter and a sunny dinette.
- The bedroom wing offers three bedrooms, including the master suite, which has a sloped ceiling, a large walk-in closet, a personal bath with whirlpool tub and a private terrace.

Plan AHP-9330

Bedrooms: 3	Baths: 2
Space:	
Main floor	1,528 sq. ft.
Total Living Area	**1,528 sq. ft.**
Basement	1,542 sq. ft.
Garage	400 sq. ft.
Exterior Wall Framing	2x4 or 2x6

Foundation options:

Standard Basement
Crawlspace
Slab
(Foundation & framing conversion diagram available—see order form.)

Blueprint Price Code   **B**

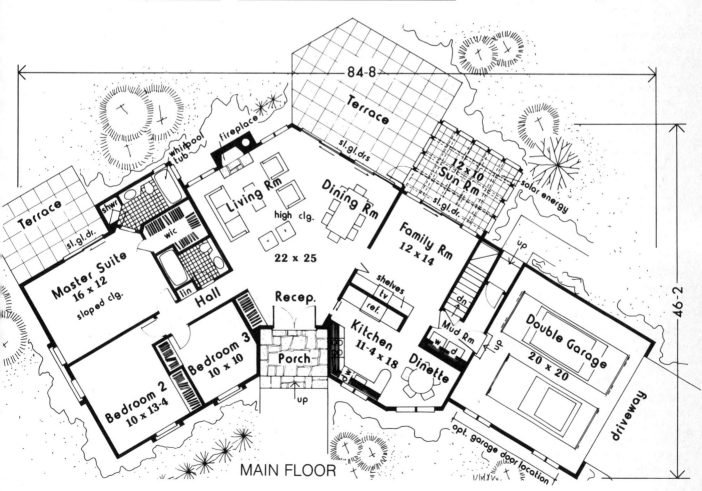

MAIN FLOOR

Open, Energy-Saving Design

- Wrapped with heavy insulation beneath elegant horizontal siding, this handsome three-bedroom ranch helps generate and conserve natural energy.
- An expansive sun roof and sliding glass doors enlighten the informal family room adjoining a lavish U-shaped kitchen with bar and connecting eating area.
- A cathedral ceiling, wood-burning fireplace, sliding glass doors and two tall windows grace the formal living room.
- The isolated master bedroom boasts a private terrace and luxury bath; the secondary bedrooms share a second full bath.

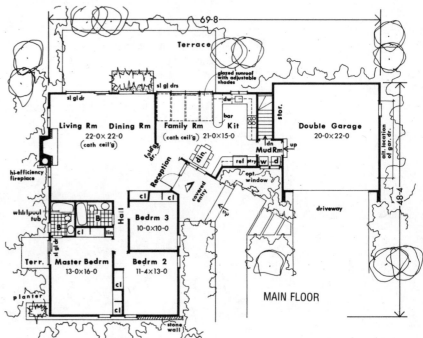

MAIN FLOOR

Plan K-538-L

Bedrooms: 3	Baths: 2

Space:	
Total living area:	1,532 sq. ft.
Optional basement:	1,570 sq. ft.
Garage, mudroom:	550 sq. ft.

Exterior Wall Framing:	2x4 or 2x6

Foundation options:
Standard basement.
Slab.
(Foundation & framing conversion diagram available — see order form.)

Blueprint Price Code:	B

L-Shaped Country-Style Home

- The classic L-shape and covered front porch with decorative railings and columns make this home reminiscent of the early 20th century farmhouse.
- The dormer windows give the home the look of a two-story, even though it is designed for convenient single-level living.
- The huge living room features ceilings that slope up to 13 feet. The beamed area of the ceiling is 8 feet high and creates a cozy atmosphere. A corner fireplace radiates warmth to both the living room and the dining room.
- The dining room overlooks the backyard patio and is open to the kitchen. Just off the kitchen is a large utility room.
- The master bedroom has a private bath. The two smaller bedrooms at the other end of the home share a full bath.

Plan E-1412

Bedrooms: 3	Baths: 2
Space:	
Main floor	1,484 sq. ft.
Total Living Area	**1,484 sq. ft.**
Exterior Wall Framing	2x6
Foundation options:	
Crawlspace	
Slab	
(Foundation & framing conversion diagram available—see order form.)	
Blueprint Price Code	**A**

Octagonal Vacation Retreat

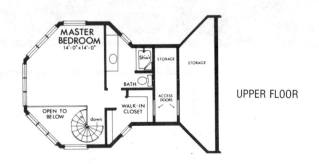

UPPER FLOOR

- Octagonal shape offers a view on all sides.
- Living, dining, and meal preparation are combined in a single Great Room, interrupted only by a provocative spiral staircase.
- Winding staircase allows continuous observance of activities below.
- Extraordinary master suite is bordered by glass, a private bath, and dressing room.
- Attached garage has room for boat, camper, or extra automobile.

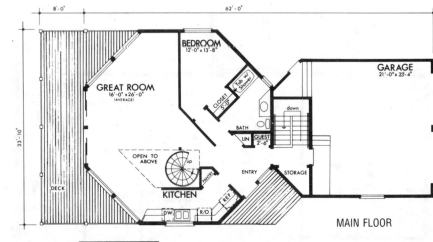

MAIN FLOOR

SCALE

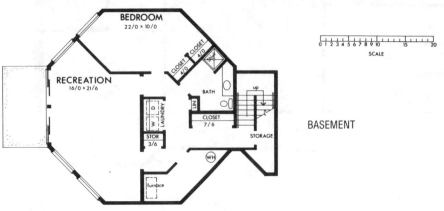

BASEMENT

Plans H-964-1A & -1B

Bedrooms: 2-3	Baths: 2-3

Space:	
Upper floor:	346 sq. ft.
Main floor:	1,067 sq. ft.

Total living area:	1,413 sq. ft.
Basement:	approx. 1,045 sq. ft.
Garage:	512 sq. ft.
Storage (2nd floor)	134 sq. ft.

Exterior Wall Framing:	2x6

Foundation options:
Daylight basement (Plan H-964-1B).
Crawlspace (Plan H-964-1A).
Foundation & framing conversion
diagram available — see order form.)

Blueprint Price Code:

Without basement:	A
With basement:	C

Angles Open Rear of Home to More Sunshine

PATIO

PORCH
12' x 6'

DINING
12' x 12'

MASTER SUITE
16' x 12'

BED RM.
14' x 12'

BAR
DW SINK

KITCHEN

REF RANGE

LIVING
18' x 16'

HALL

BATH

BATH

50'

CLO.

WASH DRY

UTIL
9' x 6'

PANT
BRM
STOR

STORAGE
10' x 6'

CLO.

ENTRY

BED RM.
14' x 12'

PORCH
8' x 4'

GARAGE
22' x 22'

56'

AREAS

Living	1415 sq. ft.
Porches	114 sq. ft.
Garage, Storage	
Equip.	565 sq. ft.
Total	2094 sq. ft.

Exterior walls are 2x6 construction.
Specify crawlspace or slab foundation.

Blueprint Price Code A

Plan E-1424

PRICES AND DETAILS
ON PAGES 12-15

Charming Traditional

- The attractive facade of this traditional home greets visitors with warmth and charm.
- The entry area features a coat closet and a commanding view of the living room and a rear porch and patio, visible through French doors. A striking corner fireplace warms the living room.
- The bayed dining room boasts patio views and an eating bar. The U-shaped kitchen offers a nearby utility room, which includes a pantry and laundry facilities.
- The master suite has an angled window, a walk-in closet and a private bath with dual-sink vanity.
- Two additional bedrooms are secluded from the living areas with double doors. A full bath services this wing.

Plan E-1428	
Bedrooms: 3	**Baths:** 2
Living Area:	
Main floor	1,415 sq. ft.
Total Living Area:	**1,415 sq. ft.**
Garage	484 sq. ft.
Storage	60 sq. ft.
Exterior Wall Framing:	2x6
Foundation Options:	
Crawlspace	
Slab	
(Typical foundation & framing conversion diagram available—see order form.)	
BLUEPRINT PRICE CODE:	A

MAIN FLOOR

PATIO

PORCH 12' x 6'

WH

HEAT & A/C

CLO.

BED RM. 14' x 12'

DINING 12' x 12'

MASTER SUITE 16' x 12'

BAR

LIVING 18' x 16'

BATH

HALL

LIN.

KITCHEN 12' x 10'

DW SINK

RANGE

REF

BATH

LIN.

CLO.

UTIL 9' x 6'

DRY WASH

PANT BRM STOR

STORAGE 10' x 6'

ENTRY

CLO.

BED RM. 14' x 12'

CLO.

SHV'S

PORCH

50'

ATTIC STAIRS

GARAGE 22' x 22'

56'

Plan E-1428

PRICES AND DETAILS ON PAGES 12-15

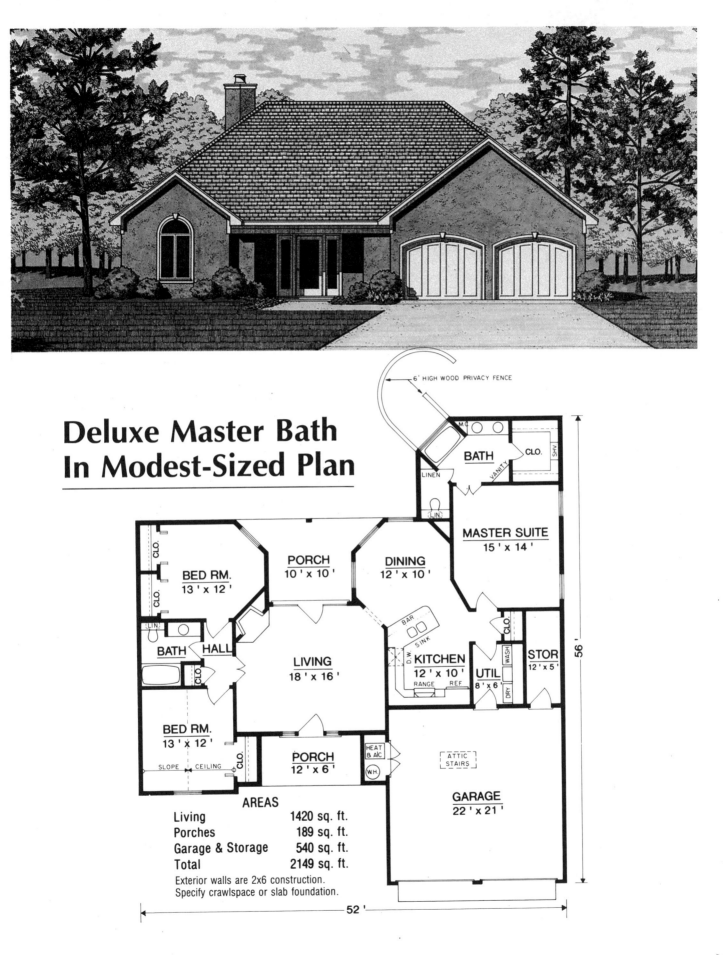

Deluxe Master Bath In Modest-Sized Plan

6' HIGH WOOD PRIVACY FENCE

BATH

CLO.

SHV

MO

LINEN

VANITY

MASTER SUITE
15 ' x 14 '

LIN

CLO.

CLO.

BED RM.
13 ' x 12 '

PORCH
10 ' x 10 '

DINING
12 ' x 10 '

CLO.

LIN

BATH

HALL

LIVING
18 ' x 16 '

BAR

SINK

D.W

KITCHEN
12 ' x 10 '

WASH

STOR
12 ' x 5 '

CLO.

UTIL
8 ' x 6 '

DRY

RANGE

REF

CLO.

BED RM.
13 ' x 12 '

CLO.

PORCH
12 ' x 6 '

HEAT & A/C

W.H.

ATTIC STAIRS

SLOPE

CEILING

GARAGE
22 ' x 21 '

56 '

52 '

AREAS

Living	1420 sq. ft.
Porches	189 sq. ft.
Garage & Storage	540 sq. ft.
Total	2149 sq. ft.

Exterior walls are 2x6 construction.
Specify crawlspace or slab foundation.

TO ORDER THIS BLUEPRINT,
CALL TOLL-FREE 1-800-547-5570

Blueprint Price Code A
Plan E-1426

PRICES AND DETAILS
ON PAGES 12-15 **53**

Eye-Catching Prow-Shaped Chalet

- Steep pitched roof lines and wide cornices give this chalet a distinct alpine appearance.
- Prowed shape, large windows, and 10′ deck provide view and enhancement of indoor/outdoor living.
- Functional division of living and sleeping areas by hallway and first floor full bath.

- Laundry facilities conveniently located near bedroom wing.
- U-shaped kitchen and spacious dining/living areas make the main floor perfect for entertaining.

UPPER FLOOR

Plans H-886-3 & -3A

Bedrooms: 3	Baths: 2

Space:

Upper floor:	486 sq. ft.
Main floor:	994 sq. ft.

Total without basement:	1,480 sq. ft.
Basement:	approx. 715 sq. ft.
Garage:	279 sq. ft.

Exterior Wall Framing:	2x6

Foundation options:
Daylight basement (Plan H-886-3).
Crawlspace (Plan H-886-3A).
(Foundation & framing conversion diagram available — see order form.)

Blueprint Price Code:	A

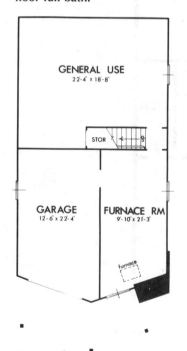

BASEMENT

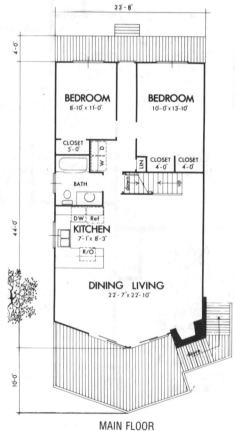

MAIN FLOOR

Plans H-886-3 & -3A

PRICES AND DETAILS ON PAGES 12-15

Compact Traditional Classic

AREAS

Living-Lower	767 sq. ft.
Living-Upper	720 sq. ft.
Total Living	1487 sq. ft.
Garage & Storage	565 sq. ft.
Atrium	72 sq. ft.
Porch	180 sq. ft.
Total	2304 sq. ft.

⬆ UPPER LEVEL

Exterior walls are 2x6 construction.
Specify crawlspace or slab foundation.

⬆ LOWER LEVEL

TO ORDER THIS BLUEPRINT,
CALL TOLL-FREE 1-800-547-5570

Unique, Dramatic Floor Plan

- An expansive and impressive Great Room, warmed by a wood stove, features an island kitchen that's completely open in design.
- A passive solar sun room is designed to collect and store heat from the sun, while also providing a good view of the surroundings.
- Upstairs, you'll see a glamorous master suite with a private bath and a huge walk-in closet.
- The daylight basement adds a sunny sitting room, a third bedroom and a large recreation room.

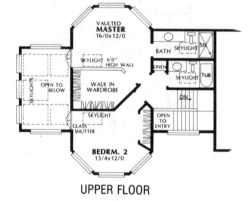

UPPER FLOOR

Plans P-536-2A & -2D

Bedrooms: 2-3	Baths: 2-3
Space:	
Upper floor:	642 sq. ft.
Main floor:	863 sq. ft.
Total living area:	**1,505 sq. ft.**
Basement:	863 sq. ft.
Garage:	445 sq. ft.
Exterior Wall Framing:	2x6

Foundation options:	Plan #
Daylight basement	P-536-2D
Crawlspace	P-536-2A

(Foundation & framing conversion diagram available — see order form.)

Blueprint Price Code:

Plan P-536-2A	B
Plan P-536-2D	C

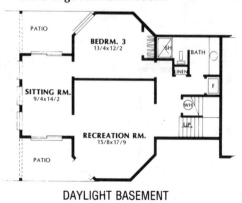

DAYLIGHT BASEMENT

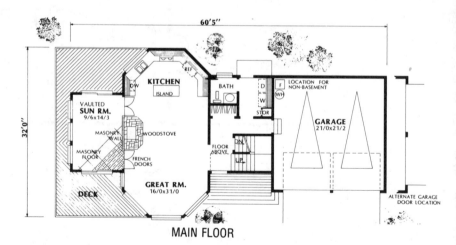

MAIN FLOOR

FRONT VIEW

REAR VIEW

Hillside Design Fits Contours

- The daylight-basement version of this popular plan is perfect for a scenic, sloping lot.
- A large, wraparound deck embraces the rear-oriented living areas, accessed through sliding glass doors.
- The spectacular living room boasts a corner fireplace, a sloped ceiling and outdoor views to the side and rear.
- The secluded master suite upstairs offers a walk-in closet, a private bath and sliders to a sun deck.
- The daylight basement (not shown) includes a fourth bedroom with private bath and walk-in closet, as well as a recreation room with fireplace and sliders to a rear patio.
- The standard basement (not shown) includes a recreation room with fireplace and a room for hobbies or child's play.
- Both basements also have a large unfinished area below the main-floor bedrooms.

UPPER FLOOR

Plans H-877-4, -4A & -4B	
Bedrooms: 3-4	**Baths:** 2-3
Living Area:	
Upper floor	333 sq. ft.
Main floor	1,200 sq. ft.
Basement (finished portion)	591 sq. ft.
Total Living Area:	**1,533/2,124 sq. ft.**
Basement (unfinished portion)	493 sq. ft.
Garage	480 sq. ft.
Exterior Wall Framing:	2x6
Foundation Options:	**Plan #**
Daylight basement	H-877-4B
Standard basement	H-877-4
Crawlspace	H-877-4A
(Typical foundation & framing conversion diagram available—see order form.)	
BLUEPRINT PRICE CODE:	**B/C**

MAIN FLOOR

PLAN H-877-4
WITH BASEMENT

PLAN H-877-4B
WITH DAYLIGHT BASEMENT

PLAN H-877-4A
WITHOUT BASEMENT

Space-Saving Floor Plan

- Easy, affordable living is the basis for this great town and country design.
- The welcoming porch and the graceful arched window give the home its curb appeal. Inside, the floor plan provides large, highly livable spaces rather than several specialized rooms.
- The foyer opens to the spacious living room. A column separates the foyer from the formal dining room, which features a bay window and an alcove that is perfect for a china hutch. The country kitchen is large enough to accommodate family and guests alike.
- A beautiful open staircase leads to the second floor, where there are three bedrooms and two baths. The master bedroom offers a tray ceiling and a luxurious bath with a sloped ceiling and a corner shower.

Plan AX-92320

Bedrooms: 3	Baths: 2½
Living Area:	
Upper floor	706 sq. ft.
Main floor	830 sq. ft.
Total Living Area:	**1,536 sq. ft.**
Standard basement	754 sq. ft.
Garage	510 sq. ft.
Exterior Wall Framing:	2x6

Foundation Options:

Standard basement
Slab

(Typical foundation & framing conversion diagram available—see order form.)

BLUEPRINT PRICE CODE:	**B**

Photo by Mark Englund/HomeStyles

**NOTE:
The above photographed home may have been modified by the homeowner. Please refer to floor plan and/or drawn elevation shown for actual blueprint details.

FRONT VIEW

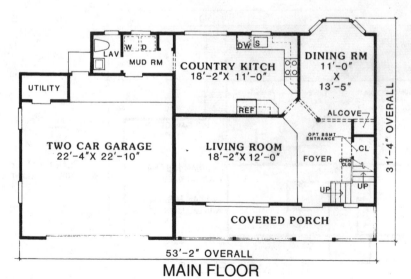

MAIN FLOOR

UTILITY

TWO CAR GARAGE
22'-4" X 22'-10"

LAV
W D
MUD RM

COUNTRY KITCH
18'-2" X 11'-0"

DW S

REF

DINING RM
11'-0" X 13'-5"

ALCOVE

LIVING ROOM
18'-2" X 12'-0"

OPT BSMT ENTRANCE

FOYER

CL

OPEN CLG

UP   UP

COVERED PORCH

31'-4" OVERALL

53'-2" OVERALL

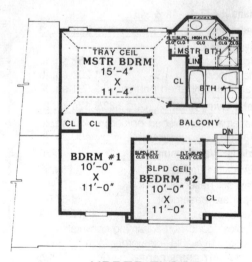

UPPER FLOOR

TRAY CEIL
MSTR BDRM
15'-4" X 11'-4"

MSTR BTH
LIN
CL
BTH #1

CL CL

BALCONY
DN

BDRM #1
10'-0" X 11'-0"

SLPD CEIL
BEDRM #2
10'-0" X 11'-0"

CL

TO ORDER THIS BLUEPRINT, CALL TOLL-FREE 1-800-547-5570

Plan AX-92320

PRICES AND DETAILS ON PAGES 12-15

BEDROOM
17'6" x 9'9"

WALK-IN
CLOSET
6'0"   down

Shwr

CLOSET
5'6"   BATH

BEDROOM
17'6" x 13'9"

DECK

UPPER FLOOR

30'0"

BEDROOM
12'0" x 13'3"

CLOSET 4'9"

CLOSET 4'9"

BATH

Shwr

DW

KITCHEN
10'3" x 8'3"

REF

up

down

DINING
10'9" x 6'6"

32'0"

LIVING ROOM
29'0" x 13'9"

ENTRY

DECK

down

MAIN FLOOR

LAUNDRY   D

W

WH

HEAT

GARAGE
14'0" x 30'9"

up   STOR

BASEMENT

Chalet for All Seasons

- Rustic exterior makes this design suitable for a lakefront, beach, or wooded setting.
- Patterned railing and wood deck edge the front and side main level, while a smaller deck assumes a balcony role.
- Designed for relaxed, leisure living, the main level features a large L-shaped Great Room warmed by a central free-standing fireplace.
- Upper level offers a second bath and added sleeping accommodations.

Plan H-858-2

Bedrooms: 3	Baths: 2
Space:	
Upper floor:	576 sq. ft.
Main floor:	960 sq. ft.
Total living area:	**1,536 sq. ft.**
Basement:	530 sq. ft.
Garage:	430 sq. ft.

Exterior Wall Framing:	2x6

Foundation options:
Daylight basement.
(Foundation & framing conversion diagram available — see order form.)

Blueprint Price Code:	B

8'-0" 30'-0" 8'-0"

44'-0"

DECK

SHELV | WH
STOR | heat

W | D
LAUNDRY

REF
DW
KITCHEN
10/8 x 12/6

PANTRY | LAV | CLOSET 5/5 | STUDY/ BEDR'M 9/0 x 8/10

R/O

STOR | STOR

DINING
10/0 x 10/6

WOOD STOVE

UP

FRENCH DOORS

SLOPED CEILING

LIVING ROOM
15/2 x 16/10
SKYLIGHTS

GUEST 4/6

AIR LOCK ENTRY

GARAGE
25/4 x 11/8

PASSIVE SUN SPACE
29/0 x 7/6

(Exterior walls are 2x6 construction)

MAIN FLOOR

down

PLAN H-970-1
WITH BASEMENT

PLAN H-970-1A
WITHOUT BASEMENT
(CRAWLSPACE FOUNDATION)

SKYLIGHTS

Tub w/ Shower | LINEN | LINEN | CLOSET 5/6 | CLOSET 5/6

BATH

BEDROOM
10/0 x 13/6

down

DESK

CLOSET 4/9

BEDROOM
15/2 x 16/6

DESK | CLOSET

SKYLIGHTS

SKYLIGHTS

STORAGE

SECOND FLOOR

First floor:	817 sq. ft.
Sunspace:	192 sq. ft.
Second floor:	563 sq. ft.
Total living area: (Not counting basement or garage)	1,572 sq. ft.
Airlock entry:	40 sq. ft.
Garage:	288 sq. ft.

The Simple Life at Its Best in a Passive Solar Design

This home's rustic exterior is suggestive of Carpenter Gothic Style homes or early barn designs. The wood shake roof and "board-and-batten" style siding help to carry out this theme. An air-lock entry provides a protected place to remove outer garments as well as serving as an energy-conserving heat loss barrier. As you pass from the entry into the cozy living room, there is an immediate perception of warmth and light. This room features a centrally located woodstove and two skylights.

Between the living room and the sun space are two double-hung windows to provide heat circulation as well as admit natural light. Further inspection of the ground floor reveals a delightful flow of space. From the dining room it is possible to view the kitchen, the wider portion of the sun space and part of the living room. An open staircase connects this room with the second floor.

The kitchen boasts modern appliances, large pantry and storage closets and a convenient peninsula open to the dining room. The remainder of the first floor includes a handy laundry room, an easily accessible half-bath and a bonus room with an unlimited number of possibilities. One such use may be as a home computer/study area. Upstairs, two bedrooms with an abundance of closet space share the fully appointed, skylighted bathroom.

A word about the passive sun room: It seems that solar design has come full circle, returning us to the concept that less is more. This sun room uses masonry floor pavers as heat storage and natural convection as the primary means of heat circulation. This serves to reduce both the potential for system failures and the heavy operating workload often found in more elaborate solar designs, not to mention the high cost of such systems.

Rustic Comfort

- While rustic in exterior appearance, this home is completely modern inside and loaded with the amenities preferred by today's builders.
- A large living room is made to seem immense by use of 16' ceilings, and an impressive fireplace and hearth dominate one end of the room.
- A formal dining room adds to the spaciousness, since it is separated from the living room only by a divider and a 6" step.
- The large U-shaped kitchen is adjoined by a convenient sewing and utility area, which in turn leads to the garage. A storage area is included in the garage, along with a built-in workbench.

- The sumptuous master suite features a sitting area, enormous walk-in closet and deluxe private bath.
- The two secondary bedrooms share another full bath and are zoned for privacy.

Plan E-1607

Bedrooms: 3	Baths: 2

Space:

Total living area:	1,600 sq. ft.
Basement:	approx. 1,600 sq. ft.
Garage:	484 sq. ft.
Storage:	132 sq. ft.
Porch:	295 sq. ft.

Exterior Wall Framing:	2x6

Foundation options:
Standard basement.
Crawlspace.
Slab.
(Foundation & framing conversion diagram available — see order form)

Blueprint Price Code:	B

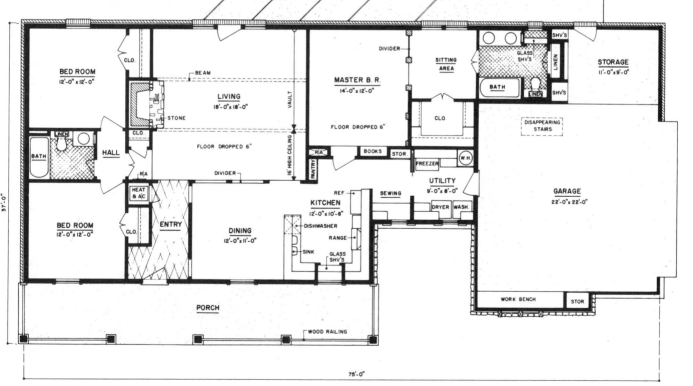

UPPER FLOOR

Cost-Saving Style

- This country-style home has a classic exterior look and an open, space-saving floor plan.
- The U-shaped kitchen flows nicely into the dining room, where an angled hall stretches to the screened-in porch and the living room.
- The deluxe master bedroom is large for a home this size, and includes a separate sink and vanity area that adjoins the main bath.
- A good-sized utility room is convenient to the garage, which features a large storage area.
- The second floor offers two bedrooms, each with extra closet space, and another full bath. Both bedrooms also have access to attic storage space.

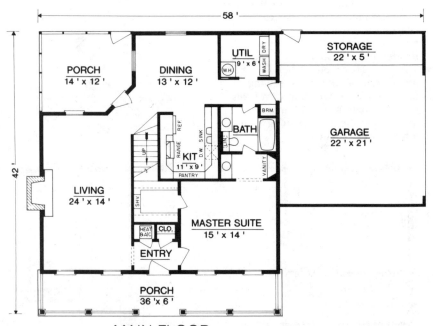

MAIN FLOOR

Plan E-1626

Bedrooms: 3	Baths: 2
Living Area:	
Upper floor	464 sq. ft.
Main floor	1,136 sq. ft.
Total Living Area:	**1,600 sq. ft.**
Garage	462 sq. ft.
Exterior Wall Framing:	2x6

Foundation Options:

Crawlspace

Slab

(Typical foundation & framing conversion diagram available—see order form.)

BLUEPRINT PRICE CODE:	**B**

**NOTE:
The above photographed home may have been modified by the homeowner. Please refer to floor plan and/or drawn elevation shown for actual blueprint details.

TO ORDER THIS BLUEPRINT,
CALL TOLL-FREE 1-800-547-5570

Plan E-1626

PRICES AND DETAILS
ON PAGES 12-15

A Home for Sun Lovers

This open plan home, brightened by a landscaped atrium, also has a vaulted, glass-ceiling solarium with an optional spa, offering a sunny garden room for sitting or soaking — a bonus in a three-bedroom home of only 1,621 sq. ft.

Intersecting hip roofs with corner notches, a clerestory dormer, vertical board siding and a covered front walkway add design interest and set the house apart from its neighbors. Inside the vaulted, skylighted entry, the hallway angles left past the atrium into the vaulted great room, which has a fireplace and a door leading out to a wood deck or patio.

The spacious L-shaped kitchen also overlooks the atrium and has an adjacent vaulted nook with solarium window and a door to the garage.

To the right of the entry hall is the bedroom wing. Double doors open into the master bedroom, with a private bath and walk-in closet. Doors lead to the solarium and the front courtyard. A second bathroom serves the other two bedrooms, one of which can double as a den and has doors opening into the great room.

In the daylight basement version of the plan, a stairway replaces the atrium.

Main floor:	1,497 sq. ft.
Solarium:	124 sq. ft.
Total living area: (Not counting basement or garage)	1,621 sq. ft.
Basement:	1,514 sq. ft.

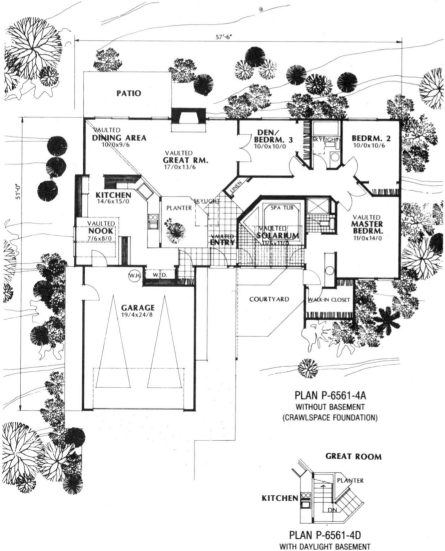

PLAN P-6561-4A
WITHOUT BASEMENT
(CRAWLSPACE FOUNDATION)

PLAN P-6561-4D
WITH DAYLIGHT BASEMENT

Blueprint Price Code B

Plans P-6561-4A & -4D

TO ORDER THIS BLUEPRINT,
CALL TOLL-FREE 1-800-547-5570

PRICES AND DETAILS
ON PAGES 12-15   **63**

Covered Wraparound Deck Featured

- A covered deck spans this home from the main entrance to the kitchen door.
- An over-sized fireplace is the focal point of the living room, which merges into an expandable dining area.
- The kitchen is tucked into one corner, but open counter space allows visual contact with living areas beyond.
- Two good-sized main-floor bedrooms are furnished with sufficient closet space.
- The basement level adds a third bedroom in an additional 673 sq. ft. of living space.

Plan H-806-2

Bedrooms: 3	Baths: 1
Living Area:	
Main floor	952 sq. ft.
Daylight basement	673 sq. ft.
Total Living Area:	**1,625 sq. ft.**
Garage	279 sq. ft.
Exterior Wall Framing:	2x6

Foundation Options:
Daylight basement
(Typical foundation & framing conversion diagram available—see order form.)

BLUEPRINT PRICE CODE:	**B**

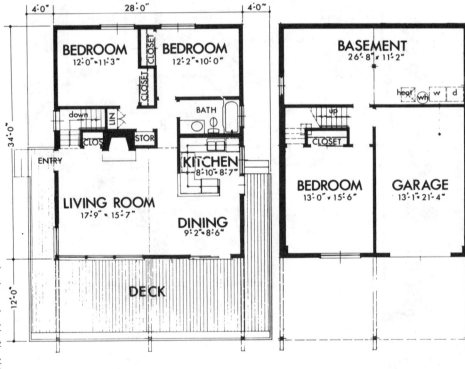

MAIN FLOOR

DAYLIGHT BASEMENT

Solarium Adds Extra Touch of Luxury

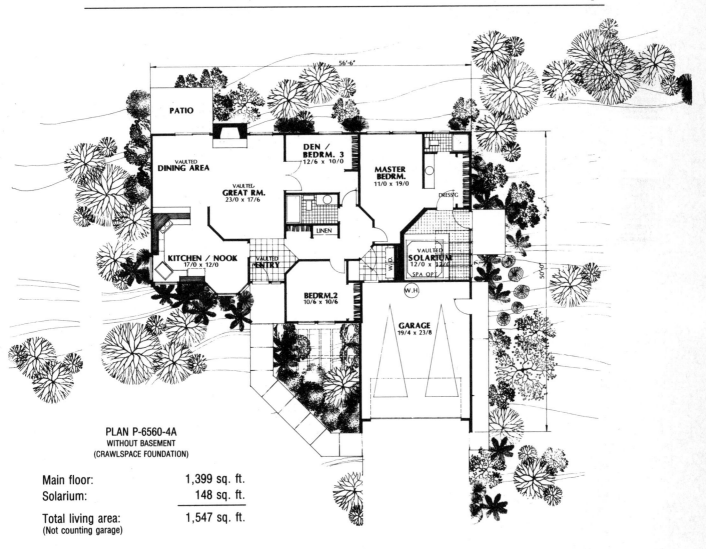

PLAN P-6560-4A
WITHOUT BASEMENT
(CRAWLSPACE FOUNDATION)

Main floor:	1,399 sq. ft.
Solarium:	148 sq. ft.
Total living area:	1,547 sq. ft.
(Not counting garage)	

Blueprint Price Code B

Plan P-6560-4A

PRICES AND DETAILS
ON PAGES 12-15

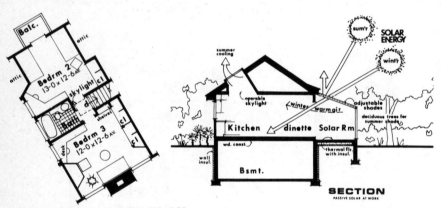

SECOND FLOOR PLAN

Balc.

attic

attic

Bedrm 2
13-0 x 12-6 AV.

skylight

shelves

Bedrm 3
12-0 x 12-6 AV.

desk

SECTION
PASSIVE SOLAR AT WORK

SOLAR ENERGY

sum'r

wint'r

summer cooling

operable skylight

winter warm air

adjustable shades

deciduous trees for summer shade

Kitchen   dinette   Solar Rm

wd. const.

wall insul.

thermal flr. with insul.

Bsmt.

Passive Solar Home Meets Modern Demands

The exterior of this two-story plan is thoroughly contemporary. The layout is angled to give it added distinction in any neighborhood. Optional orientations in relation to the street allow this plan to adapt to a variety of plot shapes. Inside, the reception hall immediately presents a pleasing view of the rear terrace and solar room. To the left is the living room, which is graced by a stone fireplace.

In winter months, light and solar heat enter through the glass and heat is stored in the ceramic tiled floor of the solar room; after the sun sets, this warmth is released to the house. In summer months, the sun rises higher and its rays are blocked by adjustable shades built into glazed ceiling panels; automatic vent guards against heat buildup.

Generously sized, the master bedroom features extensive glass to the south side, a personal bath and sliding glass doors that lead out to a private terrace.

Total living area, excluding the solar room, is 1,132 sq. ft. on the first floor and 416 sq. ft. on the second. Optional basement is 1,176 sq. ft.; garage, mud room, etc., come to 560 sq. ft. (Alternate slab-on-grade foundation plan is included.)

Total living area: 1,548 sq. ft.

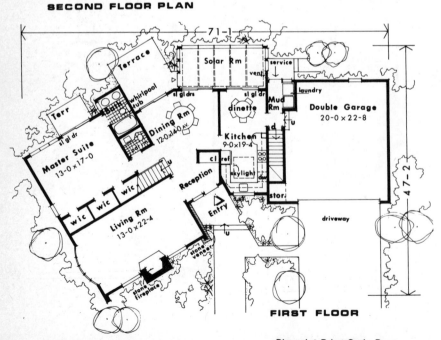

71-1

47-2

Terrace

Solar Rm

service

vent

Terr

whirlpool tub

Bath

sl gl drs

sl gl dr

Mud Rm

laundry

Double Garage
20-0 x 22-8

Dining Rm
12-0 x 14-0 AV.

dinette

Master Suite
13-0 x 17-0

sl gl dr

Kitchen
9-0 x 19-4

cl   ref

Reception

skylight

wic   wic

wic   wic

stor.

Entry

Living Rm
13-0 x 22-4

stone veneer

driveway

stone fireplace

FIRST FLOOR

Blueprint Price Code B
Plan K-513-A

PRICES AND DETAILS ON PAGES 12-15

Open Plan Includes Circular Dining Room

- Innovative architectural features and a functional, light-filled floor plan are the hallmarks of this attractive design.
- The facade is graced by a stone chimney and a circular glass bay which houses the spectacular dining room with its domed ceiling.
- A bright, sunny kitchen is set up for efficient operation and adjoins a dinette area which echoes the circular shape of the formal dining room.
- The living room features a stone fireplace, and opens to the dining room to make a great space for entertaining.
- The bedrooms are zoned to the left, with the master suite including a private bath, large walk-in closet and access to an outdoor terrace.

Plan K-663-N

Bedrooms: 3	Baths: 2

Space:	
Total living area:	**1,560 sq. ft.**
Basement:	1,645 sq. ft.
Garage:	453 sq. ft.
Mudroom & stairs:	122 sq. ft.

Exterior Wall Framing:	2x4/2x6

Foundation options:
Standard basement.
Slab.
(Foundation & framing conversion diagram available — see order form.)

Blueprint Price Code:	B

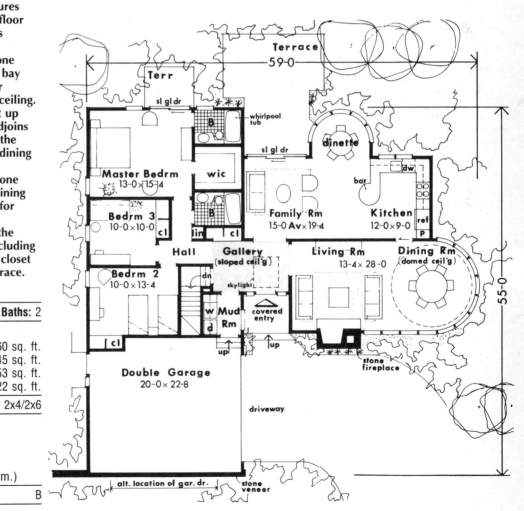

Filled with Style and Light

- A fluid floor plan highlights this stylish and practical contemporary design.
- An overhead arch and an angled half-wall separate the formal entryway from the dining room and add architectural interest that sets this plan apart.
- Another arched opening in the dining room leads to the sunken living room. A vaulted ceiling and an expansive window wall heighten and brighten this beautiful room.
- The airy, open kitchen boasts a handy island cooktop and a built-in pantry.
- An informal family room provides light, comfort and livability, with its large bay window, inviting woodstove and sliding glass doors to a patio or deck.
- A skylighted hallway illuminates the path to the private master suite, the two additional bedrooms and the hall bath.

Plan R-1066

Bedrooms: 3	Baths: 2
Living Area:	
Main floor	1,560 sq. ft.
Total Living Area:	**1,560 sq. ft.**
Garage	367 sq. ft.
Exterior Wall Framing:	2x6
Foundation Options:	
Crawlspace	
BLUEPRINT PRICE CODE:	**B**

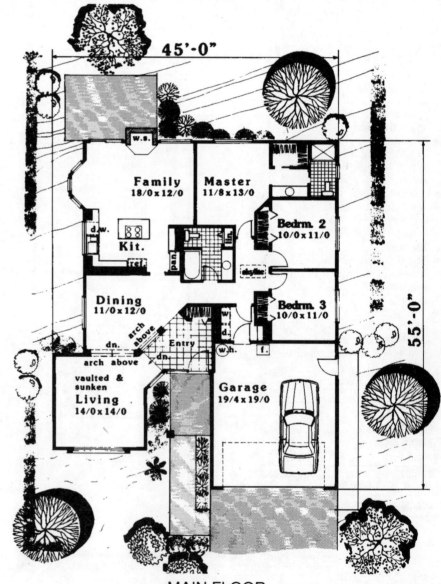

MAIN FLOOR

TO ORDER THIS BLUEPRINT, CALL TOLL-FREE 1-800-547-5570

Plan R-1066

PRICES AND DETAILS ON PAGES 12-15

Distinctive Exterior, Economical Construction

- A modest-sized and fairly simple one-story design, this home will fit the budget of many young families.
- To make optimum use of a limited space, the living and dining rooms are combined to make more space for entertaining large groups.
- The open kitchen faces a sunny nook, with bay windows to brighten the entire area.
- An adjoining family room includes a corner wood stove for heat and a cozy atmosphere on chilly days.
- A pleasant master suite includes a double-door entry, skylighted bath and large closet.
- Bedrooms 2 and 3 share another full bath, and the utility area is convenient to all three bedrooms.

Plan R-1063

Bedrooms: 3	Baths: 2
Living Area:	
Main floor	1,585 sq. ft.
Total Living Area:	**1,585 sq. ft.**
Garage	408 sq. ft.
Exterior Wall Framing:	2x6

Foundation Options:

Crawlspace
(Typical foundation & framing conversion diagram available—see order form.)

BLUEPRINT PRICE CODE: B

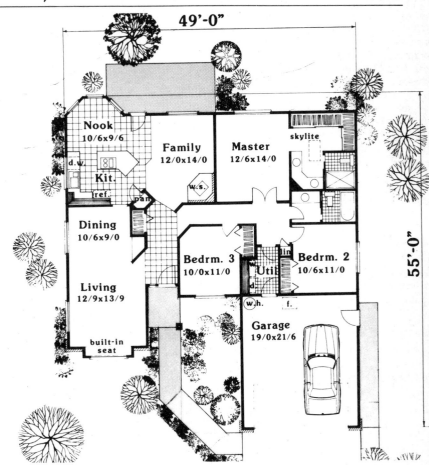

Low-Cost Comfort

- Designed for the energy-conscious, this passive solar home provides year-round comfort at much lower fuel costs.
- The open, airy interior is a delight. In winter, sunshine penetrates deeply into the living spaces. In summer, wide overhangs shade the interior.
- The family room/breakfast/kitchen combination is roomy and bright for family activities.
- The living/dining areas flow together for more bright, open space.
- The master suite includes a private bath and walk-in closet. Two other bedrooms share another full bath.

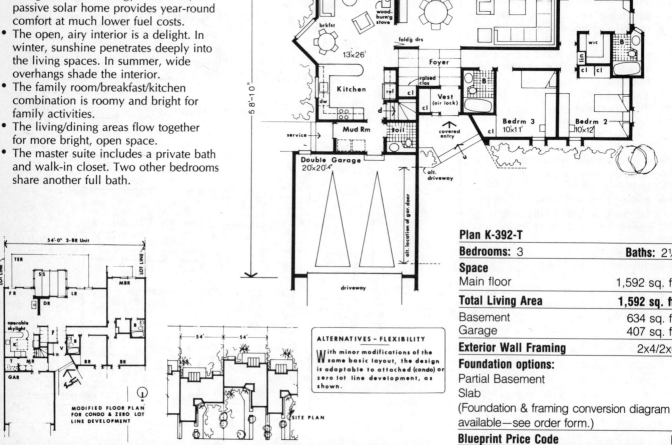

ALTERNATIVES – FLEXIBILITY

With minor modifications of the same basic layout, the design is adaptable to attached (condo) or zero lot line development, as shown.

Plan K-392-T

Bedrooms: 3	**Baths:** 2½

Space

Main floor	1,592 sq. ft.
Total Living Area	**1,592 sq. ft.**
Basement	634 sq. ft.
Garage	407 sq. ft.
Exterior Wall Framing	2x4/2x6

Foundation options:
Partial Basement
Slab
(Foundation & framing conversion diagram available—see order form.)

Blueprint Price Code B

TO ORDER THIS BLUEPRINT, CALL TOLL-FREE 1-800-547-5570   **Plan K-392-T**   **PRICES AND DETAILS ON PAGES 12-15**

Classy Touches in Compact Home

- Charming window treatments, a quality front door, covered porch and detailed railings add class to this smaller home.
- The beautiful kitchen is brightened and enlarged by a sunny bay window.
- The spacious family room enjoys easy access to a patio in the back yard.
- The roomy living room features an impressive corner fireplace and a large bay window in the front.
- The master bedroom boasts a large bathroom, dressing area and closet in addition to the sleeping area.
- Both secondary bedrooms feature cozy window seats.

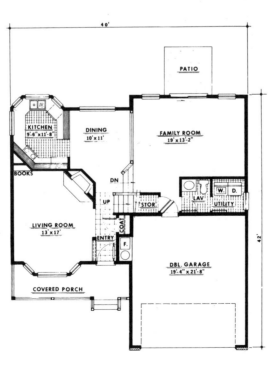

MAIN FLOOR

UPPER FLOOR

Plan NW-836

Bedrooms: 3	Baths: 2½

Space:

Upper floor:	684 sq. ft.
Main floor:	934 sq. ft.
Total living area:	1,618 sq. ft.
Garage:	419 sq. ft.

Exterior Wall Framing:	2x6

Foundation options:
Crawlspace only.
(Foundation & framing conversion diagram available — see order form.)

Blueprint Price Code:	B

Functional, Nostalgic Home Offers Choices in Floor Plans

- Your choice of first- and second-floor room arrangements and foundation plans is required when ordering this design.
- Pick from a family room/kitchen combination with a separate living room, or an expansive living/dining room adjoining a kitchen and nook with either two or three bedrooms.
- In both cases, front entry parlor has an open stairway brightened by a round glass window.
- 8' wide front porch connects with a covered walk to a detached double-car garage.

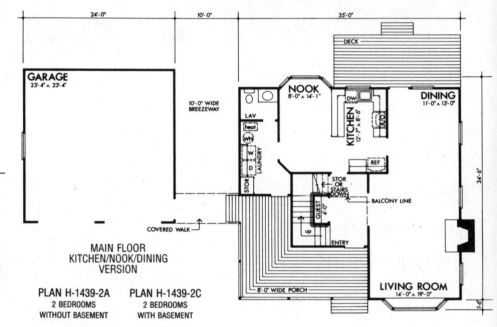

MAIN FLOOR
KITCHEN/NOOK/DINING
VERSION

PLAN H-1439-2A
2 BEDROOMS
WITHOUT BASEMENT

PLAN H-1439-2C
2 BEDROOMS
WITH BASEMENT

PLAN H-1439-3A
3 BEDROOMS
WITHOUT BASEMENT

PLAN H-1439-3C
3 BEDROOMS
WITH BASEMENT

(See facing page for alternate main floor)

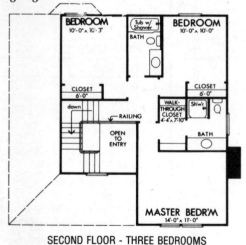

SECOND FLOOR - THREE BEDROOMS
678 SQUARE FEET

SECOND FLOOR - TWO BEDROOMS
678 SQUARE FEET

TO ORDER THIS BLUEPRINT,
CALL TOLL-FREE 1-800-547-5570

Plans H-1439-2A, -2C, -3A & -3C

PRICES AND DETAILS
ON PAGES 12-15

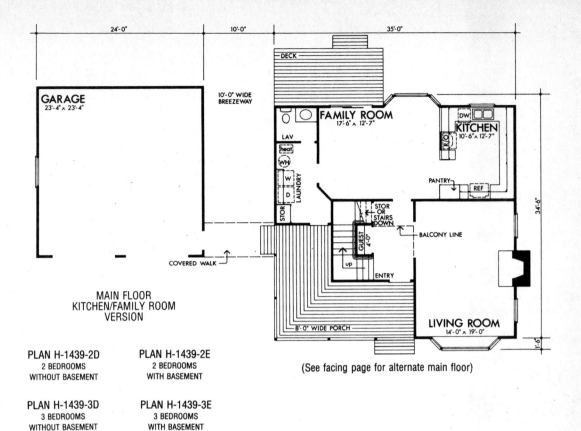

MAIN FLOOR
KITCHEN/FAMILY ROOM
VERSION

PLAN H-1439-2D
2 BEDROOMS
WITHOUT BASEMENT

PLAN H-1439-2E
2 BEDROOMS
WITH BASEMENT

PLAN H-1439-3D
3 BEDROOMS
WITHOUT BASEMENT

PLAN H-1439-3E
3 BEDROOMS
WITH BASEMENT

(See facing page for alternate main floor)

Plans H-1439-2A, -2C, -3A & -3C
Plans H-1439-2D, -2E, -3D & -3E

Bedrooms: 2-3	Baths: 2½
Space:	
Upper floor:	678 sq. ft.
Main floor:	940 sq. ft.
Total living area:	1,618 sq. ft.
Basement:	approx. 940 sq. ft.
Garage:	544 sq. ft.
Exterior Wall Framing:	2x6

Foundation options:
Standard basement (Plans H-1439-2C, -3C, -2E & -3E).
Crawlspace (Plans H-1439-2A, -3A, -2D & -3D).
(Foundation & framing conversion diagram available — see order form.)

Blueprint Price Code: B

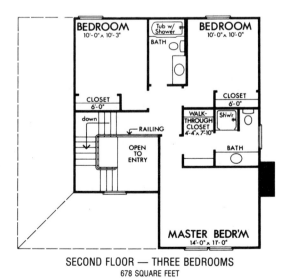

SECOND FLOOR — THREE BEDROOMS
678 SQUARE FEET

SECOND FLOOR — TWO BEDROOMS
678 SQUARE FEET

Family-Oriented Two-Story

- Accents of cedar shake siding and a covered front porch complement this traditional two-story.
- The volume entry is flanked by formal living spaces.
- The comfortable family room, kitchen and nook share a spacious, informal setting at the rear of the home. All three areas enjoy the optional fireplace and outdoor views. Sliders in the nook open to the patio. The oversized cooktop island in the ktichen can also serve as a snack counter.
- A handy laundry closet is located near the garage entrance.
- Three nice-sized bedrooms and two full baths share the upper level with a large bonus room that can be used as a playroom, TV room or extra bedroom.

Plan NW-406-A

Bedrooms: 3-4	Baths: 2½
Living Area:	
Upper floor	752 sq. ft.
Main floor	873 sq. ft.
Total Living Area:	**1,625 sq. ft.**
Garage	498 sq. ft.
Exterior Wall Framing:	2x6

Foundation Options:

Crawlspace
(Typical foundation & framing conversion diagram available—see order form.)

BLUEPRINT PRICE CODE:	**B**

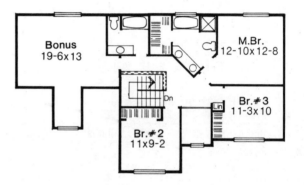

UPPER FLOOR

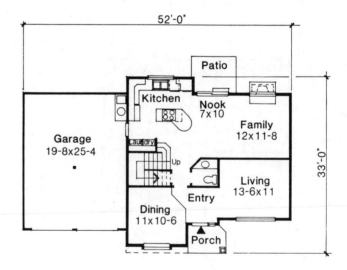

MAIN FLOOR

Southwestern Standout

- Contemporary styling with a traditional touch makes this house a standout in any neighborhood.
- The generously sized kitchen contains abundant counter space, a handy pantry and corner windows overlooking an enticing backyard patio. The kitchen is open to the family room and nook for informal living.
- The family room and kitchen can be totally closed off to provide extra privacy for the formal dining and living rooms. Both the family room and the living room feature fireplaces.
- The master bedroom has a private bath and is highlighted by a sunny alcove with a French door that opens to the patio.
- The laundry room is handy to the garage and to the bedrooms.

Plan R-1039

Bedrooms: 3	Baths: 2
Space:	
Main floor	1,642 sq. ft.
Total Living Area	**1,642 sq. ft.**
Garage	517 sq. ft.
Exterior Wall Framing	2x6
Foundation options:	
Slab	
Crawlspace	
(Foundation & framing conversion diagram available—see order form.)	
Blueprint Price Code	**B**

Floor Plan

53'-0"
64'-8"

Master 14/0x15/0
Nook 8/6x8/6
Kit.
Dining 10/0x10/0
Family 13/0x17/0
ref. pan.
Bedrm. 2 10/0x11/0
Entry
Living 13/0x17/0
w. h. f.
d w
Bedrm. 3 10/0x10/0
Garage 22/0x23/6

Elegance and Convenience

- Exterior design presents a dignified, distinctive and solid look.
- Energy-efficient, 2 x 6 exterior walls are used.
- 15' ceilings and a beautifully detailed fireplace are part of the living room decor.
- Octagonal dining room has window walls on three sides to view adjacent porches.
- Master suite features access to a private porch and an attached bath with corner marbled tub and separate shower.

Plan E-1628

Bedrooms: 3	Baths: 2

Space:

Total living area:	1,655 sq. ft.
Garage and storage:	549 sq. ft.
Porches:	322 sq. ft.

Exterior Wall Framing:	2x6

Foundation options:
Crawlspace.
Slab.
(Foundation & framing conversion diagram available — see order form.)

Blueprint Price Code:	B

TO ORDER THIS BLUEPRINT, CALL TOLL-FREE 1-800-547-5570

Plan E-1628

PRICES AND DETAILS ON PAGES 12-15

Traditional Split Level

- A traditional exterior and a compact interior characterize this split level.
- An extensive deck along the rear of the home can be entered through the dining room and master bedroom; another deck sits off the living room, which also offers a fireplace and large front windows.
- The kitchen provides a handy breakfast bar, also convenient to the dining room; both are situated above the living room.
- The master suite and two additional bedrooms complete the upper level.
- Below are laundry and utility facilities and a generous family room.

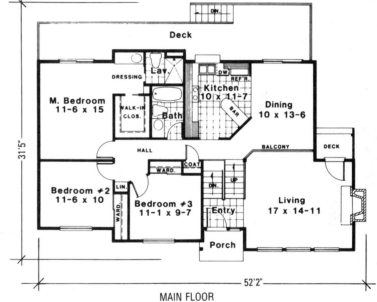

MAIN FLOOR

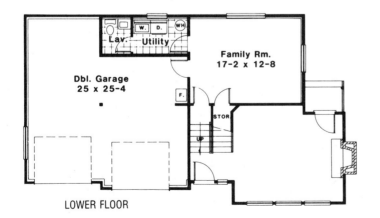

LOWER FLOOR

Plan NW-413

Bedrooms: 3	Baths: 2½

Space:	
Main/upper floor:	1,315 sq. ft.
Lower floor:	345 sq. ft.

Total living area:	1,660 sq. ft.
Garage:	633 sq. ft.

Exterior Wall Framing:	2x6

Foundation options:
Daylight basement.
(Foundation & framing conversion diagram available — see order form.)

Blueprint Price Code:	B

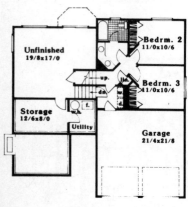

UPPER FLOOR

Plan R-4033

Bedrooms: 3	Baths: 2

Space:

Upper two levels:	1,185 sq. ft.
Lower level:	480 sq. ft.

Total living area:	1,665 sq. ft.
Bonus area:	334 sq. ft.
Garage:	462 sq. ft.
Storage:	100 sq. ft.

Exterior Wall Framing:	2x6

Foundation options:
Daylight basement only.
(Foundation & framing conversion
diagram available — see order form.)

Blueprint Price Code:	B

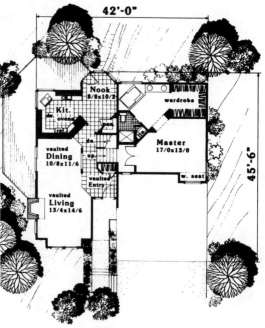

MAIN FLOOR

Exciting Design for Sloping Lot

- This design offers an exciting floor plan for a side-sloping lot.
- The vaulted foyer opens to the living room which is highlighted by a cheerful fireplace and is also vaulted.
- A half-wall with overhead arch separates the foyer and hallway from the dining room without interrupting the flow of space.
- The kitchen offers plenty of counter and cabinet space, and adjoins a brightly lit vaulted nook with a pantry in the corner.
- Separated from the rest of the household, the upper level master suite is a true haven from the day's worries, with its relaxing whirlpool tub, dual vanities and roomy closet.
- The lower level includes two bedrooms, a bath plus a large area which can be finished as a recreation room, plus a utility and storage area.

Plan R-4033

Elegant Master Suite

- This charming traditional home offers a multitude of fine features inside an attractive and stylish exterior.
- The covered entry and vaulted foyer create an inviting atmosphere.
- The vaulted Great Room features a fireplace, a covered patio, a bar and lots of windows.
- The splendid gourmet kitchen adjoins a sunny nook on one side and the dining area of the Great Room on the other.
- The master suite boasts a reading area, a large walk-in closet and a superb bath with separate tub and shower. The tray ceiling in the master bedroom soars to a height of 9 ft., 6 inches.
- Two secondary bedrooms share another full bath and are connected by a skylighted hallway.
- A utility area is positioned in the garage entryway, conveniently near the bedrooms.

Plan S-4789

Bedrooms: 3	Baths: 2
Living Area:	
Main floor	1,665 sq. ft.
Total Living Area:	**1,665 sq. ft.**
Standard basement	1,665 sq. ft.
Garage	400 sq. ft.
Exterior Wall Framing:	2x6

Foundation Options:

Standard basement

Crawlspace

Slab

(Typical foundation & framing conversion diagram available—see order form.)

BLUEPRINT PRICE CODE:	**B**

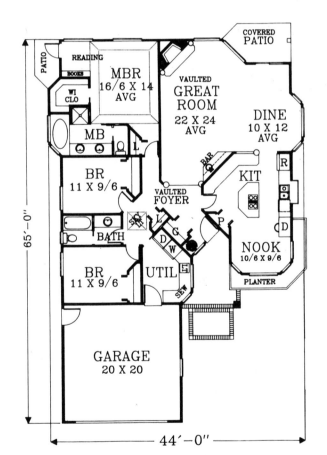

MAIN FLOOR

BASEMENT STAIRWAY LOCATION

Covered Porch Offers Three Entries

- Showy window treatments, columns and covered front and rear porches give this Southern-style home a welcoming exterior. Entry is possible through three separate front entrances.
- 12' ceilings in the living room, the dining area and the kitchen add volume to the economical 1,600+ square feet of living space.
- A corner fireplace and a rear view to the back porch are found in the living room. A counter bar separates the kitchen from the formal dining area and from the informal eating area on the opposite side.
- The private master suite offers a cathedral ceiling, a walk-in closet and a large luxury bath. Two additional bedrooms are located at the opposite end of the home and share a second bath.

Plan E-1602	
Bedrooms: 3	**Baths: 2**
Space:	
Main floor	1,672 sq. ft.
Total Living Area	**1,672 sq. ft.**
Basement	1,672 sq. ft.
Garage	484 sq. ft.
Exterior Wall Framing	2x6

Foundation options:
Standard Basement
Crawlspace
Slab
(Foundation & framing conversion diagram available—see order form.)

Blueprint Price Code	B

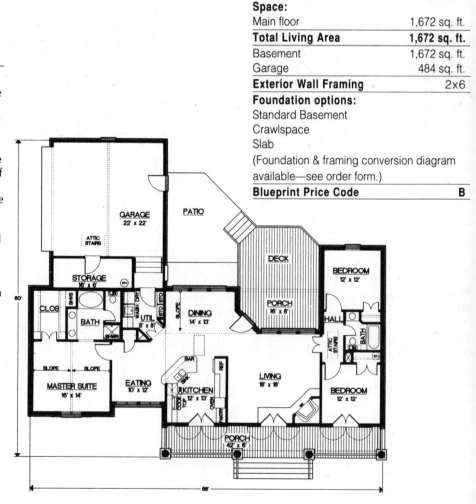

TO ORDER THIS BLUEPRINT, CALL TOLL-FREE 1-800-547-5570

Plan E-1602

PRICES AND DETAILS ON PAGES 12-15

Classic Ranch-Style

- A classic exterior facade of stone and unpainted wood distinguishes this classic ranch-style home.
- A covered front entry leads guests into a welcoming gallery. At the left is the living and dining area, with its elegant cathedral ceiling. The living room has an optional entrance to the family room via folding doors.

- The open kitchen offers an adjoining dinette, which showcases a curved wall of windows overlooking the huge backyard terrace. A screen or partition separates the dinette from the family room. The family room boasts a built-in fireplace and access to the terrace.
- To the right of the gallery lie the three bedrooms. The master suite features a skylighted dressing/vanity area, a walk-in closet and a private bath.
- The two remaining bedrooms share a convenient hall bath that features a double-sink vanity.

Plan K-162-J

Bedrooms: 3	Baths: 2

Living Area:	
Main floor	1,721 sq. ft.
Total Living Area:	**1,721 sq. ft.**
Standard basement	1,672 sq. ft.
Garage and storage	496 sq. ft.
Exterior Wall Framing:	2x4 or 2x6

Foundation Options:
Standard basement
Slab

BLUEPRINT PRICE CODE:	**B**

MAIN FLOOR

Plan K-162-J

Smart Design for Sloping Lot

- This design is perfect for a narrow, sloping lot.
- The main entry opens to a spacious, vaulted living area. A comfortable Great Room and a sunny dining area merge with corner windows that create a dramatic boxed bay. Another attention-getter is the cozy woodstove in the corner of the beautiful Great Room.
- The dining area offers sliding glass doors that extend family activities or entertaining to the adjoining deck.
- The dining area flows into the kitchen, which features a vaulted ceiling and a windowed sink that overlooks the deck.
- Two bedrooms are located at the back of the home, each with a private, skylighted bath. The master bedroom also has a walk-in wardrobe, a lovely window seat and deck access.
- A vaulted, skylighted hall leads to the stairway to the basement, where there are a third bedroom and another full bathroom. A very large shop/storage area and a two-car garage are also included. An extra bonus is the carport/storage area below the deck.

Plan P-529-2D	
Bedrooms: 3	**Baths:** 3
Living Area:	
Main floor	1,076 sq. ft.
Daylight basement	597 sq. ft.
Total Living Area:	**1,673 sq. ft.**
Tuck-under garage	425 sq. ft.
Exterior Wall Framing:	2x6
Foundation Options:	
Daylight basement	
BLUEPRINT PRICE CODE:	B

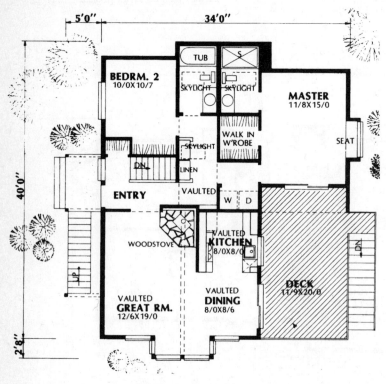

MAIN FLOOR

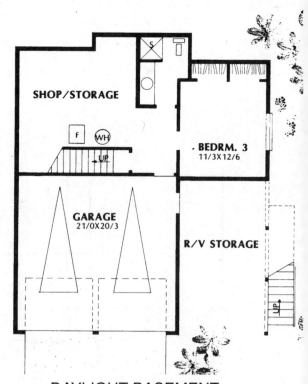

DAYLIGHT BASEMENT

Plan P-529-2D

PRICES AND DETAILS ON PAGES 12-15

FRONT VIEW

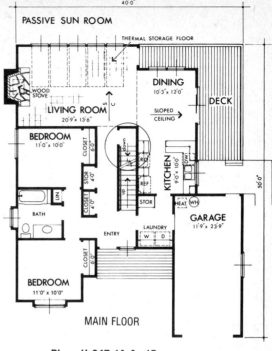

PASSIVE SUN ROOM

40'-0"

THERMAL STORAGE FLOOR

DINING
10'-3" x 12'-0"

DECK

WOOD STOVE

LIVING ROOM
20'-9" x 13'-6"

SLOPED CEILING

BEDROOM
11'-0" x 10'-0"

CLOSET 6'-0"

STOR 4'-0"

KITCHEN
9'-0" x 10'-0"

CLOSET 4'-0"

LIN

REF

STOR

HEAT WH

GARAGE
11'-9" x 23'-9"

BATH

ENTRY

LAUNDRY
W D

BEDROOM
11'-0" x 10'-0"

CLOSET 6'-0"

50'-0"

MAIN FLOOR

Sunny Family Living

- Pleasant-looking and unassuming from the front, this plan breaks into striking, sun-catching angles at the rear.
- The living room sun roof gathers passive solar heat, which is stored in the tile floor and the two-story high masonry backdrop to the wood stove.
- A 516-square-foot master suite with private bath and balcony makes up the second floor.
- The main floor offers two more bedrooms and a full bath.

PASSIVE SUN ROOM BELOW

SLOPED CEILING

BALCONY RAILING

BEDROOM
17'-3" x 13'-3"

WALK-IN CLOSET
10'-9" x 6'-6"

BATH

Shwr

UPPER FLOOR

STOR

WITHOUT BASEMENT
(CRAWLSPACE FOUNDATION)

RECREATION
20'-6" x 13'-6"

GAME AREA
10'-9" x 20'-9"

GENERAL USE
13'-0" x 14'-6"

BATH

Shwr

HEAT

WH

BASEMENT

Plans H-947-1A & -1B

Bedrooms: 3	Baths: 2-3
Space:	
Upper floor:	516 sq. ft.
Main floor:	1,162 sq. ft.
Total without basement:	1,678 sq. ft.
Daylight basement:	966 sq. ft.
Total with basement:	2,644 sq. ft.
Garage:	279 sq. ft.
Exterior Wall Framing:	2x6

Foundation options:
Daylight basement (H-947-1B).
Crawlspace (H-947-1A).
(Foundation & framing conversion diagram available — see order form.)

Blueprint Price Code:

Without basement:	B
With basement:	D

REAR VIEW

Bright, Vaulted Spaces

- The arched brick entry and the tall, arched window set the tone for the bright, vaulted spaces found within.
- A barrel-vaulted ceiling highlights the living room and adds to the striking effect of the arched window. The adjoining dining room further enhances the feeling of spaciousness.
- The kitchen is designed as an integral part of the family room and the nook. The angled counter houses the dishwasher and the sink, keeping the cook in touch with surrounding activities while providing a convenient cleanup area.
- The nook features solarium windows that flood the area with natural light. The family room has sliding glass doors opening to the backyard patio.
- The master bedroom includes a private, skylighted bath and a walk-in closet. Another bath lies between the two smaller bedrooms.

Plan R-1067

Bedrooms: 3	Baths: 2
Living Area:	
Main floor	1,685 sq. ft.
Total Living Area:	**1,685 sq. ft.**
Garage	432 sq. ft.
Exterior Wall Framing:	2x6

Foundation Options:

Crawlspace
(Typical foundation & framing conversion diagram available—see order form.)

BLUEPRINT PRICE CODE: **B**

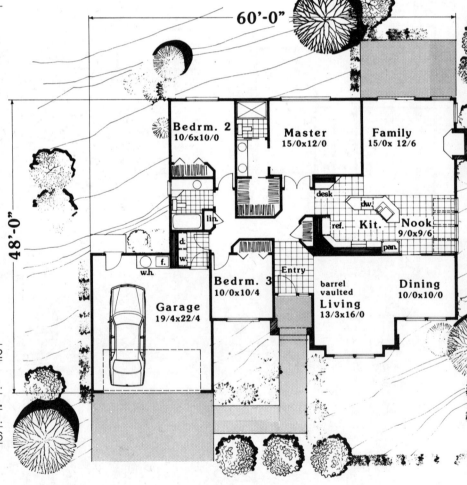

MAIN FLOOR

Two-Story with Victorian Touch

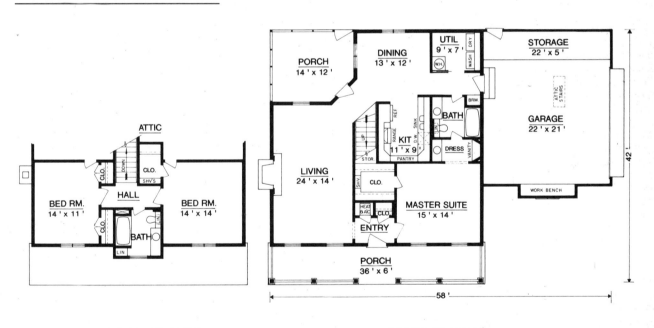

UPPER FLOOR

MAIN FLOOR

Living area:	1,686 sq. ft.
Porches:	393 sq. ft.
Garage & storage:	592 sq. ft.
Total area:	2,671 sq. ft.

Specify crawlspace or slab foundation.
Exterior walls are energy-efficient 2x6 construction.

Blueprint Price Code B

Plan E-1631

Southern Styling

- Classic Southern plantation styling is recreated with a full width covered front porch, triple roof dormers and stucco exterior.
- Once inside, the interior feels open, airy and bright with the living room merging into the dining room, both overlooked by the kitchen's serving and entertaining wet bar.
- The living room features a fireplace and three pairs of French doors.
- The dining room has rear access to a covered porch, connecting the two-car garage to the house.
- The main-floor master suite has two pairs of French doors leading to the front porch. The master bath includes a raised marble tub, sloped ceiling with skylight, and a walk-in closet.
- There are two bedrooms upstairs which share a second full bath and each feature a quaint dormer to let the light shine in.

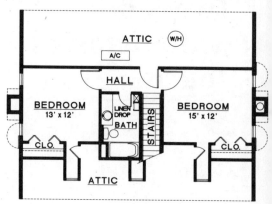

UPPER FLOOR

MAIN FLOOR

Plan E-1709

Bedrooms: 3	**Baths:** 2 ½

Space:

Upper floor	540 sq. ft.
Main floor	1,160 sq. ft.
Total Living Area	**1,700 sq. ft.**
Basement	1,160 sq. ft.
Garage	484 sq. ft.
Exterior Wall Framing	2x6

Foundation options:

Standard Basement
Crawlspace
Slab
(Foundation & framing conversion diagram available—see order form.)

Blueprint Price Code	**B**

TO ORDER THIS BLUEPRINT,
CALL TOLL-FREE 1-800-547-5570

Plan E-1709

PRICES AND DETAILS
ON PAGES 12-15

Panoramic Prow View

- A glass-filled prow gable design is almost as spectacular as the panoramic view from inside. The two-story window-wall floods the living room with light and views.
- The open-feeling corner kitchen has the right angle to enjoy the dining room and the family room, including views of the front and rear decks.

- Two main level bedrooms share a full bath.
- The entire upper floor is a private master bedroom suite with large bath, dressing area and balcony opening to the two-story glass wall, a real "good morning" view.

Plan NW-196	
Bedrooms: 3	**Baths:** 2

Space:	
Upper floor	394 sq. ft.
Main floor:	1,317 sq. ft.

Total living area:	1,711 sq. ft.

Exterior Wall Framing:	2x6

Foundation options:
Crawlspace.
(Foundation & framing conversion diagram available — see order form.)

Blueprint Price Code:	B

MAIN FLOOR

48'-0"

32'-0"

Deck   DN

Br #2
11-6 x 11

Br #3
11 x 11-3

Util.

Family
15-4 x 13-6

DN
UP

Living Rm.
25-8 x 14-6

Dining
12 x 10-6

Kit.

DN

Deck

UPPER FLOOR

M.Br
16-6 x 13-5

DN

OPEN TO BELOW

Panoramic View Embraces Outdoors

- This geometric design takes full advantage of scenic sites.
- Living area faces a glass-filled wall and wrap-around deck.
- Open dining/living room arrangement is complemented by vaulted ceilings, an overhead balcony, and a 5-ft-wide fireplace.
- 12' deep main deck offers generous space for outdoor dining and entertaining.

PLAN H-855-1A
WITHOUT BASEMENT

SCALE
20'   10' 9 8 7 6 5 4 3 2 1 0

UPPER FLOOR

BEDROOM
11'-4" x 13'-6"

BEDROOM
10'-0" x 15'-0"

BATH
8'-6" x 7'-6"

CLOSET
5'-2"

STOR

CLOSET
4'-6"

CLOSET
4'-6"

LINEN

BALCONY

down

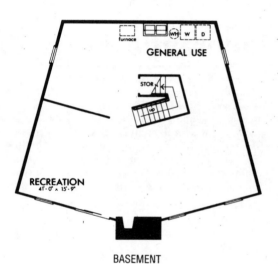

GENERAL USE

furnace   WH   W   D

STOR

RECREATION
41'-0" x 15'-9"

BASEMENT

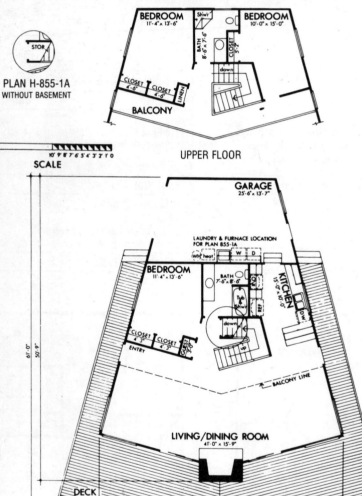

GARAGE
25'-6" x 13'-7"

LAUNDRY & FURNACE LOCATION
FOR PLAN 855-1A

WH heat   W   D

BEDROOM
11'-4" x 13'-6"

BATH
7'-6" x 8'-6"

KITCHEN
15'-0" x 10'-0"

CLOSET
3'

CLOSET
4'-6"

CLOSET

ENTRY

down

up

BALCONY LINE

LIVING/DINING ROOM
41'-0" x 15'-9"

DECK

50'-9"   61'-0"

42'-0"

56'-0"

MAIN FLOOR

Plans H-855-1 & -1A

Bedrooms: 3	Baths: 2

Space:

Upper floor:	625 sq. ft.
Main floor:	1,108 sq. ft.

Total living area:	**1,733 sq. ft.**
Basement:	approx. 1,108 sq. ft.
Garage:	346 sq. ft.

Exterior Wall Framing:	2x6

Foundation options:
Daylight basement (Plan H-855-1).
Crawlspace (Plan H-855-1A).
(Foundation & framing conversion diagram available — see order form.)

Blueprint Price Code:

Without basement	B
With basement	D

TO ORDER THIS BLUEPRINT,
CALL TOLL-FREE 1-800-547-5570

Plans H-855-1 & -1A

PRICES AND DETAILS
ON PAGES 12-15

Elevation B

Elevation A

Traditional Twosome

- This plan offers a choice of two elevations. Elevation A has an upper-level Palladian window, while Elevation B has a stately Georgian entry. Both versions are included in the blueprints.
- A vaulted entry foyer leads to formal living and dining rooms.
- The family room, nook and kitchen are combined to create one huge casual living area.
- The second-floor master suite is roomy and includes a beautiful, skylighted bath and a large closet.

Plan S-22189

Bedrooms: 3	Baths: 2½
Living Area:	
Upper floor	774 sq. ft.
Main floor	963 sq. ft.
Total Living Area:	**1,737 sq. ft.**
Standard basement	963 sq. ft.
Garage	462 sq. ft.
Exterior Wall Framing:	2x6

Foundation Options:
Standard basement
Crawlspace
Slab
(Typical foundation & framing conversion diagram available—see order form.)

BLUEPRINT PRICE CODE: **B**

UPPER FLOOR

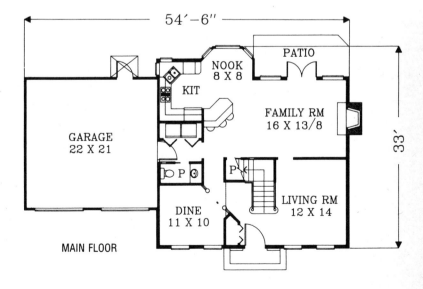

MAIN FLOOR

Colonial Has Modern Features

- This stately Colonial is as distinguished on the inside as it is on the outside.
- The dramatic entrance reveals a spacious living room with a big fireplace and a front bay window and an adjoining family room separated only by a decorative see-through wood divider. A sloped ceiling and French doors to the rear terrace are highlights in the family room.
- The high-tech kitchen has an island work area, a pantry, a handy laundry closet and a sunny, circular dinette.
- Featured in the private main-floor master suite is a cathedral ceiling and a private terrace accessed through French doors. A walk-in closet and a personal bath with whirlpool tub are other extras.
- Three other bedrooms share the upper level, which also offers a balcony that views the family room below.

Plan AHP-9121

Bedrooms: 4	Baths: 2 ½
Space:	
Upper floor	557 sq. ft.
Main floor	1,183 sq. ft.
Total Living Area	**1,740 sq. ft.**
Basement	1,183 sq. ft.
Garage	440 sq. ft.
Exterior Wall Framing	2x4 or 2x6

Foundation options:

Standard Basement

Crawlspace

Slab

(Foundation & framing conversion diagram available—see order form.)

Blueprint Price Code   B

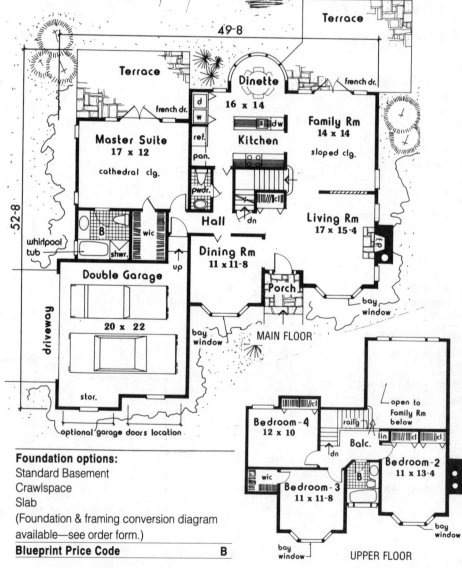

K-645-PB (Four-Bedroom Plan)

Total living area: 1,752 sq. ft.

Basement plan included in blueprints

K-645-PA (Three-Bedroom Plan)

Total living area: 1,548 sq. ft.

Flexible Design

This distinctive contemporary ranch offers a three-bedroom or a four-bedroom version of a nearly identical basic plan. Natural stone and wood finish generates an exterior appeal and requires little maintenance. Double doors at the entry open onto a wide reception hall and a stunning view of the rear garden.

A dramatic cathedral ceiling crowns the living room and the family room/kitchen area. The living room features a woodburning fireplace amid a glass wall. Overlooking the backyard is the informal area; the family room is graced with operable skylights and a second fireplace. An efficient kitchen serves both the cheerful dinette and the formal dining room.

The privately zoned sleeping wing comes with either three bedrooms or four bedrooms. The master bedroom suite boasts a private terrace, ample closet space and a full bath. Living area is 1,548 sq. ft. for the three-bedroom and 1,752 sq. ft. for the four. Garage, mud room, etc., total 563 sq. ft.

The home features 2x6 exterior walls for energy efficiency.

Blueprint Price Code B

Panoramic Rear View

- This rustic but elegant country home offers an open, airy interior.
- At the center of the floor plan is a spacious living room with a sloped ceiling, fireplace and an all-glass circular wall giving a panoramic view of the backyard.
- The adjoining dining room shares the sloped ceiling and offers sliders to the rear terrace.
- The bright kitchen has a large window, an optional skylight and a counter bar that separates it from the bayed dinette.
- The bedroom wing includes two secondary bedrooms and a large, bayed master bedroom with dual walk-in closets and a private bath with a sloped ceiling and a garden whirlpool tub.

VIEW OF LIVING AND DINING ROOMS.

Plan K-685-DA

Bedrooms: 3	Baths: 2 ½
Space:	
Main floor	1,760 sq. ft.
Total Living Area	**1,760 sq. ft.**
Basement	1,700 sq. ft.
Garage	482 sq. ft.
Exterior Wall Framing	2x4 or 2x6

Foundation options:

Standard Basement

Slab

(Foundation & framing conversion diagram available—see order form.)

Blueprint Price Code	B

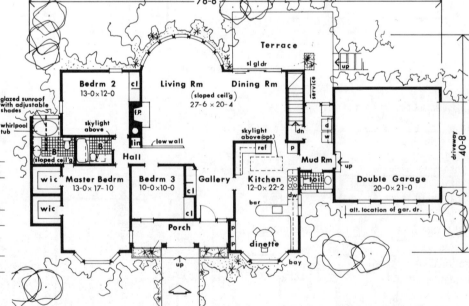

Plan K-685-DA

PRICES AND DETAILS
ON PAGES 12-15

FRONT VIEW

Sun Lovers' Hideaway

- Attractive, cozy and sunny are only three adjectives that come immediately to mind as one looks at this plan. Energy efficiency is also a major element.
- An air-lock entry helps seal heated or cooled air inside, and the home is well-insulated in walls, ceilings and floors for tight control of energy bills.
- The major portion of the main floor is devoted to a spacious living/dining/kitchen area with easy access to the large sun room.
- Two downstairs bedrooms share a full bath and include large double-glazed windows.
- Upstairs, the master suite features a private bath and large closet, plus a balcony overlook into the living room.
- An optional daylight basement offers potential for an additional bedroom as well as a large recreation room and general use area. In this version, the sun room is on the lower level, and a dramatic spiral staircase ascends to the main floor.

UPPER FLOOR

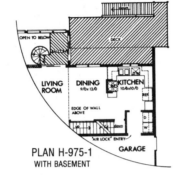

PLAN H-975-1
WITH BASEMENT

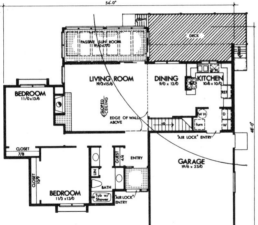

MAIN FLOOR
PLAN H-975-1A
WITHOUT BASEMENT

BASEMENT

Plans H-975-1 & -1A

Bedrooms: 3		**Baths:** 2

Space:

Upper floor	370 sq. ft.
Main floor	
(including sun room)	1,394 sq. ft.
Optional daylight basement	1,394 sq. ft.
Finished (including sun room)	782 sq. ft.
Unfinished	612 sq. ft.
Total Living Area	**1,764/2,546 sq. ft.**
Garage	448 sq. ft.
Exterior Wall Framing	**2x6**

Foundation options:	**Plan #**
Daylight Basement	H-975-1
Crawlspace	H-975-1A
(Foundation & framing conversion diagram available—see order form.)	
Blueprint Price Code	**B/D**

REAR VIEW

Ground-Hugging Design

- A clean-lined roof with wide overhangs blends this home into the landscape, and a low-walled entrance court adds to the effect.
- Inside, you'll find many sunny surprises, including bow windows in the living and dining rooms, a beautiful kitchen and a bright semi-circular dinette area.
- The large family room features a fireplace and cathedral ceiling.

- The master suite includes a private bath, large walk-in closet and a skylit dressing area.

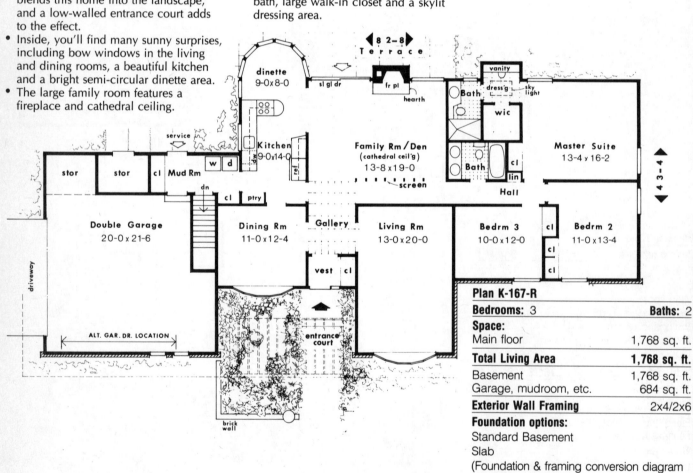

Plan K-167-R

Bedrooms: 3	Baths: 2
Space:	
Main floor	1,768 sq. ft.
Total Living Area	**1,768 sq. ft.**
Basement	1,768 sq. ft.
Garage, mudroom, etc.	684 sq. ft.
Exterior Wall Framing	2x4/2x6

Foundation options:
Standard Basement
Slab
(Foundation & framing conversion diagram available—see order form.)

Blueprint Price Code	B

TO ORDER THIS BLUEPRINT, CALL TOLL-FREE 1-800-547-5570

Plan K-167-R

PRICES AND DETAILS ON PAGES 12-15

Compact and Luxurious

- The best from the past and the present is bundled up in this compact design, reminiscent of a New England saltbox.
- The cozy kitchen has a center island with a breakfast counter and a built-in range and oven. The corner sink saves on counter space.
- A decorative railing separates the formal dining room from the sunken living room.
- The living room features a vaulted ceiling, built-in shelves, a central fireplace and access to a large rear deck.
- The upper-floor master suite boasts a spa bath, a separate shower and a walk-in closet.

Plan H-1453-1A

Bedrooms: 3	Baths: 2
Living Area:	
Upper floor	386 sq. ft.
Main floor	1,385 sq. ft.
Total Living Area:	**1,771 sq. ft.**
Garage	409 sq. ft.
Exterior Wall Framing:	2x6

Foundation Options:

Crawlspace

(Typical foundation & framing conversion diagram available—see order form.)

BLUEPRINT PRICE CODE: B

UPPER FLOOR

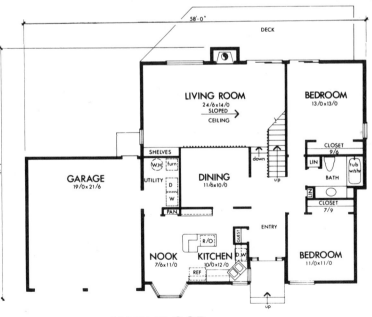

MAIN FLOOR

Dramatic Visual Impact

Rich brick accents this unique hillside home. The family room is sequestered on the lower level for informal, relaxed living and is overlooked not only by the nook and entry but the stairway landing above as well. The added height creates a dramatic visual impact and opens up the core of the house.

The landing itself presents an unusual decorating opportunity. It is light and spacious enough for plants, handsome book shelves, or perhaps your own art collection!

Upstairs, double doors lead into a spacious master suite getaway featuring a large walk-in closet.

This design features 2x6 exterior walls for energy efficiency.

Main floor:	1,048 sq. ft.
Upper floor:	726 sq. ft.
Total living area:	1,774 sq. ft.
(Not counting garage)	

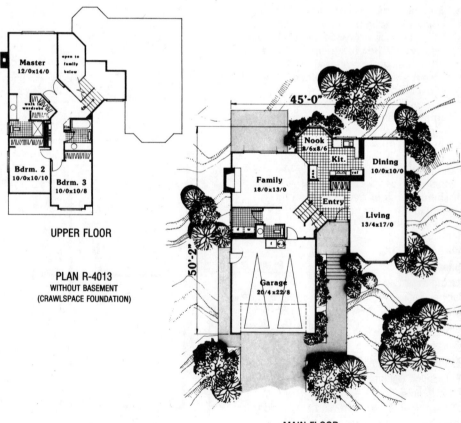

UPPER FLOOR

PLAN R-4013
WITHOUT BASEMENT
(CRAWLSPACE FOUNDATION)

MAIN FLOOR

Blueprint Price Code B
Plan R-4013

PRICES AND DETAILS
ON PAGES 12-15

Country Serenity

- The full porch gives a nice country look and homey feel to this 1,781 square foot, two-story home.
- A spacious Great Room awaits guests to the right of the entry, highlighted by a fireplace and three walls of windows.
- The kitchen is well-placed between the formal dining room, the informal breakfast eating area, and the laundry/mud room with garage access.
- The upper floor houses three bedrooms and two full baths.
- The master bedroom offers a sitting area and two options for the master bath and walk-in closet arrangement, one incorporating a separate tub and shower.

Plan GL-1781

Bedrooms: 3	Baths: 2 ½
Space:	
Upper floor	837 sq. ft.
Main floor	944 sq. ft.
Total Living Area	**1,781 sq. ft.**
Basement	944 sq. ft.
Garage	400 sq. ft.
Exterior Wall Framing	**2x6**

Foundation options:

Standard Basement

(Foundation & framing conversion diagram available—see order form.)

Blueprint Price Code	**B**

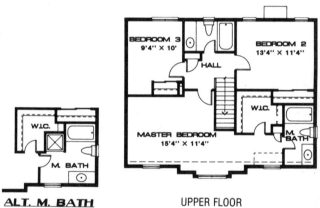

ALT. M. BATH

UPPER FLOOR

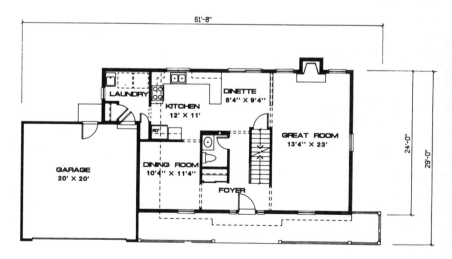

MAIN FLOOR

High in Style

Not only does this home score high in curb appeal, with its tall arched windows, brick accents and repeating gables, but it also gets high marks for a layout with outstanding livability.

The kitchen is a pure delight. No need to worry about storage space with its abundant cabinetry and built-in pantry. The cook in the family will love the sink placement with a view to the family/nook area and the outdoors beyond.

There are no dark corners in this house — heightened windows highlight the vaulted living and dining room. Together with the window above the entryway, they create a bright and cheerful interior.

The home also features energy-efficient construction, with 2x6 exterior walls.

Total living area: 1,793 sq. ft.
(Not counting garage)

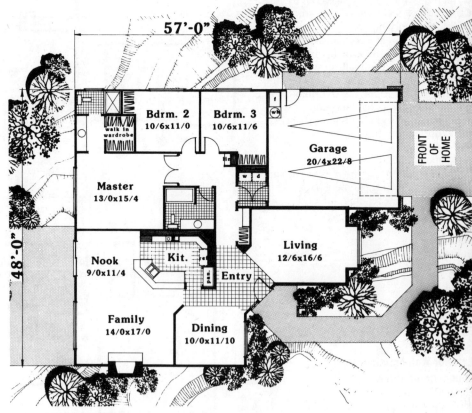

57'-0"

48'-0"

Bdrm. 2
10/6x11/0

Bdrm. 3
10/6x11/6

Garage
20/4x22/8

FRONT OF HOME

Master
13/0x15/4

walk in wardrobe

Living
12/6x16/6

Nook
9/0x11/4

Kit.

Entry

Family
14/0x17/0

Dining
10/0x11/10

PLAN R-1023
WITHOUT BASEMENT
(CRAWLSPACE FOUNDATION)

Blueprint Price Code B

Plan R-1023

TO ORDER THIS BLUEPRINT,
CALL TOLL-FREE 1-800-547-5570

PRICES AND DETAILS
ON PAGES 12-15

Fresh New Interior with an Old Favorite Exterior

This Louisiana-style raised cottage features a separate master suite with a connecting showplace bathroom fit for the most demanding taste.

Pairs of French doors in each of the front rooms invite family members and visitors to enjoy the cool and relaxing front porch. The tin roof adds to the comfort and nostalgic appeal of this Creole classic. An unusual, angled eating bar overlooks the cozy covered terrance via a bay window morning room.

The secondary bedroom wing has two full-size bedrooms, maximum closets, and a full-size bath.

This full-feature energy-efficient design is drawn on a raised crawlspace foundation. An alternate concrete slab foundation is available.

PLAN E-1823
WITHOUT BASEMENT

Areas:

Heated:	1,800 sq. ft.
Unheated:	1,100 sq. ft.
Total area:	2,900 sq. ft.

Exterior walls are 2x6 construction.
Specify crawlspace or slab foundation.

Blueprint Price Code B
Plan E-1823

PRICES AND DETAILS
ON PAGES 12-15

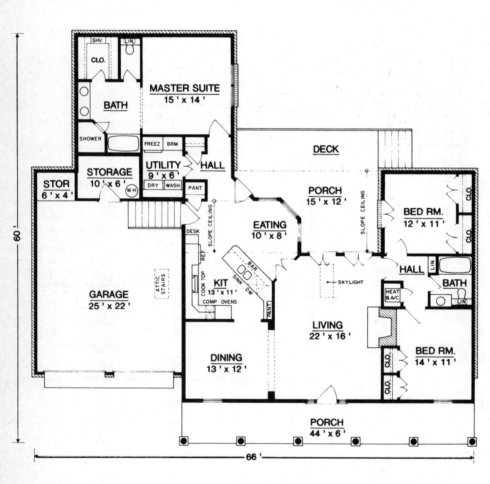

Raised Cottage Design Offers Large Covered Porches

- Twin dormers and covered porch add drama to this raised one-story.
- Large centered living room features 12' ceilings and built-in skylights.
- Kitchen has unusual but functional angular design, sloped ceilings, bar, and eating area that overlooks the adjoining deck.
- Elegant master suite is conveniently located near kitchen.

Plan E-1826

Bedrooms: 3	Baths: 2

Space:	
Total living area:	1,800 sq. ft.
Garage:	550 sq. ft.
Storage:	84 sq. ft.
Porches:	466 sq. ft.

Exterior Wall Framing:	2x6

Foundation options:
Crawlspace.
Slab.
(Foundation & framing conversion diagram available — see order form.)

Blueprint Price Code:	B

A Present From the Past

- A covered front porch with Victorian trim and an exterior with half-round windows and classic, high-pitched gables give today's homebuyers a present from the past.
- Arriving guests enjoy an open view into the Great Room with fireplace and the formal dining room with window wall.
- The kitchen incorporates a breakfast bay with rear access and adjacent laundry room.
- Up the double-stairs, lit by a round-top window, are three bedrooms and two full baths.
- All of the main-floor rooms are enhanced by 10-ft. ceilings. The upper floor has standard 8-ft. ceilings.

Plan V-1803

Bedrooms: 3	Baths: 2½
Living Area:	
Upper floor	875 sq. ft.
Main floor	928 sq. ft.
Total Living Area:	**1,803 sq. ft.**
Exterior Wall Framing:	2x6

Foundation Options:
Crawlspace
(Typical foundation & framing conversion diagram available—see order form.)

BLUEPRINT PRICE CODE:	B

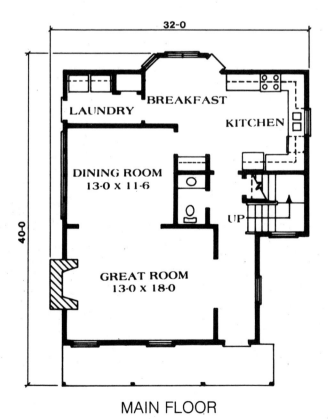

MAIN FLOOR

UPPER FLOOR

Great Value

"Lots of house for the money" is what you get with this practical plan. It efficiently utilizes every inch of space to make it a real winner. Features include a formal living room, formal dining room, kitchen with a 4-person bar, family room, master suite with a large dressing area sporting a tub and shower, two additional bedrooms and a den that doubles as a fourth bedroom.

The traffic flow is very convenient, with the sleeping rooms at one end, the work and family areas at the other, and the formal entertaining area in the middle. With the addition of two 6' x 12' sunrooms on the south side, it will score high in solar efficiency also.

This truly is a spacious house for gracious living, captured in only 1,819 sq. ft. With the traditional northwest styling that is so attractive, this house will be a good value for years to come.

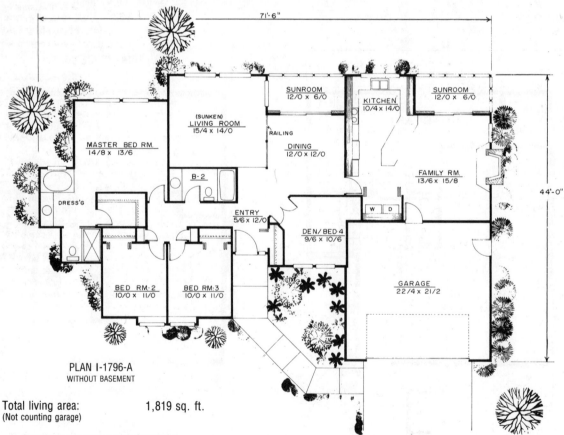

PLAN I-1796-A
WITHOUT BASEMENT

Total living area: 1,819 sq. ft.
(Not counting garage)

Specify crawlspace or slab foundation.

Blueprint Price Code B

Plan I-1796-A

PRICES AND DETAILS ON PAGES 12-15

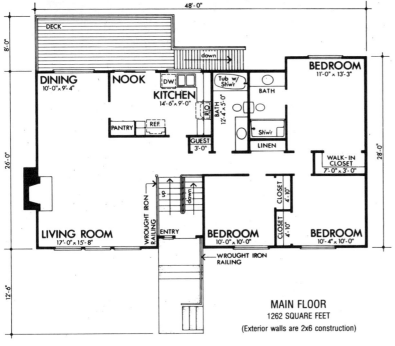

DECK

48'-0"

8'-0"

DINING
10'-0" x 9'-4"

NOOK

DW

down

KITCHEN
14'-6" x 9'-0"

Tub w/
Sh'wr

BATH

BEDROOM
11'-0" x 13'-3"

PANTRY   REF.

GUEST
3'-0"

BATH
12'-4" x 5'-0"

Sh'wr

LINEN

26'-0"

28'-0"

WALK-IN
CLOSET
7'-0" x 3'-0"

12'-6"

LIVING ROOM
17'-0" x 15'-8"

WROUGHT IRON RAILING

up

down

ENTRY

BEDROOM
10'-0" x 10'-0"

CLOSET
4'-10"

CLOSET
4'-10"

BEDROOM
10'-4" x 10'-0"

WROUGHT IRON RAILING

MAIN FLOOR
1262 SQUARE FEET
(Exterior walls are 2x6 construction)

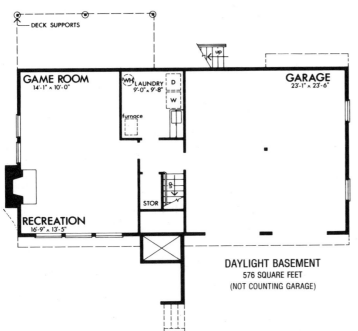

DECK SUPPORTS

GAME ROOM
14'-1" x 10'-0"

WH

LAUNDRY
9'-0" x 9'-8"

D

W

GARAGE
23'-1" x 23'-6"

up

furnace

up

STOR

RECREATION
16'-9" x 13'-5"

DAYLIGHT BASEMENT
576 SQUARE FEET
(NOT COUNTING GARAGE)

Economical Hillside Design

The solid, expansive, well-to-do appearance of this home plan belies the fact that it contains only 1,262 sq. ft. on the main floor and 1,152 sq. ft. on the lower level, including garage space.

This plan has a simple framing pattern, rectangular shape and straight roof line, and it lacks complicated embellishments. Even the excavation, only half as deep as usual, helps make this an affordable and relatively quick and easy house to build.

A split-level entry opens onto a landing between floors, providing access up to the main living room or down to the recreation and work areas.

The living space is large and open. The dining and living rooms combine with the stairwell to form a large visual space. A large 8'x20' deck, visible through the picture window in the dining room, adds visual expansiveness to this multi-purpose space.

The L-shaped kitchen and adjoining nook are perfect for daily food preparation and family meals, and the deck is also accessible from this area through sliding glass doors. The kitchen features a 48 cubic foot pantry closet.

The master bedroom has a complete private bathroom and oversized closet. The remaining bedrooms each have a large closet and access to a full-size bathroom.

A huge rec and game room is easily accessible from the entry, making it ideal for a home office or business.

Main floor:	1,262 sq. ft.
Lower level:	576 sq. ft.
Total living area:	1,838 sq. ft.

(Not counting garage)

Blueprint Price Code B

Plan H-1332-5

Unique Inside and Out

- This delightful design is as striking on the inside as it is on the outside.
- The focal point of the home is the huge Grand Room, which features a vaulted ceiling, plant shelves and lots of glass, including a clerestory window. French doors flanking the fireplace lead to the covered porch and the two adjoining sun decks.
- The centrally located kitchen offers easy access from any room in the house, and a full bath, a laundry area and the garage entrance are nearby.
- The two main-floor master suites are another unique design element of the home. Both of the suites showcase a volume ceiling, a sunny window seat, a walk-in closet, a private bath and French doors that open to a sun deck.
- Upstairs, two guest suites overlook the vaulted Grand Room below.

Plan EOF-13

Bedrooms: 4	Baths: 3
Living Area:	
Upper floor	443 sq. ft.
Main floor	1,411 sq. ft.
Total Living Area:	**1,854 sq. ft.**
Garage	264 sq. ft.
Storage	50 sq. ft.
Exterior Wall Framing:	2x6

Foundation Options:

Crawlspace

(Typical foundation & framing conversion diagram available—see order form.)

BLUEPRINT PRICE CODE:	B

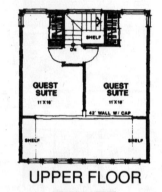

UPPER FLOOR

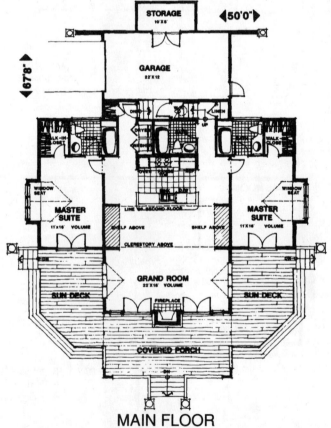

MAIN FLOOR

FRONT ELEVATION

Popular Ranch With Sun Room

This 1,859 sq. ft. ranch design features large areas of glass in the master suite and kitchen, and a sun room accessible from both the family room and breakfast room. A recessed entry and a limited amount of glass on the north wall help keep the warm air in during the winter, and over-heating during the summer months is prevented by eliminating glass from the east and west walls.

The master suite features a walk-in closet and a compartmentalized bath with linen closet, a second walk-in closet and a dressing area with double vanity. One of the two front bedrooms has a double closet and direct access to a second full bath and the other has a walk-in closet. A centrally located utility closet and two hall closets complete the left wing.

Separating the sunken living room and the foyer area is a massive stone fireplace. A formal dining room can be entered from either the living room or the kitchen. The U-shaped kitchen has a bar counter open to the breakfast area. A mud room with coat closet and access to the garage acts as a buffer from northwestern winter winds. Specify crawlspace, basement or slab foundation when ordering.

Total living area: 1,859 sq. ft.
(Not counting basement or garage)

SOUTH ELEVATION

FLOOR PLAN

67' 2"

50' 0"

SUN ROOM

PATIO

BREAKFAST

KITCHEN

MASTER BEDROOM

DRESS

LIVING ROOM

BATH

DINING

FOYER

BEDROOM

BEDROOM

GARAGE

Attainable Luxury

- This traditional ranch home offers a large, central living room with a volume ceiling, a corner fireplace and an adjoining patio.
- The U-shaped kitchen easily services both the formal dining room and the bayed eating area.
- The luxurious master suite features a large bath with separate vanities and dressing areas.
- A covered carport boasts a decorative brick wall, attic space above and two additional storage areas.

Plan E-1812

Bedrooms: 3	Baths: 2
Living Area:	
Main floor	1,860 sq. ft.
Total Living Area:	**1,860 sq. ft.**
Carport	484 sq. ft.
Exterior Wall Framing:	2x6

Foundation Options:
Crawlspace
Slab
(Typical foundation & framing conversion diagram available—see order form.)

BLUEPRINT PRICE CODE: B

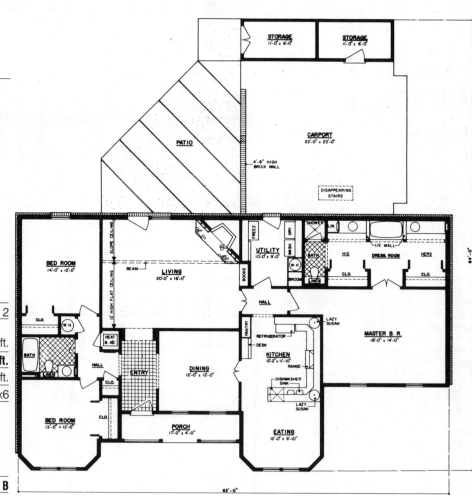

MAIN FLOOR

TO ORDER THIS BLUEPRINT, CALL TOLL-FREE 1-800-547-5570

Plan E-1812

PRICES AND DETAILS ON PAGES 12-15

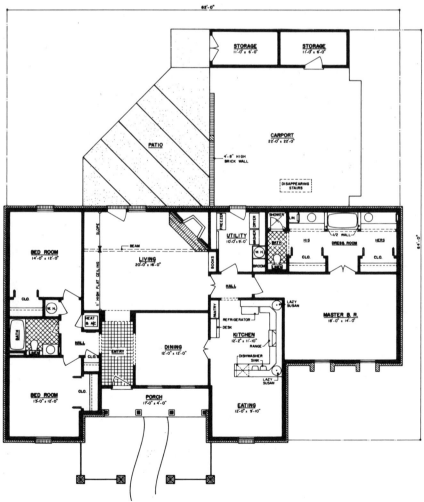

Impressive Master Bedroom Suite

- **This updated ranch features an impressive master bedroom with separate dressing areas and closets.**
- **A lovely front porch opens into a formal dining room and rear-oriented living room with fireplace and attached patio.**
- **A roomy kitchen and eating area provide plenty of space for work and casual living.**

Plan E-1818

Bedrooms: 3	Baths: 2
Space: Main floor:	1,868 sq. ft.
Total living area:	1,868 sq. ft.
Carport:	484 sq. ft.
Exterior Wall Framing:	2x6

Foundation options:
Crawlspace.
Slab.
(Foundation & framing conversion diagram available — see order form.)

Blueprint Price Code:	B

Great Bedroom/Bath Combination

- Dining room has view of entry and living room through surrounding arched openings.
- Living room features 12' ceilings, fireplace, and a view to the outdoor patio.
- Kitchen has attached eating area with sloped ceilings.
- Tray ceiling adorns the master suite; attached bath has skylight and marble enclosed tub.

Plan E-1830

Bedrooms: 3	Baths: 2
Space:	
Total living area:	1,868 sq. ft.
Garage and storage:	616 sq. ft.
Porch:	68 sq. ft.
Exterior Wall Framing:	2x6

Foundation options:
Crawlspace.
Slab.
(Foundation & framing conversion diagram available — see order form.)

Blueprint Price Code:	B

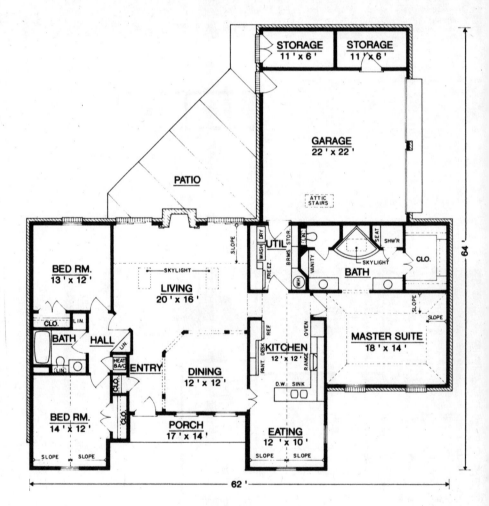

Octagonal Dining Bay

- Classic traditional styling is recreated with a covered front porch and triple dormers with half-round windows.
- Once inside, the interior feels open, airy and bright.
- The living room with fireplace leads into the formal dining room with octagonal bay windows.
- The island kitchen overlooks the breakfast bay and family room with second fireplace and sliders to the rear deck.
- A skylit hallway connects the four upstairs bedrooms and two full baths.

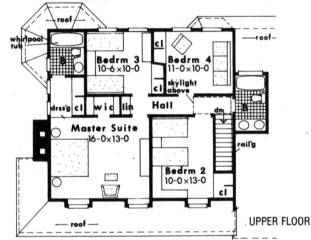

UPPER FLOOR

Bedrm 3 10-6 ×10-0
Bedrm 4 11-0 ×10-0
whirlpool tub
skylight above
drss'g cl wic lin Hall
Master Suite 16-0×13-0
Bedrm 2 10-0×13-0
rail'g

Plan K-680-R

Bedrooms: 4	Baths: 2½
Space:	
Upper floor	853 sq. ft.
Main floor	1,015 sq. ft.
Total Living Area	**1,868 sq. ft.**
Basement	1,015 sq. ft.
Garage & Mud Room	504 sq. ft.
Exterior Wall Framing	2x4 or 2x6

Foundation options:
Standard Basement
Slab
(Foundation & framing conversion diagram available—see order form.)

Blueprint Price Code	B

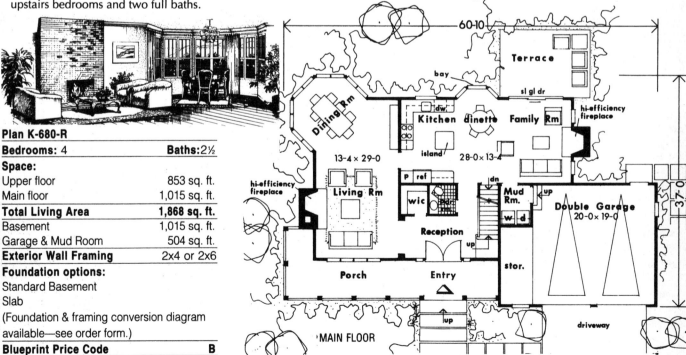

MAIN FLOOR

60-10
Terrace
bay
sl gl dr
hi-efficiency fireplace
Dining Rm
Kitchen dinette Family Rm
13-4 × 29-0
island 28-0×13-4
hi-efficiency fireplace
Living Rm
P ref
wic
dn
Mud Rm.
up
Double Garage 20-0 × 19-0
Reception
w d
up
stor.
37-0
Porch Entry
up
driveway

Roomy, Rustic Split-Level

- Horizontal wood siding, cedar shakes and paned-glass windows add rustic charm and appeal to this split-level plan, which is perfect for a sloping lot.
- The vaulted entry gives way to a majestic sunken living room with a vaulted ceiling and an intriguing boxed-out front window.
- The adjacent dining room provides a picturesque view of the backyard and easy access to the kitchen.
- A windowed sink and a serving bar are included in the kitchen's design. A vaulted nook overlooks the backyard and is separated from the family room by an open railing.
- The family room shows off a handsome fireplace and sliding glass doors that access the backyard patio.
- On the upper floor are three bedrooms and two baths. The master bedroom is entered through elegant double doors and has a private, skylighted bath with a spa tub and a separate shower.
- The secondary bedrooms, each with boxed-out windows, share a hall bath.

Plan P-7717-2A

Bedrooms: 3	Baths: 2½
Living Area:	
Upper floor	780 sq. ft.
Main floor	1,096 sq. ft.
Total Living Area:	**1,876 sq. ft.**
Garage	452 sq. ft.
Exterior Wall Framing:	2x6
Foundation Options:	
Crawlspace	
BLUEPRINT PRICE CODE:	B

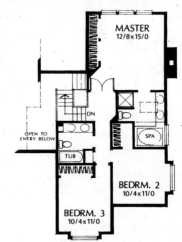

UPPER FLOOR

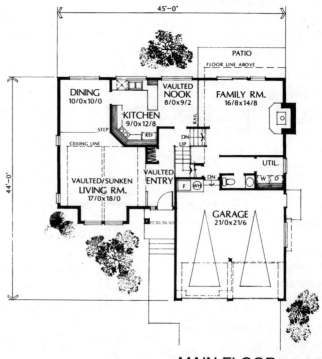

MAIN FLOOR

P-524-5D Exterior

P-524-2D Exterior

Spacious Great Room

- This same floor plan is available with two different exterior treatments, as illustrated.
- In either case, a spacious Great Room is the highlight, with its vaulted ceiling, wide windows and sliding glass doors which open to a deck, and to the view beyond.
- The dining room and kitchen also feature vaulted ceilings.
- A loft room adds another sleeping area, and the daylight basement offers even more usable space.

36'0" **10'0"**

CLERESTORY ABOVE LOFT

LOFT
19/2X8/0

LOFT
160 SQUARE FEET

BEDRM. 2
10/0X12/5

TUB

BATH

LIN

VAULTED KITCHEN
8/0X9/0

VAULTED DINING

7/0 HIGH WALL

28'0"

DECK

VAULTED GREAT RM.
15/4X27/0

BEDRM. 1
13/5X14/2

WOODSTOVE

SEAT

DN

MAIN FLOOR
1008 SQUARE FEET

(Both versions include daylight basement)

WH

W

D

F

UTILITY

GARAGE
22/0X13/0

STOR

SHOP/STORAGE
12/3X26/4

RECREATION/ BEDRM. 3
13/0X13/0

PATIO

DECK ABOVE

BASEMENT
FLOOR AREA 722 SQUARE FEET
(Not counting garage)

Plans P-524-2D & -5D

Bedrooms: 2+	**Baths:** 1

Space:	
Loft:	160 sq. ft.
Main floor:	1,008 sq. ft.
Lower level:	722 sq. ft.

Total living area:	1,890 sq. ft.
Garage:	286 sq. ft.

Exterior Wall Framing:	2x6

Foundation options:
Daylight basement.
(Foundation & framing conversion diagram available — see order form.)

Blueprint Price Code:	B

TO ORDER THIS BLUEPRINT,
CALL TOLL-FREE 1-800-547-5570

Plans P-524-2D & -5D

PRICES AND DETAILS
ON PAGES 12-15

111

Country-Style Home with Welcoming Appeal

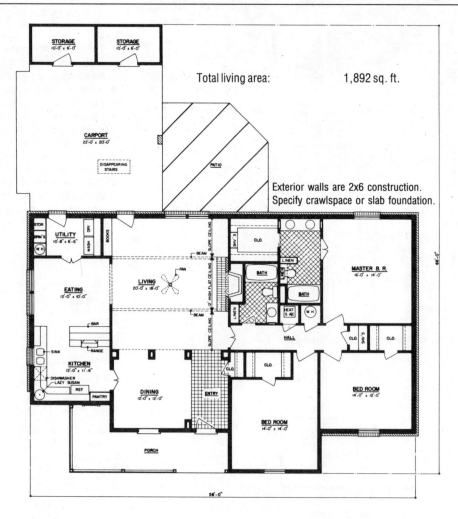

Total living area: 1,892 sq. ft.

Exterior walls are 2x6 construction.
Specify crawlspace or slab foundation.

Blueprint Price Code B

Plan E-1813

Playful Floor Plan

- High, hipped roofs and a recessed entry give this home a smart-looking exterior. A dynamic floor plan – punctuated with angled walls, high ceilings and playful window treatments – gives the home an exciting interior.
- The sunken and vaulted Great Room, the circular dining room and the angled island kitchen are the heartbeat of the home. The Great Room offers a fireplace, a built-in corner entertainment center and tall arched windows overlooking the backyard.

- An angled railing separates the Great Room from the open kitchen and dining room. An atrium door next to the glassed-in dining area opens to the backyard. The kitchen includes an island snack bar and a garden window.
- The master bedroom is nestled into one corner for quiet and privacy. This deluxe suite features two walk-in closets and a whirlpool bath. The two smaller bedrooms share another full bath.
- An extra-large laundry area, complete with a clothes-folding counter and a coat closet, is accessible from the three-car garage.
- The home is visually expanded by 9-ft. ceilings throughout, with the exception of the vaulted Great Room.

Plan PI-90-435

Bedrooms: 3	Baths: 2
Living Area:	
Main floor	1,896 sq. ft.
Total Living Area:	**1,896 sq. ft.**
Basement	1,889 sq. ft.
Garage	667 sq. ft.
Exterior Wall Framing:	2x6

Foundation Options:
Daylight basement
Standard basement
(Typical foundation & framing conversion diagram available—see order form.)

BLUEPRINT PRICE CODE:	B

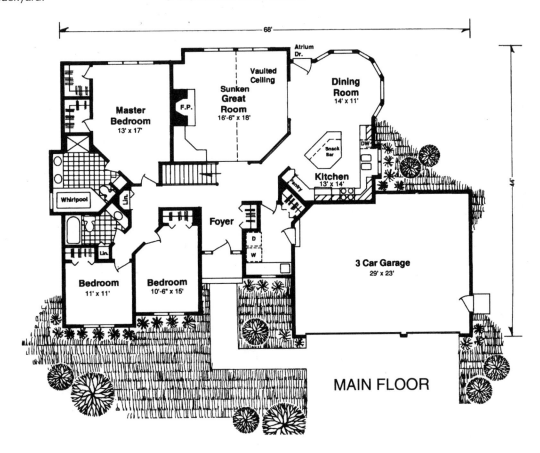

MAIN FLOOR

Spacious and Open

- A brilliant, sunken family room with rear fireplace, backyard access and vaulted ceiling is found at the center of this open floor plan.
- A cozy dinette with rear sliders and roomy island kitchen merge with the family room, creating a spacious, open atmosphere.
- Formal dining and living rooms share the front of the home.
- The main-floor master bedroom has tray ceiling, large walk-in closet and lavish bath designed for two.
- Two additional bedrooms share the upper level with a second full bath; the balcony landing overlooks the family room and foyer.

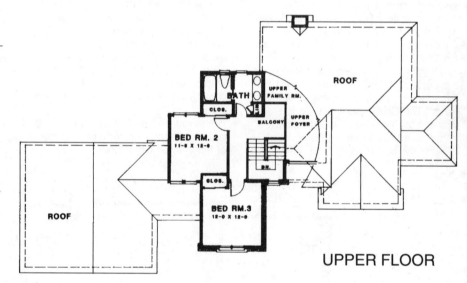

UPPER FLOOR

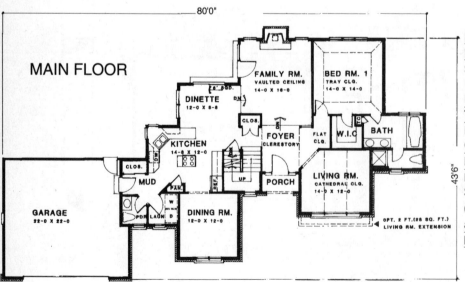

MAIN FLOOR

Plan A-2207-DS	
Bedrooms: 3	**Baths: 2 ½**
Space:	
Upper floor	518 sq. ft.
Main floor	1,389 sq. ft.
Total Living Area	**1,907 sq. ft.**
Basement	1,389 sq. ft.
Garage	484 sq. ft.
Exterior Wall Framing	2x6
Foundation options:	
Standard Basement	
(Foundation & framing conversion diagram available—see order form.)	
Blueprint Price Code	B

Soaring Design
Lifts the Human Spirit

- Suitable for level or sloping lots, this versatile design can be expanded or finished as time and budget allow.
- Surrounding deck accessible from all main living areas.
- Great living room enhanced by vaulted ceilings, second-floor balcony, skylights and dramatic window wall.
- Rear entrance has convenient access to full bath and laundry room.
- Two additional bedrooms on upper level share second bath and balcony room.

UPPER FLOOR

Plans H-930-1 & -1A

Bedrooms: 3	Baths: 2
Space:	
Upper floor:	710 sq. ft.
Main floor:	1,210 sq. ft.
Total living area:	**1,920 sq. ft.**
Basement:	605 sq. ft.
Garage/shop:	605 sq. ft.
Exterior Wall Framing:	**2x6**

Foundation options:
Daylight basement (Plan H-930-1).
Crawlspace (Plan H-930-1A).
(Foundation & framing conversion diagram available — see order form.)

Blueprint Price Code:

Without basement:	B
With basement:	D

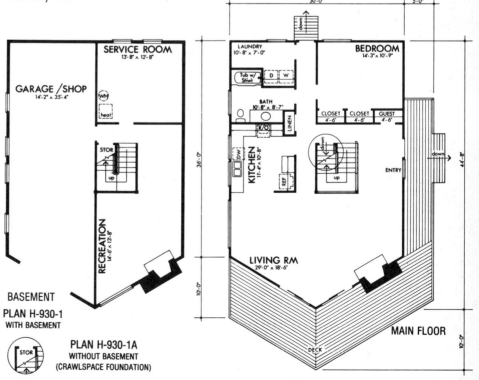

BASEMENT
PLAN H-930-1
WITH BASEMENT

PLAN H-930-1A
WITHOUT BASEMENT
(CRAWLSPACE FOUNDATION)

MAIN FLOOR

Farmhouse for Today

- An inviting veranda and charming dormer windows lend traditional warmth to this attractive design.
- An up-to-date interior includes ample space for entertaining as well as for family life.
- An elegant foyer is flanked on one side by a formal, sunken living room and a sunken family room with fireplace on the other.
- A dining room joins the living room to increase the space available for parties.
- A roomy and efficient kitchen/nook/ utility area combination with a half bath forms a spacious area for casual family life and domestic chores.
- Upstairs, a grand master suite includes a compartmentalized bath with separate tub and shower and a large closet.
- A second full bath serves the two secondary bedrooms.

Plan U-87-203

Bedrooms: 3	Baths: 2½
Space:	
Upper floor:	857 sq. ft.
Main floor:	1,064 sq. ft.
Total living area:	1,921 sq. ft.
Basement:	1,064 sq. ft.
Garage:	552 sq. ft.
Exterior Wall Framing:	2x4 & 2x6

Foundation options:
Standard basement.
Crawlspace.
Slab.
(Foundation & framing conversion diagram available — see order form.)

Blueprint Price Code:	B

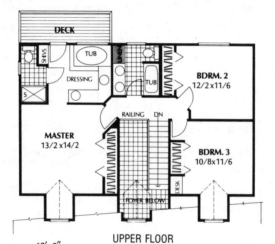

DECK
TUB
DRESSING
BDRM. 2
12/2 x11/6
S
RAILING   DN
MASTER
13/2 x14/2
TUB
BDRM. 3
10/8 x11/6
DESK
FOYER BELOW

UPPER FLOOR

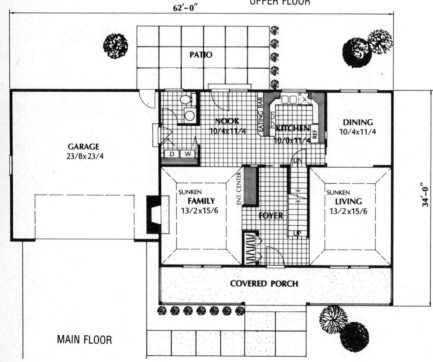

62'-0"

PATIO

GARAGE
23/8 x 23/4

NOOK
10/4 x11/4

EATING BAR

KITCHEN
10/0x11/4

REF

DINING
10/4 x11/4

D W

SUNKEN
FAMILY
13/2 x15/6

ENT CENTER

DN

FOYER

UP

SUNKEN
LIVING
13/2 x15/6

34'-0"

COVERED PORCH

MAIN FLOOR

Octagonal Home with Lofty View

- There's no better way to avoid the ordinary than by building an octagonal home and escaping from square corners and rigid rooms.
- The roomy main floor offers plenty of space for full-time family living or for a comfortable second-home retreat.
- The vaulted entry hall leads to the bedrooms on the right or down the hall to the Great Room.
- Warmed by a woodstove, the Great Room offers a panoramic view of the surrounding scenery.
- The center core of the main floor houses two baths, one of which contains a spa tub and is private to the master bedroom.
- This plan also includes a roomy kitchen and handy utility area.
- A large loft is planned as a recreation room, also with a woodstove.
- The daylight basement version adds another bedroom, a bath, a garage and a large storage area.

Plans P-532-3A & -3D

Bedrooms: 3-4	Baths: 2-3
Living Area:	
Upper floor	355 sq. ft.
Main floor	1,567 sq. ft.
Daylight basement	430 sq. ft.
Total Living Area:	**1,922/2,352 sq. ft.**
Garage and storage	1,137 sq. ft.
Exterior Wall Framing:	2x6
Foundation Options:	**Plan #**
Daylight basement	P-532-3D
Crawlspace	P-532-3A

(Typical foundation & framing conversion diagram available—see order form.)

BLUEPRINT PRICE CODE:	**B/C**

FRONT VIEW

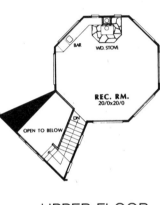

UPPER FLOOR

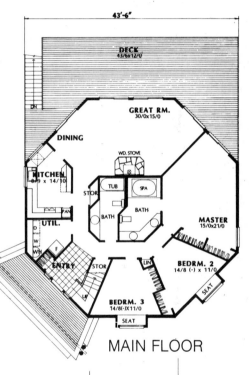

MAIN FLOOR

REAR VIEW

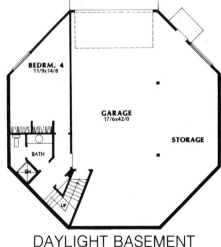

DAYLIGHT BASEMENT

Imposing Form... Outstanding Floor Plan

- Stately and imposing, this one-story design boasts an attractive wood and brick exterior.
- The focal point is a grand, spacious family room with a beamed cathedral ceiling, slate-hearth fireplace and sliding glass doors to a rear terrace.
- The large living room features a sloped ceiling and high glass panels to the front.
- The luxurious master suite includes a sky-lit dressing room, private bath and large closet.
- The beautiful kitchen adjoins a sunny dinette area which protrudes onto the rear terrace.

Plan K-278-M

Bedrooms: 3	Baths: 2½
Space:	
Main floor	1,926 sq. ft.
Total Living Area	**1,926 sq. ft.**
Basement	1,778 sq. ft.
Garage	463 sq. ft.
Exterior Wall Framing	2x4/2x6

Foundation options:
Standard Basement
Slab
(Foundation & framing conversion diagram available—see order form.)

Blueprint Price Code	**B**

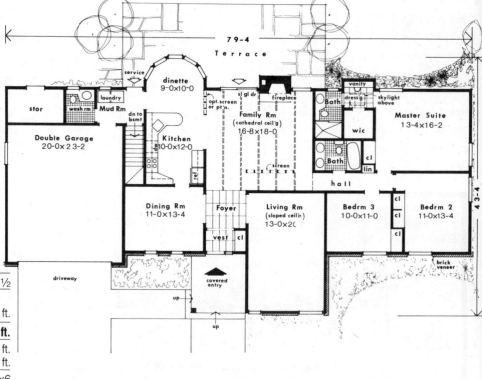

TO ORDER THIS BLUEPRINT, CALL TOLL-FREE 1-800-547-5570   Plan K-278-M   **PRICES AND DETAILS ON PAGES 12-15**

Decked Out for Fun

- Spacious deck surrounds this comfortable cabin/chalet.
- Sliding glass doors and windows blanket the living-dining area, indulged with raised hearth and a breathtaking view.
- Dining area and compact kitchen

separated by breakfast bar.
- Master bedroom, laundry room and bath complete first floor; two additional bedrooms located on second floor.
- Upper level also features impressive balcony room with exposed beams.

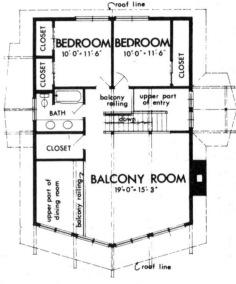

UPPER FLOOR

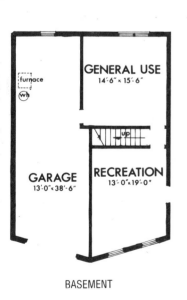

BASEMENT

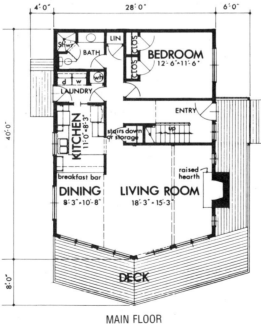

MAIN FLOOR

Plans H-919-1 & -1A

Bedrooms: 3	Baths: 2

Space:

Upper floor:	869 sq. ft.
Main floor:	1,064 sq. ft.

Total living area:	**1,933 sq. ft.**
Basement:	475 sq. ft.
Garage:	501 sq. ft.

Exterior Wall Framing:	2x6

Foundation options:
Daylight basement (Plan H-919-1).
Crawlspace (Plan H-919-1A).
(Foundation & framing conversion diagram available — see order form.)

Blueprint Price Code:

Without basement:	B
With basement:	C

Elegance Inside and Out

- The raised front porch of this brick home is finely detailed with wood columns, railings and moldings, and the transom French doors blend well with the stucco finish of the porch.
- The living room, dining room and entry have 12-ft. ceilings. Skylights illuminate the living room, which also includes a fireplace and easy access to a roomy deck.
- The master suite features a raised tray ceiling, an enormous garden bath and large walk-in closet. The large quarter-circle master tub is surrounded by a mirror wall.
- On the left, two secondary bedrooms are insulated from the more active areas of the home by an efficient hallway, and also share another full bath.

Plan E-1909

Bedrooms: 3	Baths: 2
Space:	
Main floor	1,936 sq. ft.
Total Living Area	**1,936 sq. ft.**
Garage	484 sq. ft.
Storage	132 sq. ft.
Porch	175 sq. ft.
Exterior Wall Framing	2x6

Foundation options:
Crawlspace
Slab
(Foundation & framing conversion diagram available—see order form.)

Blueprint Price Code	B

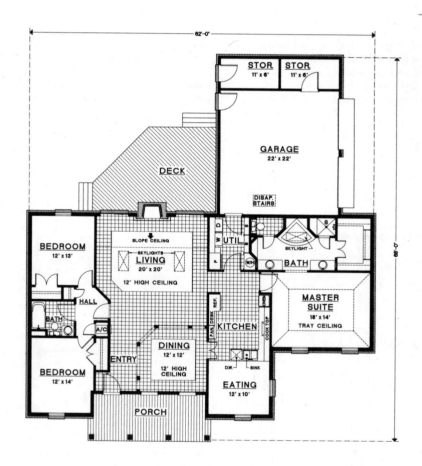

Classic Colonial

- This classic Colonial is distinguished by a curved, columned portico that leads into a breathtaking two-story gallery, highlighted by a curved staircase.
- The adjacent living room offers bright windows and an efficient fireplace.
- The sunny dining room features sliding glass doors to a rear terrace and easy access to the kitchen, which has ample counter space and an eating bar.
- The family room has its own high-efficiency fireplace, while the nearby dinette offers a circular snack bar and sliding glass doors to another terrace.
- Upstairs, the open-railed gallery leads to the spacious master suite, boasting a walk-in closet and a private bath with a whirlpool tub.
- Two additional large bedrooms share a second full bath. A fourth bedroom with built-in shelves makes an ideal den or guest room.

Plan K-655-U

Bedrooms: 4	Baths: 2½
Living Area:	
Upper floor	944 sq. ft.
Main floor	1,054 sq. ft.
Total Living Area:	**1,998 sq. ft.**
Standard basement	994 sq. ft.
Garage and storage	450 sq. ft.
Exterior Wall Framing:	2x4 or 2x6
Foundation Options:	
Standard basement	
Slab	
BLUEPRINT PRICE CODE:	**B**

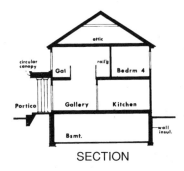

SECTION

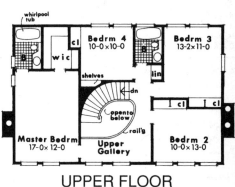

UPPER FLOOR

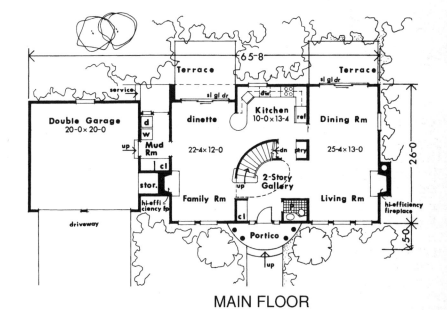

MAIN FLOOR

Updated Tudor

- Updated Tudor styling gives this home an extra-appealing exterior. Inside, the bright and open living spaces are embellished with a host of wonderfully contemporary details.

- An inviting brick arch frames the front door, which opens directly into the living room. Here, a sloped ceiling, a fireplace and a view to the covered rear porch provide an impressive welcome.

- The octagonal dining area is absolutely stunning – the perfect complement for the skylighted kitchen with an angled cooktop/snack bar and a sloped ceiling. Double doors in the kitchen lead to a roomy utility area and the cleverly disguised side-entry garage.

- No details were left out in the sumptuous master suite, which features access to a private porch with a sloped ceiling and skylights. The luxurious bath offers a platform tub, a sit-down shower, his-and-hers vanities and lots of storage and closet space.

- Two more bedrooms are situated at the opposite side of the home and share a hall bath. One bedroom features a window seat, while the other has direct access to the central covered porch.

Plan E-1912

Bedrooms: 3	Baths: 2
Living Area:	
Main floor	1,946 sq. ft.
Total Living Area:	**1,946 sq. ft.**
Garage and storage	562 sq. ft.
Exterior Wall Framing:	2x6
Foundation Options:	
Crawlspace	
Slab	
BLUEPRINT PRICE CODE:	B

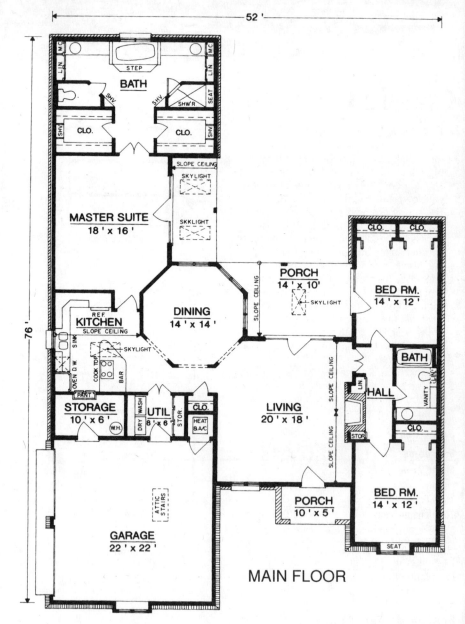

MAIN FLOOR

Plan E-1912

PRICES AND DETAILS
ON PAGES 12-15

Excellent Family Design

- Long sloping rooflines and bold design features make this home attractive for any neighborhood.
- Inside, a vaulted entry takes visitors into an impressive vaulted Great Room with a wood stove and window-wall facing the house-spanning rear deck.
- Clerestory windows flanking the stove area and large windows front and rear flood the Great Room with natural light.
- The magnificent kitchen includes a stylish island and opens to the informal dining area which in turn flows into the Great Room.
- Two bedrooms on the main floor share a full bath, and bedroom #2 boasts easy access to the rear deck which spans the width of the house.
- The upstairs comprises an "adult retreat," with a roomy master suite, luxurious bath with double sinks, and a large walk-in closet.
- A daylight basement version adds another 1,410 sq. ft. of space for entertaining and recreation, plus a fourth bedroom and a large shop/storage area.

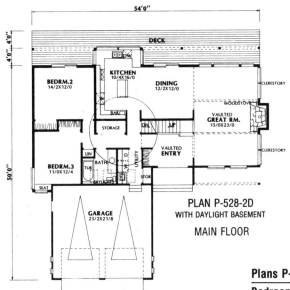

PLAN P-528-2D
WITH DAYLIGHT BASEMENT
MAIN FLOOR

UPPER FLOOR

PLAN P-528-2A
WITHOUT BASEMENT
(CRAWLSPACE FOUNDATION)

BASEMENT

Plans P-528-2A & -2D

Bedrooms: 3-4	Baths: 2-3

Space:

Upper floor:	498 sq. ft.
Main floor:	1,456 sq. ft.

Total living area:	1,954 sq. ft.
Basement:	1,410 sq. ft.
Garage:	502 sq. ft.

Exterior Wall Framing:	2x6

Foundation options:
Daylight basement (Plan P-528-2D).
Crawlspace (Plan P-528-2A).
(Foundation & framing conversion diagram available — see order form.)

Blueprint Price Code:

Without basement:	B
With basement:	E

Indoor/Outdoor Living on A Sloping Lot

- The wood siding, the front deck, and the multi-paned exterior of this Northwest contemporary will beckon you up to the entry stairs and inside.
- The two-story entry opens up to a vaulted living room with tall windows, exposed beam ceiling and adjoining dining area which accesses the hand-railed deck.
- An updated kitchen offers a walk-in pantry, eating bar and breakfast nook with sliders to a rear deck.
- A fireplace and rear patio highlight the attached family room.
- A washer/dryer in the upper level bath is convenient to all three bedrooms, making laundry a breeze.

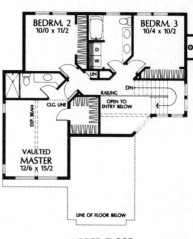

UPPER FLOOR

BEDRM. 2 10/0 x 11/2

BEDRM. 3 10/4 x 10/2

VAULTED MASTER 12/6 x 15/2

OPEN TO ENTRY BELOW

BASEMENT

CRAWLSPACE

GARAGE 25/10 x 28/6

MAIN FLOOR

37' - 0"

PATIO

STEPS

NOOK 11/0 x 10/6

FAMILY 20/0 x 12/6

DECK

EATING BAR

KITCHEN 13/4 x 11/0

PANTRY

DESK

TWO-STORY ENTRY

DINING 11/0 x 10/8

DECK

VAULTED LIVING 12/6 x 17/0

PLANTER

DRIVEWAY BELOW

Plan P-7737-4D

Bedrooms: 3	Baths: 2½
Space:	
Upper floor:	802 sq. ft.
Main floor:	1,158 sq. ft.
Total living area:	1,960 sq. ft.
Garage/basement:	736 sq. ft.
Exterior Wall Framing:	2x6

Foundation options:
Crawlspace.
(Foundation & framing conversion diagram available — see order form.)

Blueprint Price Code:	B

Updated Colonial

- This home is thoroughly Colonial outside, but it offers an updated, ultra-modern floor plan inside.
- Guests are welcomed into a formal gallery that leads to all of the main-floor living areas. A large living room and a formal dining room flank the gallery. Optional folding doors open the living room to the adjoining family room.
- The family room features an inviting fireplace as its hub and sliding-door access to a backyard terrace.
- The kitchen is located to easily service the formal dining room as well as the bayed dinette. A mudroom and a half-bath are nearby.
- Upstairs, the master suite boasts a private bath and a wall of closets. Three unique secondary bedrooms share a hall bath.

Plan K-274-M

Bedrooms: 4	Baths: 2½
Living Area:	
Upper floor	990 sq. ft.
Main floor	1,025 sq. ft.
Total Living Area:	**2,015 sq. ft.**
Standard basement	983 sq. ft.
Garage and storage	520 sq. ft.
Exterior Wall Framing:	2x4 or 2x6
Foundation Options:	
Standard basement	
Slab	
BLUEPRINT PRICE CODE:	**C**

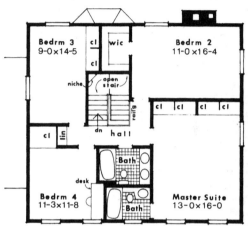

UPPER FLOOR

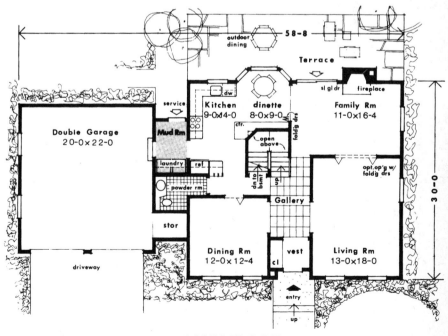

MAIN FLOOR

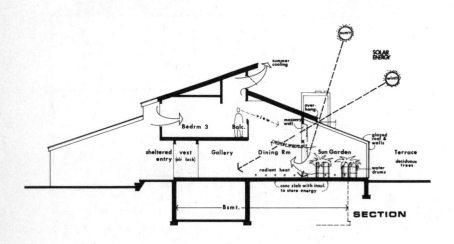

summer cooling

SOLAR ENERGY

sum'r

win't'r

overhang

masonry wall

Bedrm 3

Balc.

view

glazed roof & walls

sheltered entry

vest (air lock)

Gallery

winter warmth

Dining Rm

Sun Garden

Terrace

deciduous trees

radiant heat

water drums

conc slab with insul. to store energy

Bsmt.

SECTION

Passive Solar Design . . . from the Foundation Up

Designed to embrace the warming sun, this two-story passive solar house is constructed of standard lumber, and its dramatic exterior is finished in vertical wood siding and roof shingles. Focal point of the concept is a glass-enclosed, south-facing sun garden that is visible from the entrance gallery and is wrapped by the living, dining and family rooms. The open plan provides for a cheerful well-organized kitchen, situated to serve the dining room and family room. A library (or guest room) and bath are located off the entrance gallery.

Isolated on the second floor are three bedrooms and two baths with a balcony that overlooks the living and dining rooms. Solar energy is absorbed and stored in the masonry wall and dense floor for heating. The sun garden generates heat to the adjacent areas by opening the sliding doors. Direct heat gain is maintained through glazed walls that face south. For summer cooling, eave overhang keeps out unwanted sun. Operable vents in the clerestory draw air out of the house by convection to provide natural ventilation. Many other energy saving features are planned into the house to assure a high retention of heat, and a back-up heating system is provided for use as needed. Total living area, excluding the sun garden, is 1,214 sq. ft. on the first floor and 762 sq. ft. on the second; garage and mudroom, 536 sq. ft.; optional basement, 848 sq. ft.

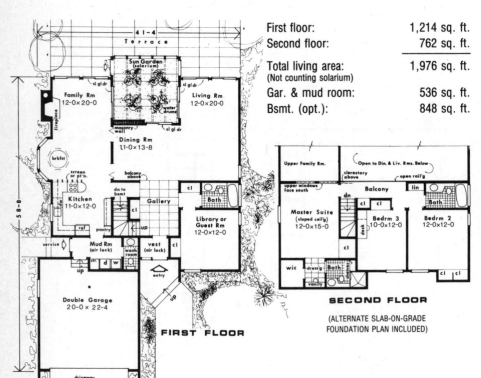

First floor:	1,214 sq. ft.
Second floor:	762 sq. ft.
Total living area: (Not counting solarium)	1,976 sq. ft.
Gar. & mud room:	536 sq. ft.
Bsmt. (opt.):	848 sq. ft.

41-4

Terrace

Sun Garden (solarium)

Family Rm 12-0×20-0

fireplace

Living Rm 12-0×20-0

sl gl dr

water drums

masonry wall

sl gl dr

Dining Rm 11-0×13-8

brkfst

screen or p't'n

balcony above

Kitchen 11-0×12-0

dn to bsmt

cl

Bath

Gallery

Upper Family Rm.

Open to Din. & Liv. Rms. Below

clerestory above

open rail'g

upper windows face south

Balcony

dn

lin

Bath

Master Suite (sloped ceil'g) 12-0×15-0

desk

Bedrm 3 10-0×12-0

Bedrm 2 12-0×12-0

wic

dress'g

Bath

vanity

cl

cl

SECOND FLOOR

(ALTERNATE SLAB-ON-GRADE FOUNDATION PLAN INCLUDED)

ref

service

Mud Rm (air lock)

wash room

ctr. d w

pantry

cl

up

vest (air lock)

cl

entry

Library or Guest Rm 12-0×12-0

Double Garage 20-0 × 22-4

up

driveway

FIRST FLOOR

Blueprint Price Code B

Plan K-279-T

TO ORDER THIS BLUEPRINT, CALL TOLL-FREE 1-800-547-5570

PRICES AND DETAILS ON PAGES 12-15

Visual Surprises

- The exterior of this two-story, four-bedroom design is boldly accented with a dramatic roof cavity, while the inside features wall angles that enhance the efficiency of the floor plan and offer visual variety.
- The double-door entry opens into a bright reception area, leading to the sloped-ceilinged living room.
- The efficient kitchen conveniently serves the formal dining room and the cheerful breakfast dinette.
- Off the reception area is a powder room and a large laundry space which could be finished to serve as a hobby room.
- Four bedrooms are isolated on the second level; a connecting balcony is open to the living room below.
- The master suite is fully equipped; sliding glass doors yield access to the open wood deck that is literally carved into the roof.

Plan K-540-L

Bedrooms: 4	Baths: 2½

Space:	
Upper floor:	884 sq. ft.
Main floor:	1,106 sq. ft.
Total living area:	**1,990 sq. ft.**
Basement:	1,106 sq. ft.
Garage:	400 sq. ft.
Storage, laundry:	254 sq. ft.

Exterior Wall Framing:	2x4/2x6

Foundation options:
Standard basement.
Slab.
(Foundation & framing conversion diagram available — see order form)

Blueprint Price Code:	B

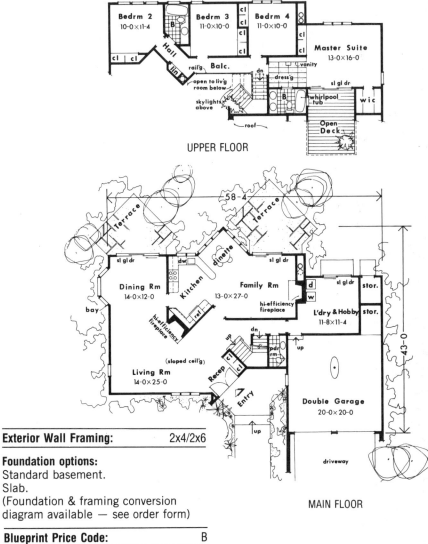

UPPER FLOOR

MAIN FLOOR

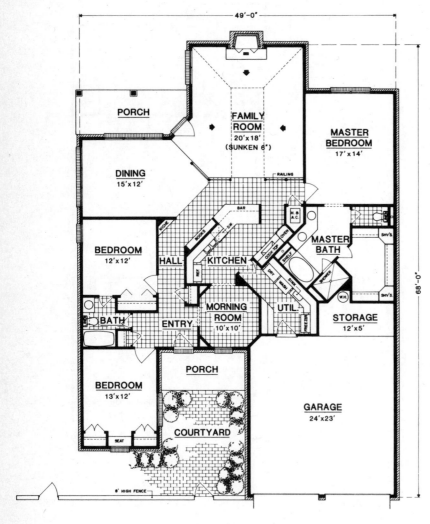

MAIN FLOOR

Designed for Private Luxury

- With its private courtyard and sheltered porch, this distinctive plan offers privacy, convenience and luxury in a design reminiscent of southern Europe.
- The focal point of the floor plan is the kitchen/morning room combination, from which radiate the bedrooms, a formal dining room and a large family room.
- The master bedroom boasts a luxurious bath and a large walk-in closet. Two secondary bedrooms share another full bath.
- The family room features a fireplace, a sunken floor and a trayed ceiling, and also adjoins a rear porch.
- This elegant design features 9' ceilings, with even higher ceilings in the family room and the front bedroom.

Plan E-1908

Bedrooms: 3	**Baths:** 2

Living Area:	
Main floor	1,994 sq. ft.
Total Living Area:	**1,994 sq. ft.**
Garage	552 sq. ft.
Exterior Wall Framing:	2x6

Foundation Options:
Crawlspace
Slab
(Typical foundation & framing conversion diagram available—see order form.)

BLUEPRINT PRICE CODE: B

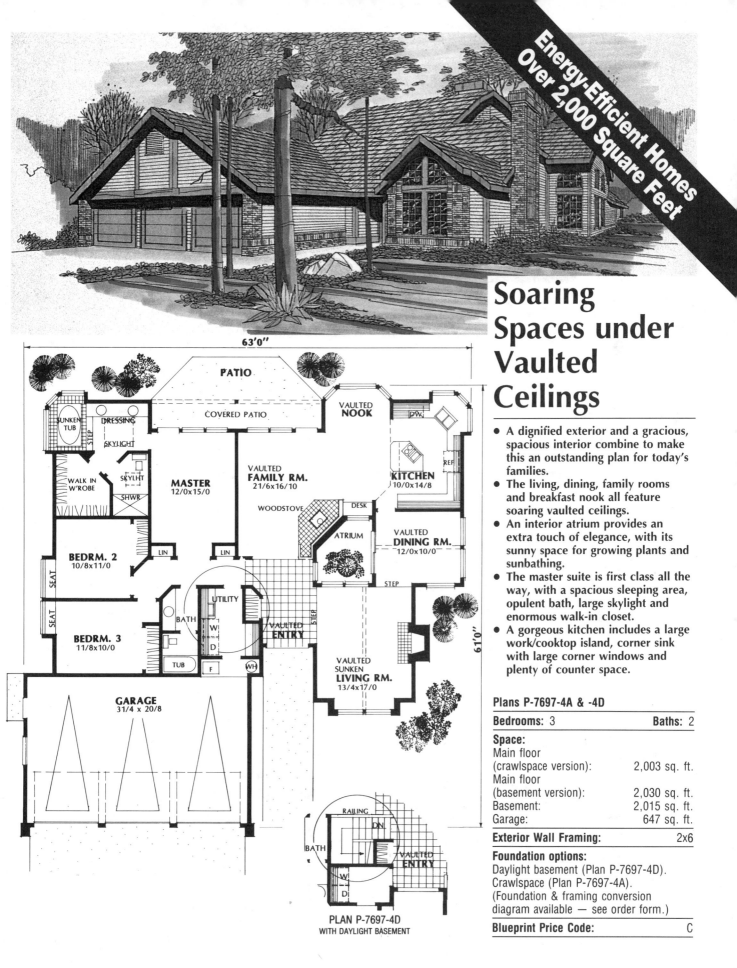

Soaring Spaces under Vaulted Ceilings

- A dignified exterior and a gracious, spacious interior combine to make this an outstanding plan for today's families.
- The living, dining, family rooms and breakfast nook all feature soaring vaulted ceilings.
- An interior atrium provides an extra touch of elegance, with its sunny space for growing plants and sunbathing.
- The master suite is first class all the way, with a spacious sleeping area, opulent bath, large skylight and enormous walk-in closet.
- A gorgeous kitchen includes a large work/cooktop island, corner sink with large corner windows and plenty of counter space.

Plans P-7697-4A & -4D

Bedrooms: 3	Baths: 2

Space:	
Main floor (crawlspace version):	2,003 sq. ft.
Main floor (basement version):	2,030 sq. ft.
Basement:	2,015 sq. ft.
Garage:	647 sq. ft.

Exterior Wall Framing:	2x6

Foundation options:
Daylight basement (Plan P-7697-4D).
Crawlspace (Plan P-7697-4A).
(Foundation & framing conversion diagram available — see order form.)

Blueprint Price Code:	C

Floor Plan Labels

63'0''

PATIO

COVERED PATIO

SUNKEN TUB

DRESSING

SKYLIGHT

WALK IN W'ROBE

SKYLHT

SHWR

MASTER
12/0x15/0

VAULTED NOOK

DW

REF

VAULTED FAMILY RM.
21/6x16/10

KITCHEN
10/0x14/8

WOODSTOVE

DESK

ATRIUM

VAULTED DINING RM.
12/0x10/0

BEDRM. 2
10/8x11/0

LIN

LIN

SEAT

STEP

SEAT

UTILITY

VAULTED ENTRY

W

D

BATH

BEDRM. 3
11/8x10/0

TUB

F

WH

VAULTED SUNKEN LIVING RM.
13/4x17/0

61'0''

GARAGE
31/4 x 20/8

RAILING

DN

BATH

VAULTED ENTRY

W

D

PLAN P-7697-4D
WITH DAYLIGHT BASEMENT

Plan E-2004

Bedrooms: 3	**Baths:** 2

Space:
Total living area:	2,023 sq. ft.
Garage:	484 sq. ft.
Storage & Porches:	423 sq. ft.

Exterior Wall Framing:	2x6

Foundation options:
Crawlspace.
Slab.
(Foundation & framing conversion
diagram available — see order form.)

Blueprint Price Code:	C

Exciting Floor Plan In Traditional French Garden Home

- Creative, angular design permits an open floor plan.
- Living and dining rooms open to a huge covered porch.
- Kitchen, living and dining rooms feature impressive 12' ceilings accented by extensive use of glass.
- Informal eating nook faces a delightful courtyard.
- Luxurious master bath offers a whirlpool tub, shower, and walk-in closet.
- Secondary bedrooms also offer walk-in closets.

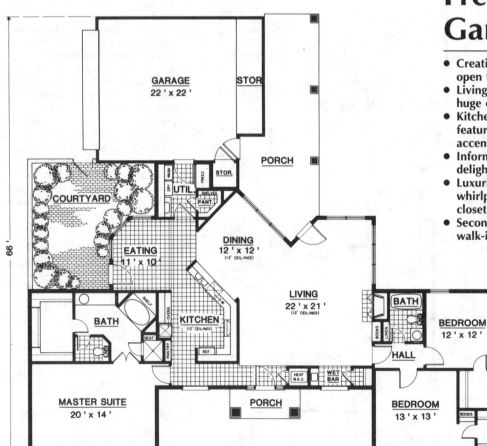

**NOTE:
The above photographed home may have been modified by the homeowner. Please refer to floor plan and/or drawn elevation shown for actual blueprint details.

Colonial Design Alive with Solar Energy

This gracious colonial home combines traditional design with contemporary passive solar efficiency. Southern exposure at the rear provides maximum sunshine in the kitchen, dinette, family room, and cheerful sun room. Heat energy, accumulated in the insulated thermal flooring, is later released for night-time comfort. An air-lock vestibule, which minimizes heat loss, adds the elegance we associate with a center-hall colonial.

Upstairs, there are four comfortable bedrooms and two luxury baths — one accented by a whirlpool tub. Also, there is an electrically operated skylight that aids in natural cooling.

Total living area of the first floor, excluding sun room, comes to 1,030 sq. ft.; second floor adds 1,003 sq. ft. Garage, mud room, etc. are 500 sq. ft., and optional basement is 633 sq. ft.

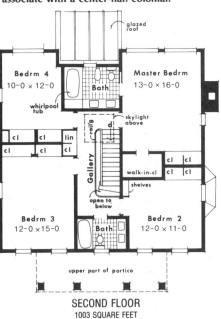

SECOND FLOOR
1003 SQUARE FEET

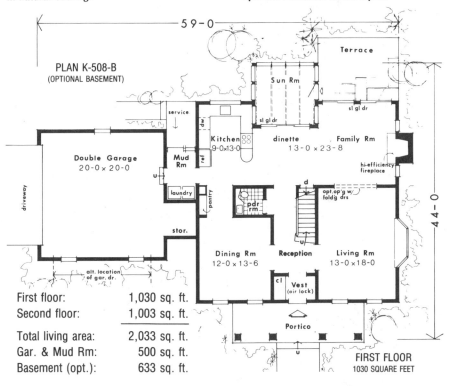

First floor:	1,030 sq. ft.
Second floor:	1,003 sq. ft.
Total living area:	2,033 sq. ft.
Gar. & Mud Rm:	500 sq. ft.
Basement (opt.):	633 sq. ft.

FIRST FLOOR
1030 SQUARE FEET

Blueprint Price Code C

Plan K-508-B

TO ORDER THIS BLUEPRINT,
CALL TOLL-FREE 1-800-547-5570

PRICES AND DETAILS
ON PAGES 12-15 **131**

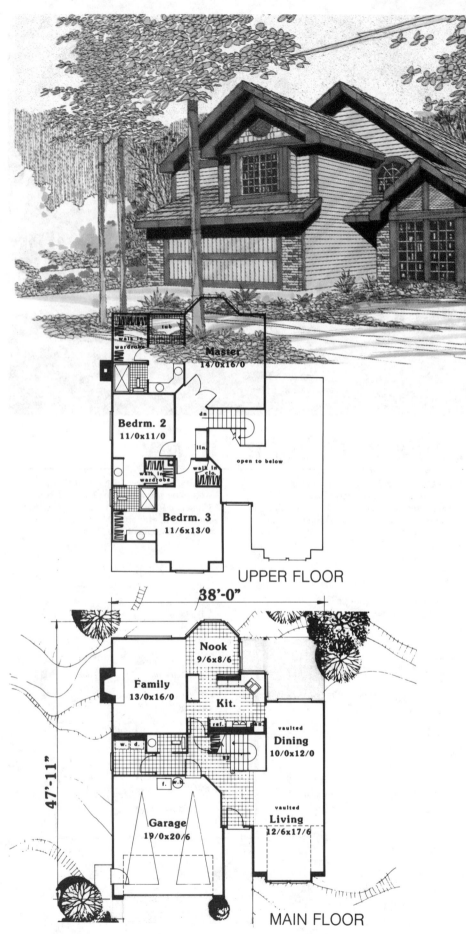

UPPER FLOOR

Master
14/0x16/0

Bedrm. 2
11/0x11/0

Bedrm. 3
11/6x13/0

walk in wardrobe

tub

dn

lin.

walk in clo.

open to below

38'-0"

47'-11"

Nook
9/6x8/6

Family
13/0x16/0

Kit.

ref.

w. d.

vaulted
Dining
10/0x12/0

f. w. h.

Garage
19/0x20/6

vaulted
Living
12/6x17/6

MAIN FLOOR

Spacious Narrow-Lot Design

- Soaring vaults and open living areas add to this spacious narrow-lot design.
- Sunlight streams through the many windows in the kitchen, nook and family room. This casual area boasts a pantry, a corner sink, a large fireplace, a bayed eating area and sliders to the backyard.
- Upstairs, all three bedrooms have walk-in closets. The master suite features a bayed sitting area and a luxurious bath. The remaining bedrooms share a connecting bath.

Plan R-2052	
Bedrooms: 3	**Baths:** 2½
Living Area:	
Upper floor	974 sq. ft.
Main floor	1,078 sq. ft.
Total Living Area:	**2,052 sq. ft.**
Garage	387 sq. ft.
Exterior Wall Framing:	2x6
Foundation Options:	
Crawlspace	
(Typical foundation & framing conversion diagram available—see order form.)	
BLUEPRINT PRICE CODE:	C

Plan R-2052

PRICES AND DETAILS
ON PAGES 12-15

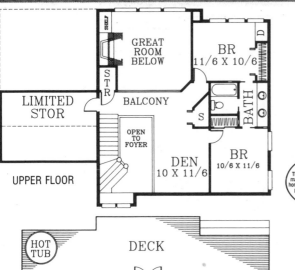

GREAT
ROOM
BELOW

STR

BALCONY

LIMITED
STOR

OPEN
TO
FOYER

UPPER FLOOR

BR
11/6 X 10/6

D

BATH

S

DEN
10 X 11/6

BR
10/6 X 11/6

**NOTE:
The above photographed home
may have been modified by the
homeowner. Please refer to floor
plan and/or drawn elevation
shown for actual
blueprint details.

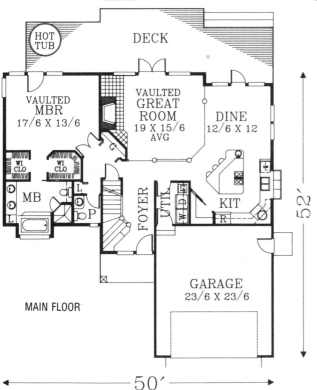

HOT
TUB

DECK

VAULTED
MBR
17/6 X 13/6

VAULTED
GREAT
ROOM
19 X 15/6
AVG

DINE
12/6 X 12

WI
CLO

WI
CLO

MB

FOYER

UTIL

KIT

W D

P

52'

GARAGE
23/6 X 23/6

MAIN FLOOR

50'

Vaulted Great Room

- While the exterior has traditional overtones, this plan is thoroughly modern both inside and out.
- The vaulted Great Room with adjacent kitchen and dining room gives the home an open and spacious feeling.
- The vaulted master suite on the first floor includes walk-in closets and a sumptuous master bath.
- The upper floor includes two more bedrooms, which share a continental bath.
- Also note the den and balcony overlooking the foyer and Great Room below.
- A huge deck with a hot tub can be reached easily from the master suite, the Great Room or the dining room.

Plan S-2100	
Bedrooms: 3	**Baths:** 2½
Living Area:	
Upper floor:	660 sq. ft.
Main floor	1,440 sq. ft.
Total Living Area:	**2,100 sq. ft.**
Standard basement	1,440 sq. ft.
Garage	552 sq. ft.
Exterior Wall Framing:	2x6

Foundation Options:

Standard basement
Crawlspace
Slab
(Typical foundation & framing conversion diagram available—see order form.)

BLUEPRINT PRICE CODE: C

Home with High Style

- Sweeping rooflines attract attention to this stylish contemporary home.
- The vaulted entry is enhanced by a clerestory window above.
- Sunlight invades the main floor by way of a window wall in the living room and a sunspace off the patio or deck.
- A main-floor den could serve as a handy guest bedroom.
- The open family room shares a woodstove with the kitchen and nook.
- A formal dining room looks out on the home's natural surroundings.
- Upstairs, a large master bedroom features a private deck, a walk-in closet and a master bath with corner tub, separate shower and dual vanities.

Plan S-2001

Bedrooms: 3-4	Baths: 2½
Living Area:	
Upper floor	890 sq. ft.
Main floor	1,249 sq. ft.
Total Living Area:	**2,139 sq. ft.**
Basement	1,249 sq. ft.
Garage	399 sq. ft.
Exterior Wall Framing:	2x6

Foundation Options:
Daylight basement
Standard basement
Crawlspace
Slab
(Typical foundation & framing conversion diagram available—see order form.)

BLUEPRINT PRICE CODE:	C

UPPER FLOOR

MAIN FLOOR

Today's Tradition

- The traditional two-story design is brought up to today's standards with this exciting new design.
- The front half of the main floor is devoted to formal entertaining. The living and dining rooms offer symmetrical bay windows overlooking the wrap-around front porch.
- The informal living zone faces the rear deck and yard. It includes a family room with fireplace and beamed ceiling as well as a modern kitchen with cooktop island and snack bar.
- There are four large bedrooms and two full baths on the upper sleeping level.

Plan AGH-2143

Bedrooms: 4	Baths: 2½
Space:	
Upper floor:	1,047 sq. ft.
Main floor:	1,096 sq. ft.
Total living area:	2,143 sq. ft.
Daylight basement:	1,096 sq. ft.
Garage:	852 sq. ft.
Exterior Wall Framing:	2x6

Foundation options:
Daylight basement.
(Foundation & framing conversion diagram available — see order form.)

Blueprint Price Code:	C

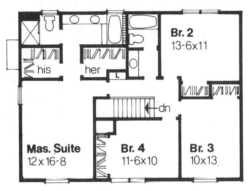

UPPER FLOOR

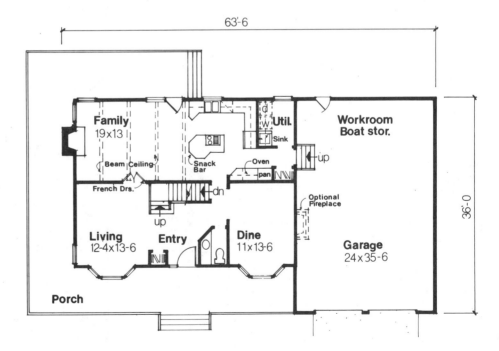

MAIN FLOOR

Colonial with a Contemporary Touch

- Open, flowing rooms highlighted by a two-story round-top window combine to give this colonial design a contemporary, today touch.
- To the left of the elegant, two-story foyer lies the living room, which flows into the rear-facing family room with fireplace.
- The centrally located kitchen serves both the formal dining room and the dinette, with a view of the family room beyond.
- All four bedrooms are located upstairs. The master suite includes a walk-in closet and private bath with double vanities, separate shower and whirlpool tub under skylights.

Plan AHP-9020

Bedrooms: 4	Baths: 2 ½
Space:	
Upper floor	1,021 sq. ft.
Main floor	1,125 sq. ft.
Total Living Area	**2,146 sq. ft.**
Basement	1,032 sq. ft.
Garage	480 sq. ft.
Exterior Wall Framing	**2x6**

Foundation options:

Standard Basement

Slab

(Foundation & framing conversion diagram available—see order form.)

Blueprint Price Code	**C**

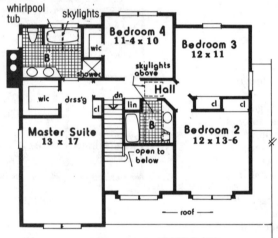

UPPER FLOOR

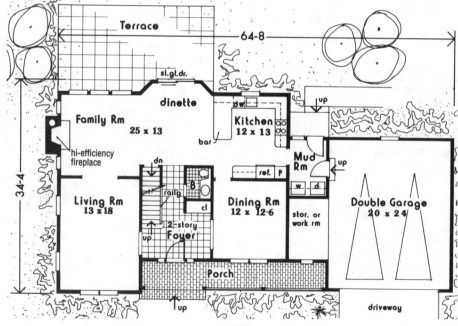

MAIN FLOOR

Striking Vertical Design

- Unique roof deck and massive wrap-around main level deck harbor an equally exciting interior.
- Large sunken living room is brightened by a three-window skylight and also features a log-sized fireplace.
- U-shaped kitchen is just off the entry, adjacent to handy laundry area.
- Second-story balcony overlooks the large living room and entryway below.

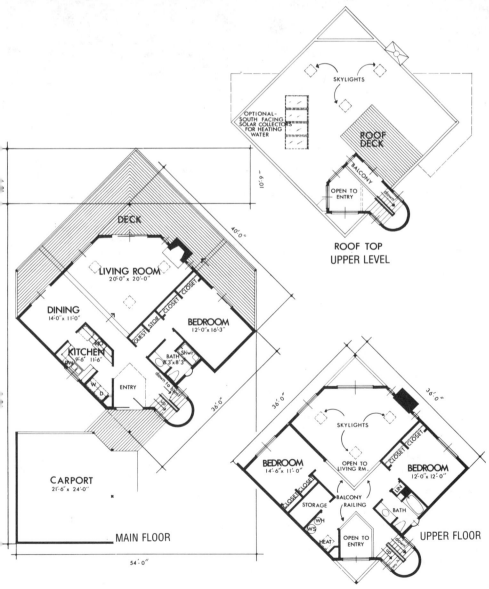

ROOF TOP
UPPER LEVEL

MAIN FLOOR

UPPER FLOOR

Plans H-935-1 & -1A

Bedrooms: 3	Baths: 2
Space:	
Upper floor:	844 sq. ft.
Main floor:	1,323 sq. ft.
Total living area:	2,167 sq. ft.
Basement:	approx. 1,323 sq. ft.
Carport:	516 sq. ft.
Exterior Wall Framing:	2x6

Foundation options:
Standard basement (Plan H-935-1).
Crawlspace (Plan H-935-1A).
(Foundation & framing conversion diagram available — see order form.)

Blueprint Price Code:	C

Sunny Indoor or Outdoor Dining

- This cozy country-style home offers an inviting front porch and an interior just as welcoming.
- A spacious living room features a warming fireplace and windows that overlook the porch.
- The living room opens to the dining area, which leads to a rear porch and patio.
- The island kitchen has plenty of counter space, a sink view and an adjoining sun room that could be used as a sunny formal dining area.
- The private master suite is secluded to the rear. Dual walk-in closets, vanities and a large windowed tub are nice features in the master bath.

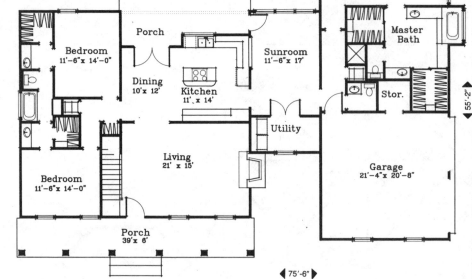

Plan J-90014

Bedrooms: 3	Baths: 2 ½
Space:	
Main floor	2,190 sq. ft.
Total Living Area	**2,190 sq. ft.**
Basement	2,190 sq. ft.
Garage	465 sq. ft.
Storage	34 sq. ft.

Exterior Wall Framing   2x6

Foundation options:
Standard Basement
Crawlspace
Slab
(Foundation & framing conversion diagram available—see order form.)

Blueprint Price Code   C

Distinctive One-Level Sunshine Special

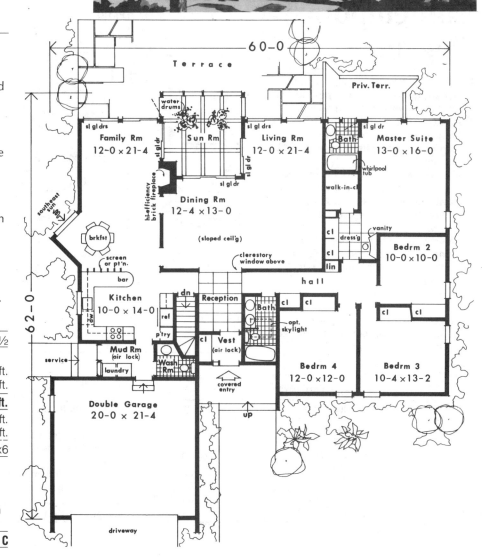

- With its solarium and window walls across the rear, this home offers a real treat for sun lovers.
- In winter, the solar features capture and distribute free heat. In summer, overhangs and clerestory windows provide shade, circulation and heat venting.
- Besides its technical features, this home offers a dramatic floor plan. The kitchen/nook/family room is big and open, and the living and dining rooms flow together to create a huge space.
- The master suite includes a private bath and a large walk-in closet, in addition to easy access to a private deck or terrace.
- Three other bedrooms share another full bath and the entire bedroom wing is insulated from the more active areas.

Plan K-502-J

Bedrooms: 4	Baths: 2½
Space:	
Main floor	2,052 sq. ft.
Sun room (approx)	144 sq. ft.
Total Living Area	**2,196 sq. ft.**
Basement	1,264 sq. ft.
Garage	426 sq. ft.
Exterior Wall Framing	2x4 or 2x6

Foundation options:

Standard Basement

Slab

(Foundation & framing conversion diagram available—see order form.)

Blueprint Price Code	**C**

Contemporary Elegance

- This contemporary design includes elegant traditional overtones, and is finished in vertical cedar siding.
- An expansive space is devoted to the vaulted living room and adjoining family/dining room and kitchen.
- A convenient utility area is located between the kitchen and the garage, and includes a clothes sorting counter, deep sink and ironing space.
- The master suite is spacious for a home of this size, and includes a sumptuous master bath and large walk-in closet.
- A loft area can be used for an additional bedroom, playroom, exercise area or hobby space.
- An optional sunroom can be added to the rear at any time.

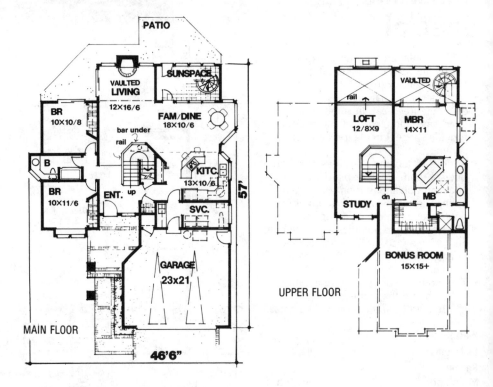

Plan LRD-1971

Bedrooms: 3-4	Baths: 2

Space:

Upper floor:	723 sq. ft.
Main floor:	1,248 sq. ft.
Bonus area:	225 sq. ft.

Total living area:	**2,196 sq. ft.**
Basement:	approx. 1,248 sq. ft.
Garage:	483 sq. ft.

Exterior Wall Framing:	2x6

Foundation options:
Standard basement.
Crawlspace.
(Foundation & framing conversion diagram available — see order form.)

Blueprint Price Code:	C

Isolated Master Bedroom Suite

Exterior walls are 2x6 construction.
Specify basement, crawlspace or slab foundation.

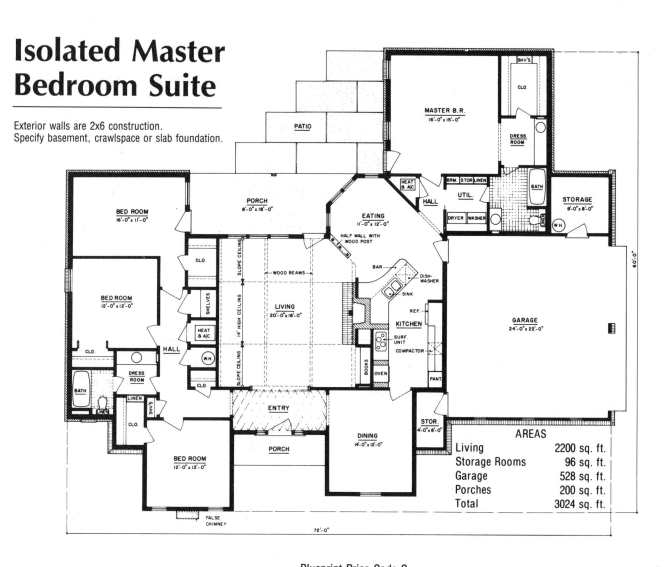

AREAS	
Living	2200 sq. ft.
Storage Rooms	96 sq. ft.
Garage	528 sq. ft.
Porches	200 sq. ft.
Total	3024 sq. ft.

TO ORDER THIS BLUEPRINT,
CALL TOLL-FREE 1-800-547-5570

Blueprint Price Code C
Plan E-2206

PRICES AND DETAILS
ON PAGES 12-15 141

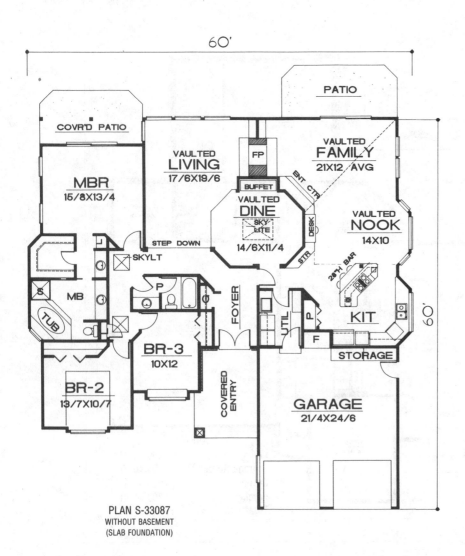

60'

PATIO

COVR'D PATIO

VAULTED LIVING
17/6X19/6

FP

VAULTED FAMILY
21X12 AVG

BUFFET

ENT CTR

MBR
15/8X13/4

VAULTED DINE
14/6X11/4

SKY LITE

DESK

STR

VAULTED NOOK
14X10

STEP DOWN

SKYLT

MB

FOYER

24" BAR

TUB

P

UTIL

P

KIT

F

BR-3
10X12

STORAGE

BR-2
13/7X10/7

COVERED ENTRY

GARAGE
21/4X24/6

60'

PLAN S-33087
WITHOUT BASEMENT
(SLAB FOUNDATION)

Separate Formal and Casual Areas

Traditional styling with contemporary overtones, cedar siding and brick accents, make this 2,215 sq. ft., three-bedroom home especially attractive.

The plan was expressly designed to separate the active informal uses from the formal sections of the home. The hip vaulted family room and nook areas are accented by the fireplace with an angular entertainment/desk/storage wall.

The raised dining space is enhanced by a centrally located sky well that incorporates a built-in light fixture.

The privately located master bedroom suite has its own covered patio area for outdoor relaxation. Separate vanities are featured in the walk-in closet and bath area. The platform tub is accented by a stained glass window.

Exterior walls are 2x6 for energy efficiency.

Total living area: 2,215 sq. ft.
(Not counting garage)

Blueprint Price Code C
Plan S-33087

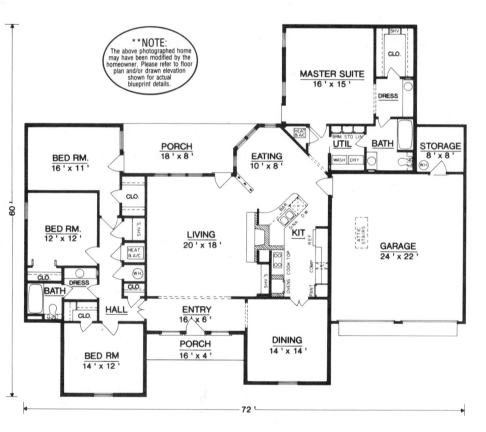

**NOTE:
The above photographed home may have been modified by the homeowner. Please refer to floor plan and/or drawn elevation shown for actual blueprint details.

MASTER SUITE
16' x 15'

CLO.

DRESS

HEAT & A/C

BRM STO LIN

UTIL

BATH

STORAGE
8' x 8'

WASH DRY

PORCH
18' x 8'

EATING
10' x 8'

BED RM.
16' x 11'

CLO.

SHV'S

BED RM.
12' x 12'

HEAT & A/C

W H

LIVING
20' x 18'

KIT

REF

COOK TOP

OVENS

SHV'S

COMP

PANT

ATTIC STAIRS

GARAGE
24' x 22'

CLO.

DRESS

BATH

CLO.

HALL

ENTRY
16' x 6'

BED RM
14' x 12'

PORCH
16' x 4'

DINING
14' x 14'

60'

72'

Luxury Living on One Level

- Exterior presents a classic air of quality and distinction in design.
- Spacious one-story interior provides space for family life and entertaining.
- The large central living room boasts a 13' ceiling and large hearth.
- A roomy formal dining room adjoins the foyer.
- The gorgeous kitchen/nook combination provides a sunny eating area along with an efficient and attractive kitchen with eating bar and abundant counter space.
- The master suite is isolated from the other bedrooms for more privacy, and includes a luxurious bath and dressing area.
- Three additional bedrooms make up the left side of the plan, and share a second bath.
- The garage is off the kitchen for maximum convenience in carrying in groceries; also note the storage space off the garage.

Plan E-2208

Bedrooms: 4		**Baths:** 2

Total living area:	2,252 sq. ft.
Garage:	528 sq. ft.
Storage:	64 sq. ft.
Exterior Wall Framing:	2x6

Typical Ceiling Heights:
8' unless otherwise noted.

Foundation options:
Standard basement.
Crawlspace.
Slab.
(Foundation & framing conversion diagram available — see order form.)

Blueprint Price Code: C

Modern Traditional-Style Home

- Covered porch and decorative double doors offer an invitation into this three or four bedroom home.
- Main floor bedroom may be used as a den, home office, or guest room, with convenient bath facilities.
- Adjoining dining room makes living room seem even more spacious; breakfast nook enlarges the look of the attached kitchen.
- Brick-size concrete block veneer and masonry tile roof give the exterior a look of durability.

UPPER FLOOR

PLAN H-1351-M1A
WITHOUT BASEMENT
(CRAWLSPACE FOUNDATION)

Plans H-1351-M1 & -M1A

Bedrooms: 3-4	**Baths:** 3

Space:	
Upper floor:	862 sq. ft.
Main floor:	1,383 sq. ft.
Total living area:	2,245 sq. ft.
Basement:	1,383 sq. ft.
Garage:	413 sq. ft.

Exterior Wall Framing:	2x6

Foundation options:
Standard basement (Plan H-1351-M1).
Crawlspace (Plan H-1351-M1A).
(Foundation & framing conversion diagram available — see order form.)

Blueprint Price Code:	C

MAIN FLOOR

TO ORDER THIS BLUEPRINT,
CALL TOLL-FREE 1-800-547-5570

Plans H-1351-M1 & -M1A

PRICES AND DETAILS
ON PAGES 12-15

Farmhouse with Modern Touch

- This classic center-hall design features an All-American Farmhouse exterior wrapped around a super-modern interior.
- A large family room features a built-in entertainment center and adjoins a convenient dinette for quick family meals.
- The spacious living and dining rooms adjoin to provide abundant space for large gatherings.
- An inviting porch leads into a roomy foyer which highlights a curved staircase.
- The second floor features a deluxe master suite and three secondary bedrooms.

VIEW INTO LIVING ROOM FROM FOYER.

UPPER FLOOR

BED RM 4
10' x 10'

DRESS RM.

BATH

vanity

BED RM 3
12'-6"x11'-4"

HALL

LIN.

BED RM 2
12'-6" x 11'-4"

dn

rail

open

MASTER BED RM
16'-8"x11'-4"

BATH

Plan HFL-1040-MB

Bedrooms: 4	Baths: 2½
Space:	
Upper floor	936 sq. ft.
Main floor	1,094 sq. ft.
Total Living Area	**2,030 sq. ft.**
Basement	1,022 sq. ft.
Garage	420 sq. ft.
Exterior Wall Framing	2x6

Foundation options:
Standard Basement
Slab
(Foundation & framing conversion diagram available—see order form.)

Blueprint Price Code   C

60'-0"

35'-6"

TERRACE

sliding glass doors

s. dw

range

sliding glass doors

service entry

MUD RM

cl

KITCHEN
10'-8" x 10'

DINETTE
8'-8" x 8'-8"

LAUNDRY

d. w.

DINING RM
12'-6"x 11'-6"

ref.

LAV.

heat-circulating fireplace

dn

railing

open

FAMILY RM
16' x 12'-2" (avg.)

entertainment center

TWO CAR GARAGE
21'-4" x 19'-8"

LIVING RM
19'-8"x 12'-6"

FOYER

up

high ceiling

cl

PORCH

MAIN FLOOR

Sunken Great Room Opens to Inviting Veranda

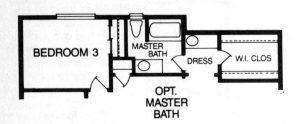

BEDROOM 3

MASTER BATH

DRESS

W.I. CLOS

OPT. MASTER BATH

PLAN GL-4161
WITH BASEMENT

First floor:	1,074 sq. ft.
Second floor:	978 sq. ft.
Total living area:	2,052 sq. ft.

(Not counting basement or garage)

Exterior walls are 2x6 for energy efficiency.

38'-0"

28'-0"

BEDROOM 3
11'-2" x 10'-4"

BATH 1

DRESSING

W.I. CLOS.

HALL

BATH 2

MASTER BEDROOM
14'-4" x 17'-0"

BEDROOM 2
13'-10" x 10'-4"

LOFT/LIBRARY

SECOND FLOOR

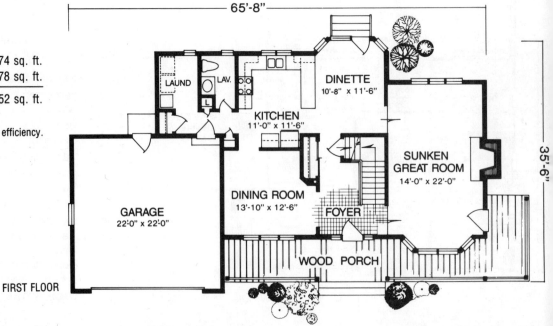

65'-8"

35'-6"

LAUND

LAV.

DINETTE
10'-8" x 11'-6"

KITCHEN
11'-0" x 11'-6"

DINING ROOM
13'-10" x 12'-6"

SUNKEN GREAT ROOM
14'-0" x 22'-0"

FOYER

GARAGE
22'-0" x 22'-0"

WOOD PORCH

FIRST FLOOR

Blueprint Price Code C

Plan GL-4161

Light-Filled Interior

- A stylish contemporary exterior and an open, light-filled interior define this two-level home.
- The covered entry leads to a central gallery. A huge living room and dining room combine to generate a spacious charm that includes a cathedral ceiling and an energy-saving fireplace.
- Oriented to the rear and overlooking the terrace and backyard landscaping are the informal spaces. The family room, sunny semi-circular dinette and modern kitchen share a snack counter and a private terrace.
- The master suite is also located on the main level. It boasts a sloped ceiling, a private terrace and a personal bath with dressing area and whirlpool tub.
- Two to three extra bedrooms on the upper level share a skylighted bath.

Plan K-683-D

Bedrooms: 3-4	Baths: 2½-3
Space:	
Upper floor	491 sq. ft.
Main floor	1,562 sq. ft.
Total Living Area	**2,053 sq. ft.**
Basement	1,425 sq. ft.
Garage	400 sq. ft.
Exterior Wall Framing	2x4 or 2x6

Foundation options:
Standard Basement
Slab
(Foundation & framing conversion diagram available—see order form.)

Blueprint Price Code	C

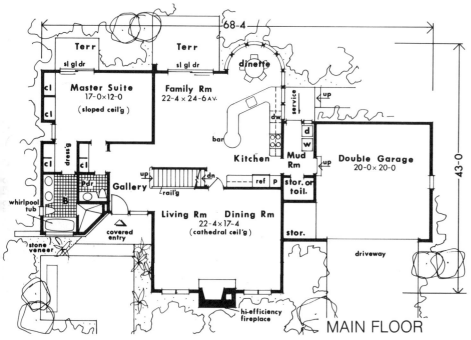

UPPER FLOOR

MAIN FLOOR

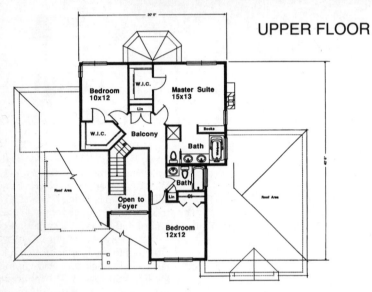

UPPER FLOOR

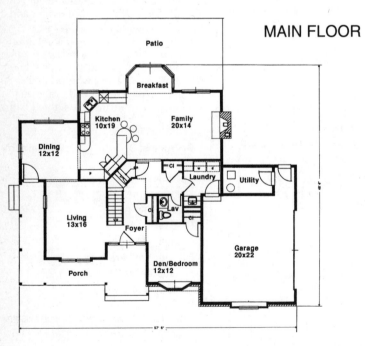

MAIN FLOOR

Intriguing Country Look

- The look of this modern and intriguing country home is enhanced by circle-top windows and a lovely front covered entry and porch.
- Off the entry is a functional den, extra bedroom or study with a bay window.
- The formal living areas merge to the left of the foyer.
- A spacious walk-through kitchen adjoins a bright, bayed breakfast nook and a large family room at the rear. A handy snack counter serves the three rooms, which also share views of the family room fireplace and the outdoor patio.
- Two full baths and abundant closet space serve the three bedrooms on the upper floor.

Plan CAR-9201

Bedrooms: 3-4	Baths: 2½
Living Area:	
Upper floor	822 sq. ft.
Main floor	1,278 sq. ft.
Total Living Area:	**2,100 sq. ft.**
Standard basement	1,278 sq. ft.
Garage	440 sq. ft.
Exterior Wall Framing:	2x6

Foundation Options:
Standard basement
Slab
(Typical foundation & framing conversion diagram available—see order form.)

BLUEPRINT PRICE CODE:	C

Upstairs Suite Creates Adult Retreat

● This multi-level design is ideal for a gently sloping site with a view to the rear.

● Upstairs master suite is a sumptuous "adult retreat" complete with magnificent bath, vaulted ceiling, walk-in closet, private deck and balcony loft.

● Living room includes wood stove area and large windows to the rear. Wood bin can be loaded from outside.

● Main floor also features roomy kitchen and large utility area.

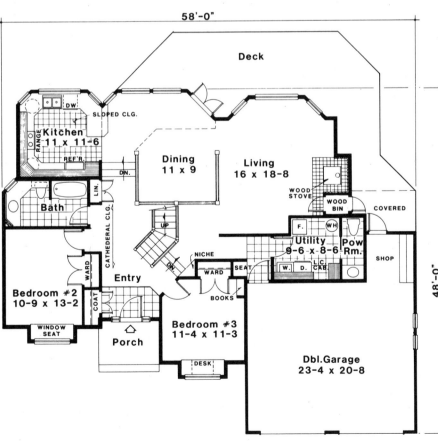

Plan NW-544-S

Bedrooms: 3	Baths: 2½
Space:	
Upper floor:	638 sq. ft.
Main floor:	1,500 sq. ft.
Total living area:	2,138 sq. ft.
Garage:	545 sq. ft.
Exterior Wall Framing:	2x6

Foundation options:
Crawlspace only.
(Foundation & framing conversion diagram available — see order form.)

Blueprint Price Code: C

A Colonial for Today

- Designed for a growing family, this handsome traditional home offers four bedrooms plus a den and three complete baths. The Colonial exterior is updated by a covered front entry porch topped off with a fanlight window above.
- The dramatic tiled foyer is two stories high and provides direct access to all the home's living areas. The spacious living room has an inviting brick fireplace and sliding pocket doors to the adjoining dining room.
- Overlooking the backyard, the huge combination kitchen/family room is the home's hidden charm. The family room has a window wall with sliding glass doors that open to an enticing terrace. The kitchen features a peninsula breakfast bar with seating for six. A built-in entertainment center and bookshelves line one wall of the family room.
- The adjacent mudroom is just off the garage entrance and includes a pantry closet. A full bath and a large den complete the first floor.
- The second floor is highlighted by a beautiful balcony that is open to the foyer below. The luxurious master suite is brightened by a skylight and boasts two closets, including an oversized walk-in closet. The master bath has a whirlpool tub and dual-sink vanity.
- The three remaining bedrooms are generously sized and have plenty of storage space. Another full bath serves these bedrooms.

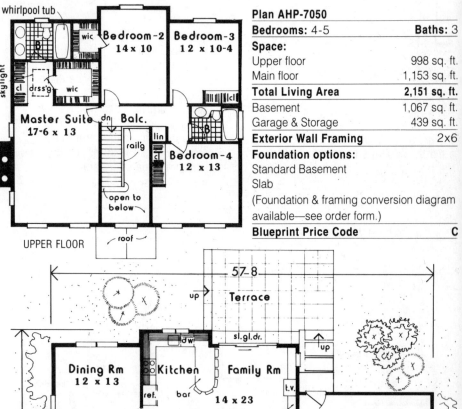

Plan AHP-7050

Bedrooms: 4-5	Baths: 3
Space:	
Upper floor	998 sq. ft.
Main floor	1,153 sq. ft.
Total Living Area	**2,151 sq. ft.**
Basement	1,067 sq. ft.
Garage & Storage	439 sq. ft.
Exterior Wall Framing	2x6

Foundation options:
Standard Basement
Slab
(Foundation & framing conversion diagram available—see order form.)

Blueprint Price Code	C

UPPER FLOOR

MAIN FLOOR

TO ORDER THIS BLUEPRINT, CALL TOLL-FREE 1-800-547-5570   Plan AHP-7050   **PRICES AND DETAILS ON PAGES 12-15**

Front Porch Invites Visitors

- This neat and well-proportioned design exudes warmth and charm.
- The roomy foyer connects formal dining and living rooms for special occasions, and the living and family rooms join together to create abundant space for large gatherings.
- The large kitchen, dinette and family room flow from one to the other for great casual family living.
- Upstairs, you'll find two master bath options in the blueprints, along with an optional fourth bedroom that replaces the library and adds 23 sq. ft. to the second floor.

Plan GL-2161

Bedrooms: 3-4	Baths: 2½
Space:	
Upper floor	991 sq. ft.
Main floor	1,170 sq. ft.
Total Living Area	**2,161 sq. ft.**
Basement	1,170 sq. ft.
Garage	462 sq. ft.
Exterior Wall Framing	2x6

Foundation options:

Standard Basement
(Foundation & framing conversion diagram available—see order form.)

Blueprint Price Code	**C**

UPPER FLOOR

OPT. MSTR. BATH

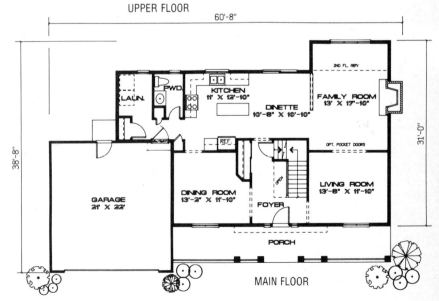

MAIN FLOOR

Country Charm

- Two story bay windows, a wrap-around porch and a half-round window theme adds up to country charm.
- Interior charm begins with a two-story entry at the stairwell, with a view into the living/dining room with fireplace, bay windows and sliders to the side porch.
- The kitchen serves the formal dining room and the breakfast bay, and enjoys the family room fireplace.
- There are four large bedrooms upstairs, including a master suite that features a walk-in closet and private bath.

Plans P-7748-2A & -2D

Bedrooms: 4	Baths: 2½
Space:	
Upper floor:	1,010 sq. ft.
Main floor:	1,157 sq. ft.
Total living area:	**2,167 sq. ft.**
Basement:	1,157 sq. ft.
Garage:	498 sq. ft.
Exterior Wall Framing:	2x6

Foundation options:
Daylight basement.   (P-7748-2D)
Crawlspace.   (P-7748-2A)
(Foundation & framing conversion diagram available — see order form.)

Blueprint Price Code:	C

UPPER FLOOR

BASEMENT

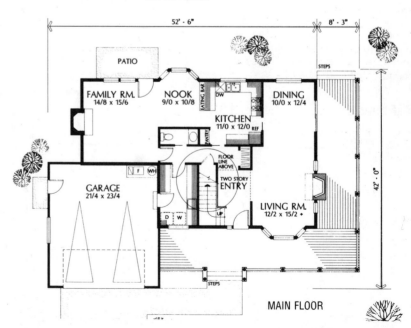

MAIN FLOOR

Plans P-7748-2A & -2D

PRICES AND DETAILS ON PAGES 12-15

Chalet Style for Town or Country

- The exterior features exposed beams, board siding and viewing decks with cut-out railings to give this home the look of a mountain chalet.
- Inside, the design lends itself equally well to year-round family living or part-time recreational enjoyment.
- An expansive Great Room features an impressive fireplace and includes a dining area next to the well-planned kitchen.
- The upstairs offers the possibility of an adult retreat, with a fine master bedroom with private bath and large closets, plus a loft area available for many uses.
- Two secondary bedrooms are on the main floor, and share another bath.
- The daylight basement level includes a garage and a large recreation room with a fireplace and a half-bath.

Plan P-531-2D

Bedrooms: 3	Baths: 2½
Living Area:	
Upper floor	573 sq. ft.
Main floor	1,120 sq. ft.
Daylight basement	532 sq. ft.
Total Living Area:	**2,225 sq. ft.**
Garage	541 sq. ft.
Exterior Wall Framing:	2x6
Foundation Options:	
Daylight basement	
(Typical foundation & framing conversion diagram available—see order form.)	
BLUEPRINT PRICE CODE:	C

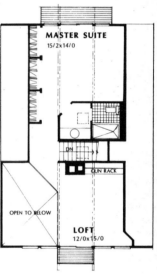

UPPER FLOOR

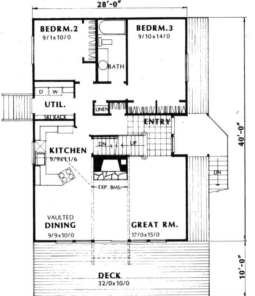

MAIN FLOOR

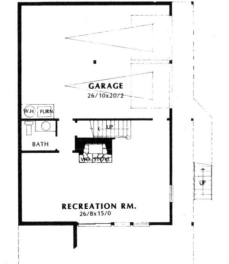

DAYLIGHT BASEMENT

Distinctive Contemporary

- Distinctive rooflines and elegant windows give this home an eye-catching, contemporary look.
- The interior offers a vaulted family room with fireplace, built-in shelving, a rear patio and an open stairway to the upper level.
- The nook and island kitchen share an eating bar and patio of their own.
- Formal living and dining rooms combine at the front of the home, both with raised ceilings.
- The main-floor master suite is entered through elegant double doors; it has a nearby washer/dryer and private bath with isolated toilet, separate shower and step-up spa.
- A study/loft shares the upper level with two additional bedrooms.

Plans P-7750-3A & -3D

Bedrooms: 3	Baths: 2 ½
Space:	
Upper floor	616 sq. ft.
Main floor	1,685 sq. ft.
Total Living Area	**2,301 sq. ft.**
Daylight Basement	1,685 sq. ft.
Garage	699 sq. ft.
Exterior Wall Framing	2x6
Foundation options:	**Plan #**
Crawlspace	P-7750-3A
Daylight Basement	P-7750-3D
(Foundation & framing conversion diagram available—see order form.)	
Blueprint Price Code	C

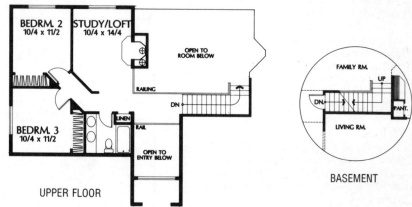

UPPER FLOOR

BASEMENT

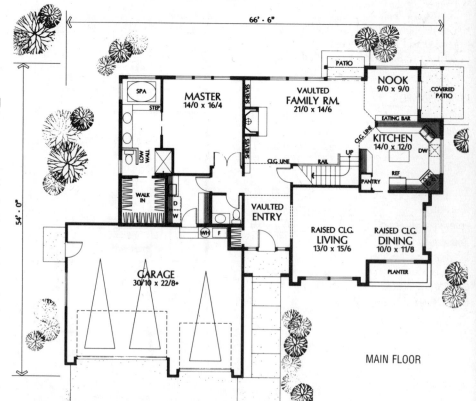

MAIN FLOOR

Plans P-7750-3A & -3D

Grand Colonial Home

- This grand Colonial home boasts a porch entry framed by bay windows and gable towers.
- The two-story foyer directs guests to the adjoining dining room and the living room with fireplace.
- At the rear, the family room features a media wall, a bar and terrace access through French doors.
- Connected to the family room is a high-tech kitchen with an island work area, a pantry, a work desk and a circular dinette.
- A private terrace, a romantic fireplace, a huge walk-in closet and a lavish bath with whirlpool tub are featured in the main-floor master suite.
- Three bedrooms and two full baths share the upper floor.

Plan AHP-9120

Bedrooms: 4	Baths: 3½
Space:	
Upper floor	776 sq. ft.
Main floor	1,551 sq. ft.
Total Living Area	**2,327 sq. ft.**
Basement	1,580 sq. ft.
Garage	440 sq. ft.
Exterior Wall Framing	2x4 or 2x6
Foundation options:	
Standard Basement	
Crawlspace	
Slab	
(Foundation & framing conversion diagram available—see order form.)	
Blueprint Price Code	C

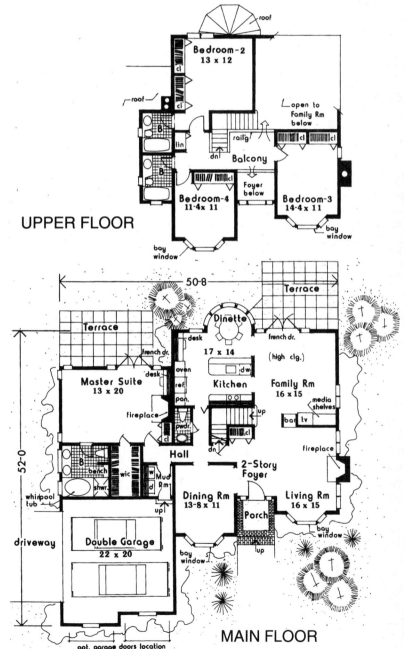

UPPER FLOOR

MAIN FLOOR

Deluxe Master Bedroom Suite

A balanced exterior with rich brick accents and arched windows sets off this home and creates plenty of street appeal.

The vaulted foyer is overlooked by the balcony upstairs for a dramatic first impression. Once inside, an arched entryway opens off the foyer and visually frames the handsome fireplace located in the vaulted living room. Sliding glass doors open off the adjoining vaulted dining room onto a fantastic deck with built-in benches.

The open family room, nook, and kitchen arrangement is a real winner. You'll discover a handy island and convenient walk-in pantry for extra storage in the kitchen. The sunny alcove provides a light and airy nook for informal dining. A trio of windows brightens the family room and a cheerful woodstove provides a warm glow on cold winter nights.

Accessible off the main entry, the den is easily converted to a fourth bedroom.

The laundry room includes abundant cabinet space for storage as well as a deep sink for those big clean-up jobs.

Upstairs, you'll find a fantastic master suite. An alcove provides a private sitting area for quiet conversations, while the luxurious master bath offers a relaxing interlude in a spa tub. Two skylights brighten the main bath.

Exterior walls are 2x6 for energy efficiency.

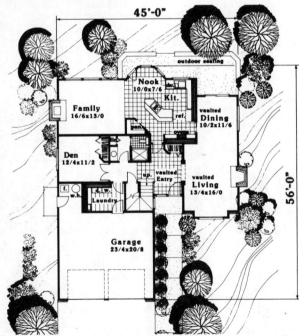

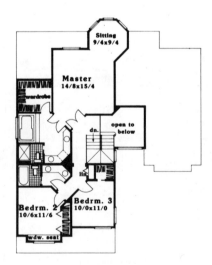

PLAN R-2112
WITHOUT BASEMENT
(CRAWLSPACE FOUNDATION)

Main floor:	1,360 sq. ft.
Upper floor:	980 sq. ft.
Total living area:	2,340 sq. ft.

Blueprint Price Code C

Plan R-2112

TO ORDER THIS BLUEPRINT, CALL TOLL-FREE 1-800-547-5570

PRICES AND DETAILS ON PAGES 12-15

Design for Steep Terrain

- A railing separates the sunken living room from the vaulted dining room for a great visual flow of space.
- The kitchen is highlighted by a corner window sink, an island and a walk-in pantry.
- The master suite includes a luxury bath illuminated by a skylight and a spacious walk-in closet.
- The partial basement could be omitted for building on flat lots.

UPPER FLOOR

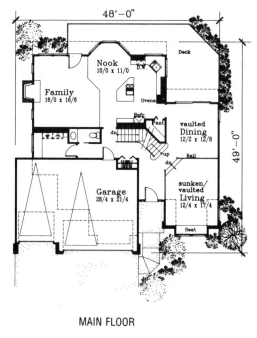

MAIN FLOOR

BASEMENT

Plan CDG-2009	
Bedrooms: 3	**Baths:** 2½
Living Area:	
Upper floor	1,113 sq. ft.
Main floor	1,230 sq. ft.
Total Living Area:	**2,343 sq. ft.**
Partial daylight basement	606 sq. ft.
Garage	604 sq. ft.
Exterior Wall Framing:	2x6
Foundation Options:	
Partial daylight basement (Typical foundation & framing conversion diagram available—see order form.)	
BLUEPRINT PRICE CODE:	C

You Asked For It!

- Our most popular plan in recent years, E-3000, has now been downsized for affordability, without sacrificing character or excitement.
- Exterior appeal is created with a covered front porch with decorative columns, triple dormers and rail-topped bay windows.
- The floor plan has combined the separate living and family rooms available in E-3000 into one spacious family room with corner fireplace, which flows into the dining room through a columned gallery.
- The kitchen serves the breakfast eating room over an angled snack bar, and features a huge walk-in pantry.
- The stunning main-floor master suite offers a private sitting area, a walk-in closet and a dramatic, angled master bath.
- There are two large bedrooms upstairs accessible via a curved staircase with bridge balcony.

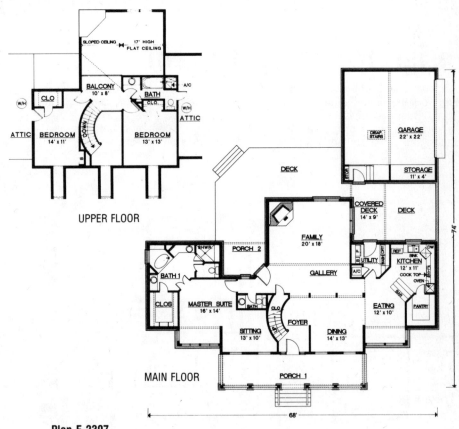

UPPER FLOOR

MAIN FLOOR

Plan E-2307

Bedrooms: 3	Baths: 2½

Space:

Upper floor:	595 sq. ft.
Main floor:	1,765 sq. ft.
Total living area:	**2,360 sq. ft.**
Basement:	1,765 sq. ft.
Garage:	484 sq. ft.
Storage area:	44 sq. ft.

Exterior Wall Framing: 2x6

Foundation options:
Standard basement.
Crawlspace.
Slab.
(Foundation & framing conversion diagram available — see order form.)

Blueprint Price Code: C

Great Room for Entertaining

- The focal point of this stylish contemporary home is its central sunken Great Room with luxurious features. Guests are easily served at a handy wet bar or at an angled counter by the kitchen and breakfast area. Open beams above and a woodstove to the left add a rustic ambience. A rear window wall gives sweeping views of the outdoors.
- A wraparound deck or patio expands the entertaining area.
- The main-floor master suite boasts a raised tub, a separate shower, a walk-in closet and outdoor access. A sunspace may be added if desired.
- Two bedrooms and a bath are located upstairs.

Plan LRD-22884

Bedrooms: 3	Baths: 2½
Living Area:	
Upper floor	674 sq. ft.
Main floor	1,686 sq. ft.
Total Living Area:	**2,360 sq. ft.**
Standard basement	1,686 sq. ft.
Garage	450 sq. ft.
Exterior Wall Framing:	2x6

Foundation Options:

Standard basement
Crawlspace

(Typical foundation & framing conversion diagram available—see order form.)

BLUEPRINT PRICE CODE:	**C**

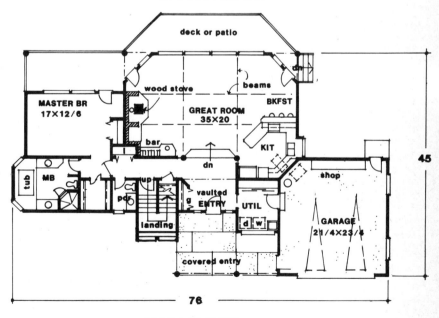

UPPER FLOOR

MAIN FLOOR

Classic Lines, Elegant Flair

- The rich brick arches and classic lines of this home lend an elegant air which will never be outdated.
- Inside, graceful archways lead from the vaulted entry to the living and dining rooms, which both feature heightened ceilings.
- The kitchen offers abundant counter space, an expansive window over the kitchen sink, large island, desk and pantry.
- The kitchen also is open to the nook and family room, which combine to make a great space for family living.
- The master suite is a pure delight, with a luxurious whirlpool tub and his-and-hers walk-in closets.
- The room marked for storage could also be an exercise or hobby room.

Plan R-2083

Bedrooms: 3	Baths: 2½
Living Area:	
Upper floor	926 sq. ft.
Main floor	1,447 sq. ft.
Total Living Area:	**2,373 sq. ft.**
Garage	609 sq. ft.
Storage	138 sq. ft.
Exterior Wall Framing:	2x6

Foundation Options:

Crawlspace
(Typical foundation & framing conversion diagram available—see order form.)

BLUEPRINT PRICE CODE: C

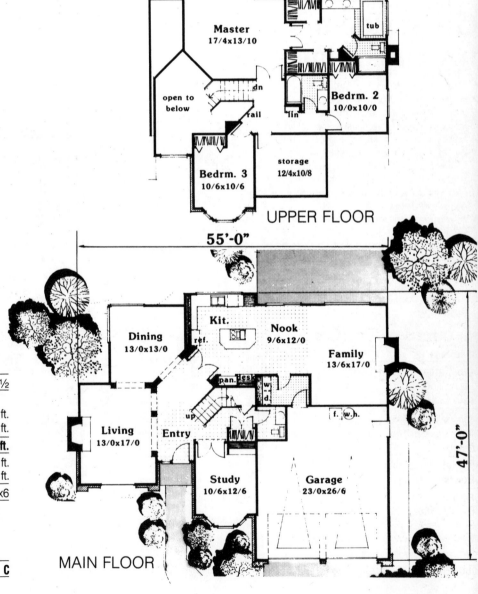

UPPER FLOOR

Master 17/4x13/10

open to below

rail

dn

lin

Bedrm. 2 10/0x10/0

tub

Bedrm. 3 10/6x10/6

storage 12/4x10/8

MAIN FLOOR

55'-0"

47'-0"

Dining 13/0x13/0

Kit.

ref.

Nook 9/6x12/0

Family 13/6x17/0

pan. desk

w/d

f. w.h.

Living 13/0x17/0

up

Entry

Study 10/6x12/6

Garage 23/0x26/6

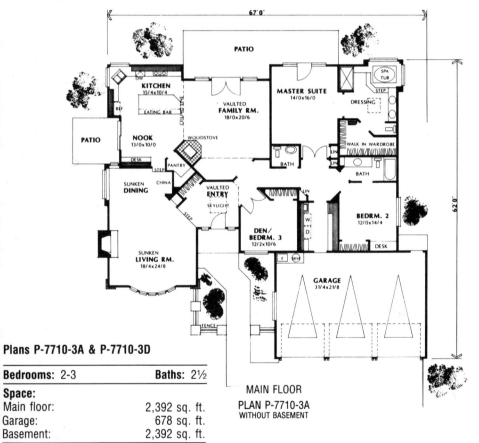

Plans P-7710-3A & P-7710-3D

Bedrooms: 2-3	**Baths:** 2½

Space:

Main floor:	2,392 sq. ft.
Garage:	678 sq. ft.
Basement:	2,392 sq. ft.

Exterior Wall Framing:	2x6

Foundation options:
Daylight basement, Plan P-7710-3D.
Crawlspace, Plan P-7710-3A.
(Foundation & framing conversion
diagram available — see order form.)

Blueprint Price Code:	C

MAIN FLOOR
PLAN P-7710-3A
WITHOUT BASEMENT

PLAN P-7710-3D
WITH DAYLIGHT BASEMENT

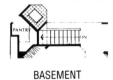

BASEMENT

Deluxe Living Spaces

- Visitors approaching the front entry are welcomed by a courtyard with a wrought-iron fence and brick columns.
- The front door opens to a large entry magnified by a vaulted ceiling and skylight.
- The large, sunken living/dining area is great for formal entertaining.
- A huge kitchen/nook combination includes an island eating bar which adjoins the spacious, vaulted family room.
- The magnificent master suite includes an incredible bath with spa tub, separate shower and a large walk-in wardrobe closet.
- Daylight basement version doubles the space.

High Luxury in One Story

- Beautiful arched windows lend a luxurious feeling to the exterior of this one-story home.
- Twelve-foot-high ceilings add volume to both the wide entry area and the central living room, which boasts a large fireplace and access to a covered porch and the patio beyond.
- Double doors separate the formal dining room from the corridor-style kitchen. Features of the kitchen include a pantry, a trash compactor, garage access and an angled eating bar with double sinks and a dishwasher. The sunny, bayed eating area is perfect for casual family meals.
- The plush master suite has amazing amenities: patio access, a walk-in closet, a skylighted, angled whirlpool tub, a separate shower, and private access to the laundry/utility room.
- Three bedrooms and a full bath are situated on the opposite side of the home.

Plan E-2302

Bedrooms: 4	Baths: 2
Living Area:	
Main floor	2,396 sq. ft.
Total Living Area:	**2,396 sq. ft.**
Standard basement	2,396 sq. ft.
Garage	484 sq. ft.
Exterior Wall Framing:	2x6

Foundation Options:
Standard basement
Crawlspace
Slab
(Typical foundation & framing conversion diagram available—see order form.)

BLUEPRINT PRICE CODE: C

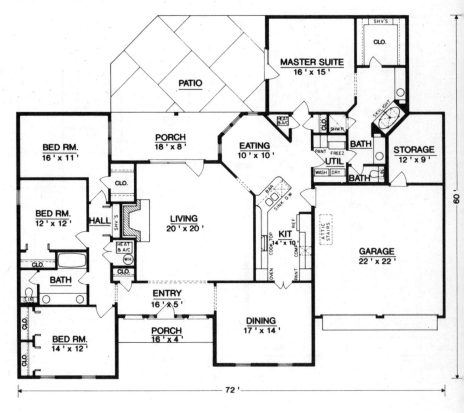

MAIN FLOOR

Charming Economy

- This plan is economical to construct, but still charming in its visual appeal and restful interior.
- The interior presents abundant space for family or informal entertaining.
- A roomy Great Room adjoining the breakfast nook includes a handsome fireplace.
- A formal dining room is available for dressier occasions.
- The downstairs guest bedroom would make a great home office if not needed for sleeping.
- Note the full bath downstairs, in addition to two baths upstairs.
- The large master suite includes a sumptuous private bath with separate tub and shower.
- Bedrooms 2 and 3 are roomy and share access to a compartmentalized bath.

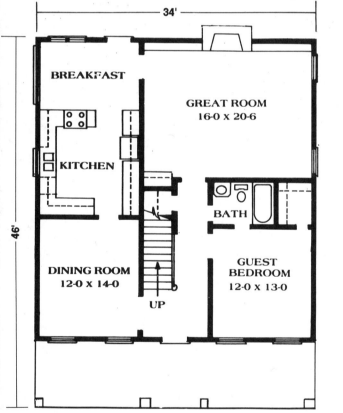

Plan V-2398	
Bedrooms: 3-4	**Baths:** 3
Space:	
Upper floor:	1,174 sq. ft.
Main floor:	1,224 sq. ft.
Total living area:	2,398 sq. ft.
Exterior Wall Framing:	2x6

Ceiling Heights:
Upper floor: 9'
Main floor: 9'

Foundation options:
Crawlspace only.
(Foundation & framing conversion diagram available — see order form.)

Blueprint Price Code: C

Old-Fashioned Charm

- A trio of dormers add old-fashioned charm to this modern design.
- Both the living room and the dining room offer vaulted celings, and the two rooms flow together to create a sense of even more spaciousness.
- The open kitchen, nook and family room combination features a sunny alcove, a walk-in pantry and an inviting wood stove.
- A first-floor den and a walk-through utility room are other big bonuses.
- Upstairs, the master suite includes a walk-in closet and a deluxe bath with a spa tub and a separate shower and water closet.
- Two more bedrooms, each with a window seat, and a bonus room complete this stylish design.

Plan CDG-2004

Bedrooms: 4	**Baths:** 2½

Living Area:	
Upper floor	928 sq. ft.
Main floor	1,317 sq. ft.
Bonus room	192 sq. ft.
Total Living Area:	**2,437 sq. ft.**
Partial daylight basement	780 sq. ft.
Garage	537 sq. ft.
Exterior Wall Framing:	2x6

Foundation Options:

Partial daylight basement
Crawlspace
(Typical foundation & framing conversion diagram available—see order form.)

BLUEPRINT PRICE CODE:	C

UPPER FLOOR

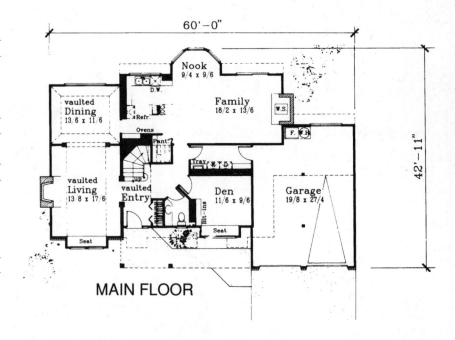

MAIN FLOOR

  Plan CDG-2004

Design Exudes Warmth and Comfort

- This plan represents a return to traditional styling with the open-concept interior so much in demand today.
- A vaulted entry and living room with an adjacent dining room make up the formal portion of this plan.
- A spacious hall leads to the large informal entertaining area composed of the kitchen, nook and family room.

- The second floor offers a large master suite and two additional bedrooms with a bonus room that can be left unfinished until needed.
- Exterior rooflines are all gabled for ease of construction and lower framing costs. The brick veneer garage face echoes the brick columns supporting the covered entry.

Plan S-8389	
Bedrooms: 3-4	**Baths:** 2½
Living Area:	
Upper floor	932 sq. ft.
Main floor	1,290 sq. ft.
Bonus room	228 sq. ft.
Total Living Area:	**2,450 sq. ft.**
Standard basement	1,290 sq. ft.
Garage	429 sq. ft.
Exterior Wall Framing:	2x6
Foundation Options:	
Standard basement	
Crawlspace	
Slab	
(Typical foundation & framing conversion diagram available—see order form.)	
BLUEPRINT PRICE CODE:	C

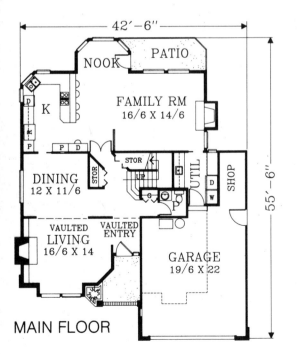

MAIN FLOOR

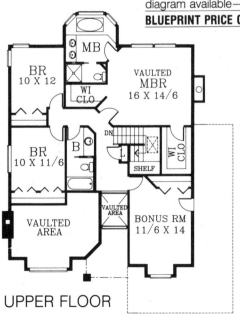

UPPER FLOOR

Elegantly Different

Arched brickwork and windows lend a uniqueness and elegance that is immediately noticeable in this three-bedroom home.

A covered entry leads to a vaulted foyer opening to the formal living and dining room area. Here you'll find large windows and a vaulted ceiling that add a light airiness to the room, balanced by the coziness of a warm fireplace.

With skylights and a windowed nook opening onto the back deck, the kitchen is bright and sunny — perfect for those who enjoy cooking and entertaining. An angled island with convenient eating bar highlight the kitchen, along with a handy pantry and a centrally located desk that is ideal for household planning. A generous family room with a practical wood stove off the kitchen is certain to make this part of your home the center of family activity.

A hallway from the garage passes a utility room designed with the emphasis on "utility." The counter space lends itself to many projects, and a built-in ironing board provides convenience and saves space.

The secluded study on the lower level provides a place for work or quiet leisure activities.

Upstairs, the two children's bedrooms show their individuality — one with a window seat and the other with a bay window. The master bedroom is a treat, with an octagonal sitting area to capture the view, a large walk-in closet, and a bath area with a step-up spa tub and double vanity.

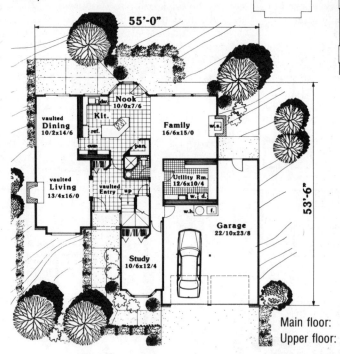

Exterior walls are 2x6 construction.
Crawlspace foundation only.

Main floor: 1,460 sq. ft.
Upper floor: 1,005 sq. ft.

Total living area: 2,465 sq. ft.
(Not counting garage)

Blueprint Price Code C
Plan R-2117

TO ORDER THIS BLUEPRINT, CALL TOLL-FREE 1-800-547-5570

PRICES AND DETAILS ON PAGES 12-15

All-American Country Home

- Romantic, old-fashioned and spacious living areas combine to create this modern home.
- Off the entryway is the generous living room with fireplace and French doors which open onto the traditional rear porch.
- Country kitchen features an island table for informal occasions, while the adjoining family room is ideal for family gatherings.
- Practically placed, a laundry/mud room lies off the garage for immediate disposal of soiled garments.
- This plan is available with garage (H-3711-1) or without garage (H-3711-2) and with or without basement.

PLANS H-3711-2 & H-3711-2A
(WITHOUT GARAGE)

PLANS H-3711-1 & H-3711-1A
(WITH GARAGE)

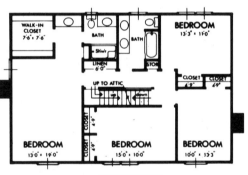

UPPER FLOOR

Plans H-3711-1/1A & -2/2A	
Bedrooms: 4	Baths: 2½

Space:

Upper floor:	1,176 sq. ft.
Main floor:	1,288 sq. ft.
Total living area:	**2,464 sq. ft.**
Basement:	approx. 1,288 sq. ft.
Garage:	505 sq. ft.

Exterior Wall Framing:	2x6

Foundation options:
Standard basement (Plans H-3711-1 & -2).
Crawlspace (Plans H-3711-1A & -2A).
(Foundation & framing conversion diagram available — see order form.)

Blueprint Price Code:	C

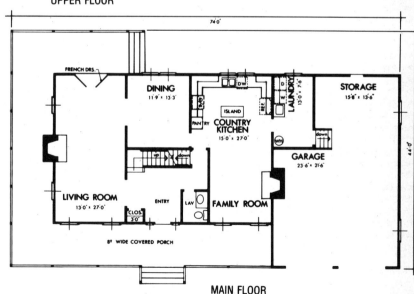

MAIN FLOOR

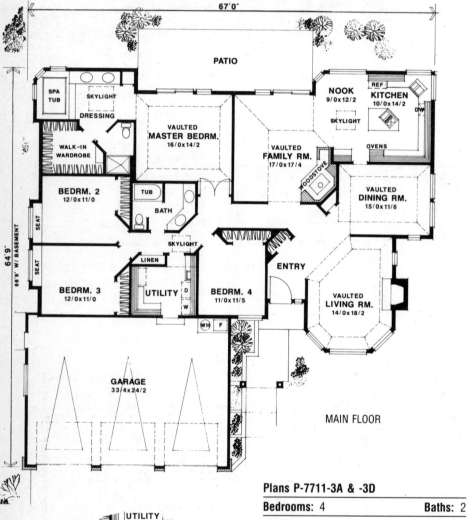

PATIO

SPA TUB

SKYLIGHT

DRESSING

WALK-IN WARDROBE

VAULTED MASTER BEDRM.
16/0 x 14/2

NOOK
9/0 x 12/2

REF

KITCHEN
10/0 x 14/2

DW

SKYLIGHT

OVENS

BEDRM. 2
12/0 x 11/0

TUB

BATH

VAULTED FAMILY RM.
17/0 x 17/4

WOODSTOVE

VAULTED DINING RM.
15/0 x 11/6

SEAT

SEAT

SKYLIGHT

LINEN

BEDRM. 3
12/0 x 11/0

UTILITY

D

W

BEDRM. 4
11/0 x 11/5

ENTRY

VAULTED LIVING RM.
14/0 x 18/2

WH

F

GARAGE
33/4 x 24/2

MAIN FLOOR

UTILITY

W

DN

GARAGE

PLAN P-7711-3D
WITH DAYLIGHT BASEMENT

67'0"

64'9"

66'9" W/ BASEMENT

Full of Surprises

- While dignified and reserved on the outside, this plan presents delightful surprises throughout the interior.
- Interesting angles, vaulted ceilings, surprising spaces and bright windows abound everywhere you look in this home.
- The elegant, vaulted living room is off the expansive foyer, and includes an imposing fireplace and large windows areas.
- The delightful kitchen includes a handy island and large corner windows in front of the sink.
- The nook is brightened not only by large windows, but also by a skylight.
- The vaulted family room includes a corner wood stove area plus easy access to the outdoors.
- A superb master suite includes an exquisite bath with a skylighted dressing area and large walk-in closet.
- Three secondary bedrooms share another full bath, and the large laundry room is conveniently positioned near the bedrooms.

Plans P-7711-3A & -3D

Bedrooms: 4	Baths: 2

Space:

Main floor (non-basement version):	2,510 sq. ft.
Main floor (basement version):	2,580 sq. ft.
Basement:	2,635 sq. ft.
Garage:	806 sq. ft.

Exterior Wall Framing:	2x6

Foundation options:
Daylight basement (Plan P-7711-3D).
Crawlspace (Plan P-7711-3A).
(Foundation & framing conversion diagram available — see order form.)

Blueprint Price Code: D

"Down-Home" Country Flavor

AREAS	
Living	2522 sq. ft.
Garage	484 sq. ft.
Porches	444 sq. ft.
Storage Rooms	90 sq. ft.
Total	3540 sq. ft.

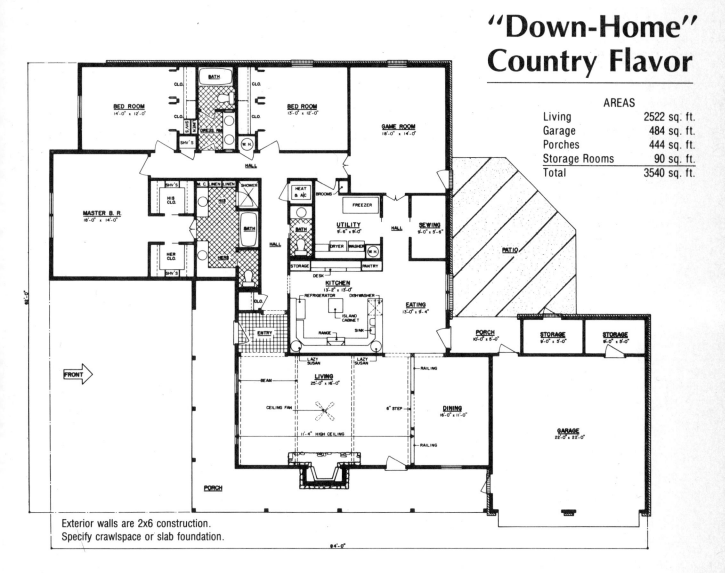

Exterior walls are 2x6 construction.
Specify crawlspace or slab foundation.

Blueprint Price Code D
Plan E-2502

TO ORDER THIS BLUEPRINT,
CALL TOLL-FREE 1-800-547-5570

PRICES AND DETAILS
ON PAGES 12-15   169

Difficult Site, No Problem

- Designed to accommodate an irregular site, this traditionally styled exterior has an interior with modern conveniences.
- The kitchen is well-planned to serve both the dining room and a spacious octagonal breakfast nook.
- A large living room with window seat and fireplace and a generous-sized family room provide ample space for entertaining and family activities.
- The master bedroom suite features a large bath with step-up jacuzzi tub, walk-in closet, and a private study entered through double doors.
- Room for three additional bedrooms and a full bath are located on the upper floor.

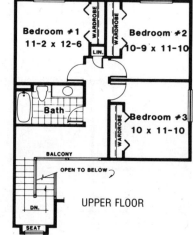

Bedroom #1 11-2 x 12-6
Bedroom #2 10-9 x 11-10
Bedroom #3 10 x 11-10
WARDROBE
LIN.
Bath
BALCONY
OPEN TO BELOW
DN.
SEAT

UPPER FLOOR

Plan NW-660	
Bedrooms: 4	**Baths:** 2½

Space:	
Upper floor:	700 sq. ft.
Main floor:	1,720 sq. ft.
Lower/basement:	106 sq. ft.
Total living area:	2,526 sq. ft.
Garage:	659 sq. ft.

Exterior Wall Framing:	2x6

Foundation options:
Daylight basement.
(Foundation & framing conversion diagram available — see order form.)

Blueprint Price Code:	D

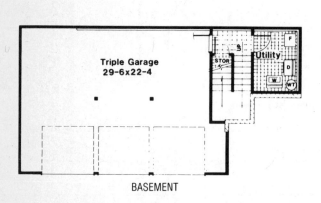

Triple Garage 29-6x22-4
STOR.
Utility
F
D
W

BASEMENT

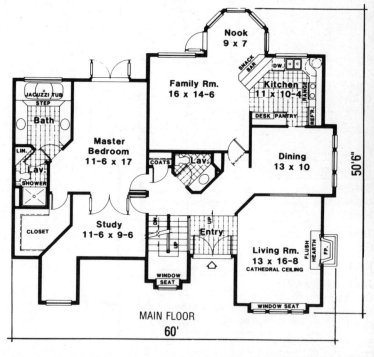

Nook 9 x 7
Family Rm. 16 x 14-6
Kitchen 11 x 10-4
SNACK BAR
DW.
RANGE
REFR.
DESK PANTRY
JACUZZI TUB
STEP
Bath
LIN.
Lav.
SHOWER
Master Bedroom 11-6 x 17
COATS
Lav.
Dining 13 x 10
Study 11-6 x 9-6
CLOSET
Entry
WINDOW SEAT
Living Rm. 13 x 16-8
CATHEDRAL CEILING
FLUSH HEARTH
FP.
WINDOW SEAT

50'6"

MAIN FLOOR
60'

Three-Sided Porch Adds Country Charm

- This inviting wrap-around porch invites visitors to come up and say "Howdy."
- The interior is just as welcoming, with its large family room with a fireplace, and the adjoining dining/living rooms.
- The open-design kitchen includes a convenient work island and adjoins a bright breakfast nook.
- A den off the foyer would make a nice home office, if needed, or a fourth bedroom as well.
- Upstairs, note the majestic master suite with a big walk-in closet and luxury bath.
- Bedrooms 2 and 3 are served by a second full bath and include large closets.

Plan I-2531-A

Bedrooms: 3-4	Baths: 2½

Space:	
Upper floor:	1,064 sq. ft.
Main floor:	1,467 sq. ft.
Total living area:	2,531 sq. ft.
Garage:	608 sq. ft.

Exterior Wall Framing:	2x6

Foundation options:
Crawlspace.
(Foundation & framing conversion diagram available — see order form.)

Blueprint Price Code:	D

UPPER FLOOR

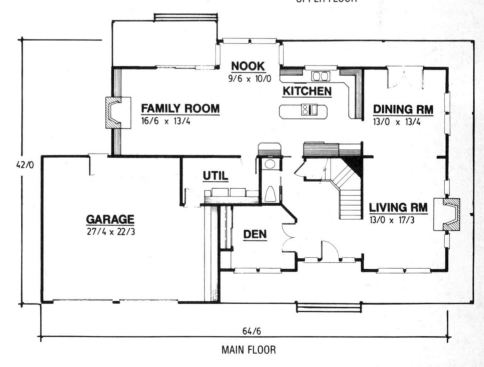

MAIN FLOOR

Hill-Hugging Design

- This angled ranch design with an expandable basement makes the most of a rear-sloping hillside site.
- Strong angles, trapezoid windows and diagonal wood siding create a contemporary appeal.
- The bright foyer unfolds to a dynamic Great Room with 12-ft. walls, corner transom windows and a fireplace.
- The island kitchen and the skylighted dinette adjoin the Great Room to the right. A windowed sink allows a view of the backyard deck, which is accessed through the dinette.
- A huge walk-in closet and a private garden bath serve the master bedroom, which is also found on the main floor. The nearby den could be used as an extra bedroom or a reading room.
- The partially finished lower level offers two more bedrooms and a full bath. There is sufficient space to add a rec room or another bedroom later.

Plan PM-691

Bedrooms: 3+	Baths: 2½
Living Area:	
Main floor	1,947 sq. ft.
Basement (finished)	587 sq. ft.
Total Living Area:	**2,534 sq. ft.**
Basement (unfinished)	1,360 sq. ft.
Garage	580 sq. ft.
Exterior Wall Framing:	2x6

Foundation Options:
Daylight basement
Standard basement
(Typical foundation & framing conversion diagram available—see order form.)

BLUEPRINT PRICE CODE:	D

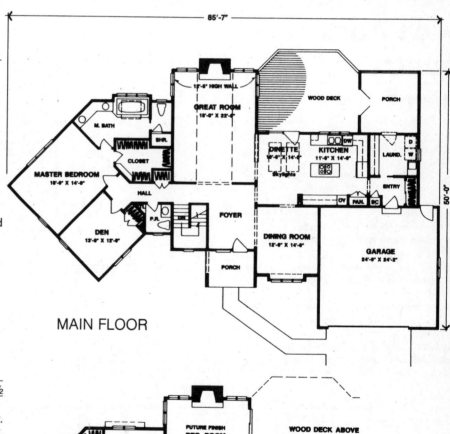

MAIN FLOOR

BASEMENT

Striking and Stylish

- A striking roofline, vertical wood siding and brick accents set this home apart from the rest. Inside, the unusual floor plan is full of high-fashion features.
- A spectacular vaulted entry with a wide, open stairway makes a strong first impression. The sunken living room is also vaulted and has a fireplace that can be enjoyed from the adjoining formal dining room.

- The efficiently designed kitchen features a boxed-out window, a curved island counter and a large breakfast nook.
- Angled off the nook, the large family room displays a handsome fireplace. A handy den is just off the family room.
- The light-filled stairway leads to the upper floor, where double doors open to the gorgeous master suite. Features here include a tiled shower, double sinks, a spa tub and an enormous walk-in closet.
- Two more generous-sized bedrooms include built-in desks set beneath windows for plenty of natural light.

Plan R-2122

Bedrooms: 3+	Baths: 2½
Living Area:	
Upper floor	1,060 sq. ft.
Main floor	1,475 sq. ft.
Total Living Area:	**2,535 sq. ft.**
Garage	440 sq. ft.
Exterior Wall Framing:	2x6
Foundation Options:	
Crawlspace	
BLUEPRINT PRICE CODE:	**D**

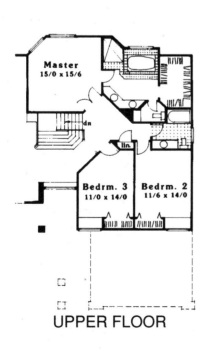

UPPER FLOOR

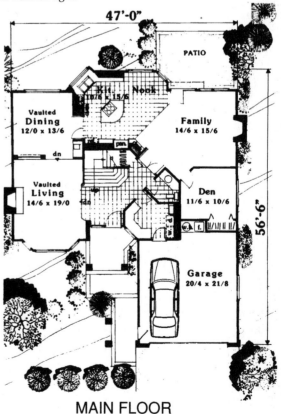

MAIN FLOOR

TO ORDER THIS BLUEPRINT,
CALL TOLL-FREE 1-800-547-5570

Plan R-2122

PRICES AND DETAILS
ON PAGES 12-15

173

Luxury Home with Outdoor Orientation

- Courtyards, patios and a sun room orient this multi-level home to the outdoors.
- Interior design is carefully zoned for informal family living and formal entertaining.
- Expansive kitchen includes large island and plenty of counter space, and a sunny nook adjoins the kitchen.

- Soaring entry area leads visitors to the vaulted living room with fireplace, or to the more casual family room.
- An optional fourth bedroom off the foyer would make an ideal home office.
- Upstairs master suite includes luxury bath and big walk-in closet.
- Daylight basement version adds nearly 1,500 more square feet of space.

Plans P-7659-3A & -3D

Bedrooms: 3-4	Baths: 3

Space:	
Upper floor:	1,050 sq. ft.
Main floor:	1,498 sq. ft.

Total living area:	2,548 sq. ft.
Basement:	1,490 sq. ft.
Garage:	583 sq. ft.

Exterior Wall Framing:	2x4

Foundation options:
Daylight basement, Plan P-7659-3D.
Crawlspace, Plan P-7659-3A.
(Foundation & framing conversion diagram available — see order form.)

Blueprint Price Code:	D

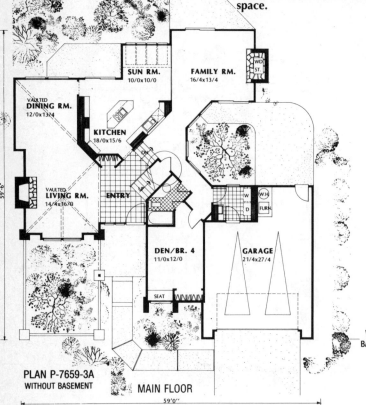

SUN RM.
10/0x10/0

FAMILY RM.
16/4x13/4

VAULTED DINING RM.
12/0x13/4

KITCHEN
18/0x15/6

VAULTED LIVING RM.
14/4x16/0

ENTRY

DEN/BR. 4
11/0x12/0

GARAGE
21/4x27/4

SEAT

PLAN P-7659-3A
WITHOUT BASEMENT

MAIN FLOOR
59'0"

PLAN P-7659-3D
WITH DAYLIGHT BASEMENT
BASEMENT LEVEL: 1490 sq. ft.

SEAT

MASTER
16/4x13/4

TUB   DRESS'G

WALK-IN WARDROBE

OPEN TO BELOW

BEDRM. 2
11/0x11/0

BEDRM. 3
11/0x12/0

SEAT

UPPER FLOOR

Gracious Open-Concept Floor Plan

- A striking and luxurious contemporary, this home offers great space and modern styling.
- A covered entry leads to a spacious foyer, which flows into the sunken dining and Great Room area.
- The vaulted Great Room boasts a spectacular two-story-high fireplace, dramatic window walls and access to a rear deck or patio.
- A bright nook adjoins the open kitchen, which includes a corner window above

the sink.
- The den, which could be a guest bedroom, features a bay window overlooking the deck.
- The majestic master bedroom on the second floor offers a 10-ft.-high coved ceiling, a splendid bath, a large closet and a private deck.
- Two other upstairs bedrooms share a second bath and a balcony hallway overlooking the Great Room and entry below.

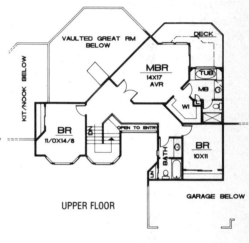

UPPER FLOOR

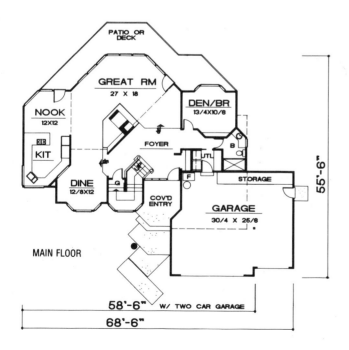

MAIN FLOOR

58'-6" W/ TWO CAR GARAGE

68'-6"

Plan S-41587

Bedrooms: 3-4	Baths: 3
Living Area:	
Upper floor:	1,001 sq. ft.
Main floor	1,550 sq. ft.
Total Living Area:	**2,551 sq. ft.**
Basement	1,550 sq. ft.
Garage (three-car)	773 sq. ft.
Exterior Wall Framing:	2x6

Foundation Options:
Daylight basement
Standard basement
Crawlspace
Slab
(Typical foundation & framing conversion diagram available—see order form.)

BLUEPRINT PRICE CODE:	D

Classic Four-Bedroom

- This classic design has a lot to offer a family of five or more.
- Large formal living areas provide an abundance of windows and space.
- The rear-oriented, sunken family room has a fireplace, sliders and optional expansion room.
- A bayed dinette joins the generous island kitchen with pantry; convenient main-floor washer/dryer are nearby.
- The upper balcony overlooks the foyer and accesses four roomy bedrooms; the master suite offers beautiful double doors and a private bath with dual vanities, large walk-in closet and separate shower and glassed bath.

Plan A-2247-DS

Bedrooms: 4	Baths: 2 ½
Space:	
Upper floor	1,220 sq. ft.
Main floor	1,339 sq. ft.
Total Living Area	**2,559 sq. ft.**
Basement	1,339 sq. ft.
Garage	576 sq. ft.
Exterior Wall Framing	2x6
Foundation options:	
Standard Basement	
(Foundation & framing conversion diagram	
available—see order form.)	
Blueprint Price Code	**D**

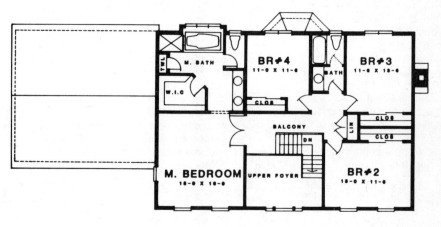

UPPER FLOOR

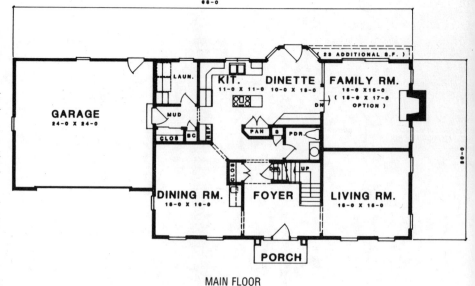

MAIN FLOOR

Plan A-2247-DS

PRICES AND DETAILS
ON PAGES 12-15

UPPER FLOOR

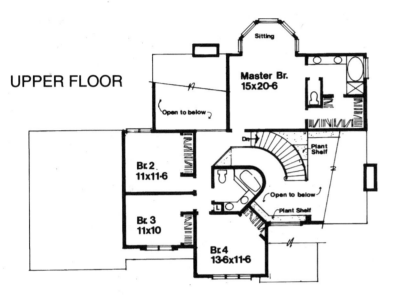

Sitting

Master Br.
15x20-6

Open to below

Br 2
11x11-6

Plant Shelf

Open to below

Plant Shelf

Br 3
11x10

Br 4
13-6x11-6

MAIN FLOOR

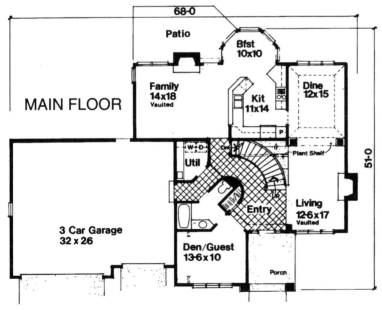

68-0

Patio

Bfst
10x10

Family
14x18
Vaulted

Kit
11x14

Dine
12x15

51-0

W + D

Util

Plant Shelf

3 Car Garage
32 x 26

Entry

Living
12-6x17
Vaulted

Den/Guest
13-6x10

Porch

Trendy Transitional Design

- This striking transitional design offers a combination of staggered hip and gable rooflines, arched transoms, brick trim and a three-car garage with decorative facade.
- The dramatic vaulted entry focuses on circular walls and a curved staircase.
- To the right, a large, vaulted living room with fireplace combines with a formal dining room for a spacious setting. The two rooms are separated by a decorative plant shelf and columns.
- Open to the walk-through kitchen are a gazebo breakfast area and a vaulted family room with corner window and second fireplace.
- The main-floor guest room can be used as a den or library.
- The upper-level master bedroom is separated from the three other bedrooms. A private master bath and octagonal sitting area are featured.

Plan AG-9104

Bedrooms: 4-5	**Baths:** 3
Living Area:	
Upper floor:	1,128 sq. ft.
Main floor	1,456 sq. ft.
Total Living Area:	**2,584 sq. ft.**
Standard basement	1,456 sq. ft.
Garage	832 sq. ft.
Exterior Wall Framing:	2x6

Foundation Options:
Standard basement
(Typical foundation & framing conversion diagram available—see order form.)

BLUEPRINT PRICE CODE:	D

Grand One-Story

- A covered entry, arched windows and stucco siding create a look and feel of grandeur for this exciting one-story.
- Inside, the rooms are bright and open, maintaining the drama of the exterior.
- The open dining room has a vaulted ceiling and columns that connect the decorative railings that surround it.
- The spacious sunken living room is recessed from the foyer and features an inviting fireplace, a coved ceiling and a boxed window with arched transoms.
- The gourmet kitchen shares a large, informal area with the breakfast nook and the family room. The family can enjoy a warm fireplace, a wet bar and a convenient snack counter without interrupting activities. Two walk-in pantries and a patio door to the adjoining deck are also featured.
- Double doors lead to the luxurious master suite, which is removed from the secondary bedrooms. The oversized master bath features two walk-in closets and an oversized garden Jacuzzi set in a bay window that overlooks the deck.

Plan S-122089

Bedrooms: 3+	Baths: 2½
Living Area:	
Main floor	2,591 sq. ft.
Total Living Area:	**2,591 sq. ft.**
Standard basement	2,580 sq. ft.
Garage	556 sq. ft.
Exterior Wall Framing:	2x6

Foundation Options:
Standard basement
Crawlspace
Slab
(Typical foundation & framing conversion diagram available—see order form.)

BLUEPRINT PRICE CODE: D

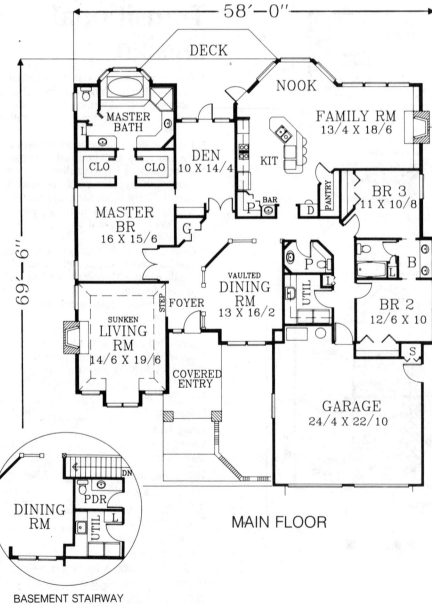

MAIN FLOOR

BASEMENT STAIRWAY LOCATION

Plan S-122089

PRICES AND DETAILS
ON PAGES 12-15

Deck Wraps Home with Plenty of Views

- A full deck and an abundance of windows surround this exciting two-level contemporary.
- Skywalls are found in the kitchen and the dining room; the kitchen also features an island cooktop.
- The brilliant living room boasts a huge fireplace and a cathedral ceiling, plus a stunning window wall.
- The master bedroom offers private access to the deck and an attached bath with a dual-sink vanity, a large tub and a walk-in closet.
- A generous-sized family room and two extra bedrooms share the lower level with a two-car garage and a shop or storage area.

Plan NW-579

Bedrooms: 4	Baths: 3
Living Area:	
Main floor	1,707 sq. ft.
Daylight basement	901 sq. ft.
Total Living Area:	**2,608 sq. ft.**
Tuck-under garage	588 sq. ft.
Shop	162 sq. ft.
Exterior Wall Framing:	2x6

Foundation Options:

Daylight basement
(Typical foundation & framing conversion diagram available—see order form.)

BLUEPRINT PRICE CODE:	D

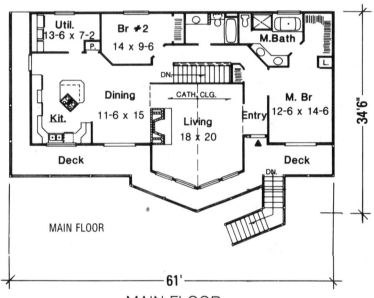

MAIN FLOOR

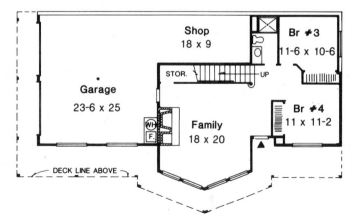

DAYLIGHT BASEMENT

Privacy and Luxury

- This home's large roof planes and privacy fences enclose a thoroughly modern, open floor plan.
- A beautiful courtyard greets guests on their way to the secluded entrance. Inside, a vaulted entry area leads directly into the living and dining rooms, which also boast a vaulted ceiling, plus floor-to-ceiling windows, a fireplace and a wall-length stone hearth.
- A sun room next to the spacious, angular kitchen offers passive solar heating and natural brightness.
- The vaulted family room features access to a rear patio through sliding glass doors.
- The main-floor master bedroom boasts sliders to a secluded portion of the front courtyard. The vaulted master bath includes a walk-in closet, a raised tub, a separate shower and access to a private sun deck with a hot tub.
- Upstairs, two bedrooms are separated by a bridge hallway that overlooks the rooms below.

Plans P-7663-3A & -3D

Bedrooms: 3 +	Baths: 3
Living Area:	
Upper floor	569 sq. ft.
Main floor	2,039 sq. ft.
Total Living Area:	**2,608 sq. ft.**
Daylight basement	2,039 sq. ft.
Garage	799 sq. ft.
Exterior Wall Framing:	2x4
Foundation Options:	**Plan #**
Daylight basement	P-7663-3D
Crawlspace	P-7663-3A
(Typical foundation & framing conversion diagram available—see order form.)	
BLUEPRINT PRICE CODE:	**D**

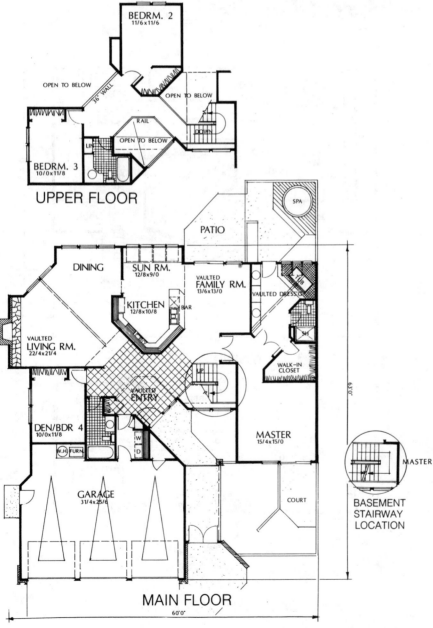

UPPER FLOOR

BEDRM. 2
11/6 x 11/6

OPEN TO BELOW

3'6" WALL

OPEN TO BELOW

RAIL

OPEN TO BELOW

DOWN

LIN

BEDRM. 3
10/0 x 11/8

MAIN FLOOR
60'0"

SPA

PATIO

DINING

SUN RM.
12/8 x 9/0

VAULTED
FAMILY RM.
13/6 x 13/0

VAULTED DRESS

KITCHEN
12/8 x 10/8

BAR

VAULTED
LIVING RM.
22/4 x 21/4

WALK-IN
CLOSET

VAULTED
ENTRY

MASTER
15/4 x 15/0

DEN/BDR 4
10/0 x 11/8

W.H. FURN.

GARAGE
31/4 x 25/6

COURT

63'0"

BASEMENT
STAIRWAY
LOCATION

MASTER

Plans P-7663-3A & -3D

PRICES AND DETAILS
ON PAGES 12-15

Well-Planned Walkout

- A dramatic double-back stair atrium descending from the Great Room to the bonus family room below ties the main floor design to the walkout lower level.
- A traditional exterior leads into a dramatic, open-feeling interior.
- The vaulted Great Room and dining room are separated by stylish columns.
- A see-thru fireplace is shared by the Great Room and the exciting kitchen with octagonal breakfast bay.
- A double-doored den/guest room opens off the Great Room.
- The spacious main floor master suite includes a huge walk-in closet and lavish master bath.

Plan AG-9105

Bedrooms: 3-4	Baths: 2½
Space:	
Main floor:	1,838 sq. ft.
Daylight basement:	800 sq. ft.
Total living area:	2,638 sq. ft.
Unfinished basement area:	1,038 sq. ft.
Garage:	462 sq. ft.
Exterior Wall Framing:	2x6

Foundation options:
Daylight basement.
(Foundation & framing conversion diagram available — see order form.)

Blueprint Price Code:	D

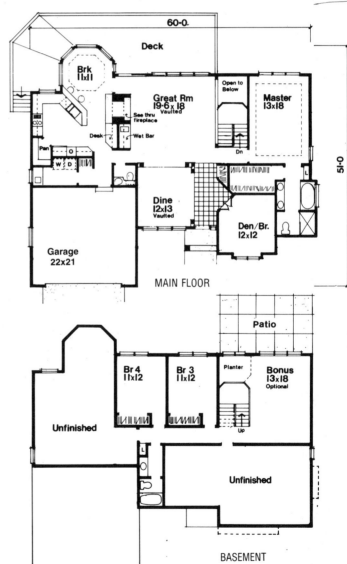

MAIN FLOOR

BASEMENT

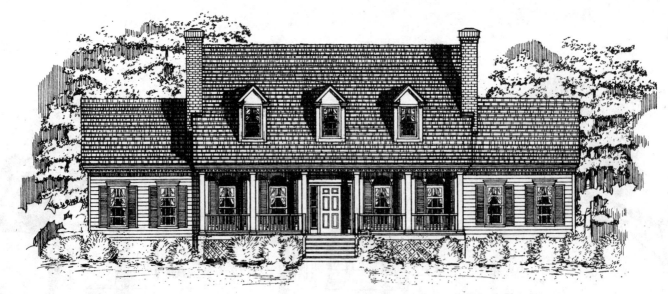

Innovative Floor Plan

- The wide, covered front porch, arched windows and symmetrical lines of this traditional home conceal the modern, innovative floor plan found within.
- The vaulted foyer guides guests to the formal living and dining rooms. The hotspot of the home is the Great Room, island kitchen and glassed-in eating nook, all of which overlook a large backyard deck. The main floor is also enhanced by 9-ft. ceilings.
- Three fireplaces add to the home's aura of warmth and hospitality, including a fireplace in the master suite. This private oasis also boasts a cathedral ceiling and a delicious bath with a garden tub.
- The largest of the four bedrooms upstairs has a sloped ceiling and a private bath, making it an ideal guest suite. Another full bath is centrally located for the remaining bedrooms.

Plan AHP-9360

Bedrooms: 5	Baths: 3½
Living Area:	
Upper floor	970 sq. ft.
Main floor	1,688 sq. ft.
Total Living Area:	**2,658 sq. ft.**
Standard basement	1,550 sq. ft.
Garage and utility area	443 sq. ft.
Exterior Wall Framing:	2x6

Foundation Options:

Standard basement
Crawlspace
Slab
(Typical foundation & framing conversion diagram available—see order form.)

BLUEPRINT PRICE CODE:	D

UPPER FLOOR

MAIN FLOOR

Simple Exterior, Luxurious Interior

- Modest and unassuming on the exterior, this design provides an elegant and spacious interior.
- Highlight of the home is undoubtedly the vast Great Room/ Dining area, with its vaulted ceiling, massive hearth and big bay windows.
- An exceptionally fine master suite is also included, with a large sleeping area, luxurious bath and big walk-in closet.
- A beautiful kitchen is joined by a bright bay-windowed breakfast nook; also note the large pantry.
- The lower level encompasses two more bedrooms and a generously sized game room and bar.

MAIN FLOOR

BASEMENT

Plan P-6595-3D

Bedrooms: 3	Baths: 2½

Space:

Main floor:	1,530 sq. ft.
Lower level:	1,145 sq. ft.
Total living area:	**2,675 sq. ft.**
Garage:	462 sq. ft.

Exterior Wall Framing:	2x6

Foundation options:
Daylight basement only.
(Foundation & framing conversion diagram available — see order form.)

Blueprint Price Code:	D

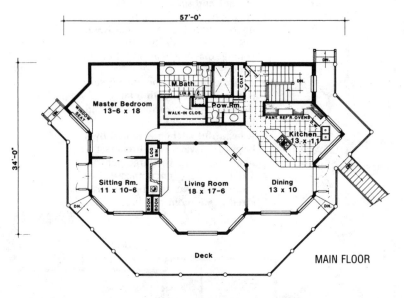

57'-0"

34'-0"

Master Bedroom
13-6 x 18

WALK-IN CLOS.

M.Bath

LIN. L.C.

COAT

Pow.Rm.

PANT. REF'R. OVENS

DN.

DN.

Kitchen
13 x 11

Sitting Rm.
11 x 10-6

LOG BIN

BOOK BOOK

Living Room
18 x 17-6

Dining
13 x 10

DN.

DN.

Deck

MAIN FLOOR

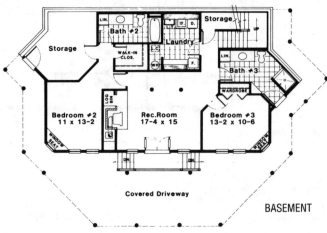

LIN.

Bath #2

Storage

W.D.

Storage

Laundry

UP

Storage

WALK-IN CLOS.

LC

LIN.

F

WH

Bath #3

Bedroom #2
11 x 13-2

LOG BIN

WINDOW SEAT

Rec.Room
17-4 x 15

WARDROBE

Bedroom #3
13-2 x 10-6

WINDOW SEAT

DN.

DN.

Covered Driveway

BASEMENT

Panoramic View for Scenic Site

- Large deck offers a panoramic view and plenty of space for outdoor living.
- Sunken living room features big windows and impressive fireplace.
- Living room is set off by railings, not walls, to create visual impact of big space.
- Master suite includes private bath, large closet, sitting area and access to deck.
- Lower level includes rec room with fireplace, two bedrooms, two baths and large utility area.

Plan NW-779

Bedrooms: 3	Baths: 3½
Space:	
Main floor:	1,450 sq. ft.
Lower floor:	1,242 sq. ft.
Total living area:	2,692 sq. ft.
Exterior Wall Framing:	2x6

Foundation options:
  Daylight basement only.
  (Foundation & framing conversion diagram available — see order form.)

Blueprint Price Code:	D

Exceptional Multi-Level

- A dramatic circular stairway sets a tone of elegance and intrigue in this stunning contemporary home.
- The double-door entry flows into the bright living room, which features a railed overlook to the formal dining room below. An angled fireplace warms both rooms.
- Three steps down, the kitchen offers a curved eating bar that is echoed by a breakfast nook set into a curved wall of sunny windows.
- The large family room boasts a corner woodstove to warm indoor activities, while a two-level deck with a hot tub provides outdoor fun.
- Upstairs, the unique master suite features a secluded den, a whirlpool tub, a shower and a private deck.
- The circular stairway continues up to a railed roof deck. This large open-air entertainment space is highlighted by a barbecue that cleverly utilizes the fireplace chimney.

Plan I-2700

Bedrooms: 3	Baths: 2½
Living Area:	
Upper floor	715 sq. ft.
Main floor	1,985 sq. ft.
Total Living Area:	**2,700 sq. ft.**
Standard basement	1,985 sq. ft.
Garage	582 sq. ft.
Exterior Wall Framing:	2x6

Foundation Options:
Standard basement
Crawlspace
Slab

BLUEPRINT PRICE CODE: D

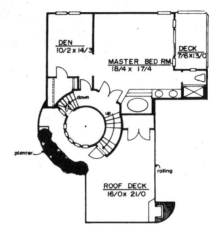

UPPER FLOOR

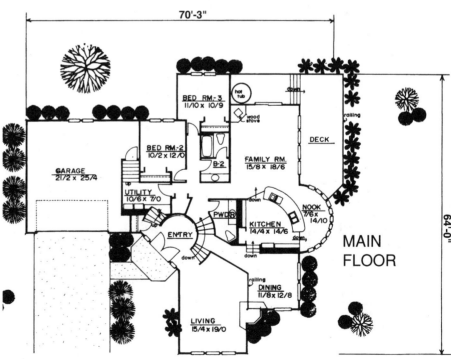

MAIN FLOOR

FRONT VIEW

REAR VIEW

Popular Plan for Any Setting

- City, country, or casual living is possible in this versatile two-story design.
- A spa room and sunning area lie between the master suite and Great Room, all encased in an extended eating and viewing deck.
- U-shaped kitchen, nook, and dining area fulfill your entertaining and dining needs.
- Two additional bedrooms and a balcony hall are located on the second level.
- Daylight basement option provides a fourth bedroom, shop, and recreation area.

UPPER FLOOR

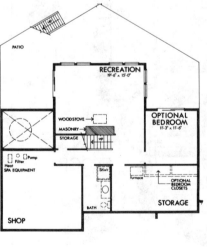

BASEMENT

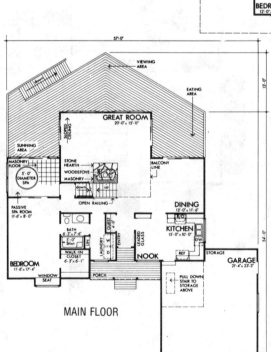

MAIN FLOOR

Plans H-952-1A &-1B

Bedrooms: 3-4	Baths: 2-3
Space:	
Upper floor:	470 sq. ft.
Main floor:	1,207 sq. ft.
Passive spa room:	102 sq. ft.
Total living area:	1,779 sq. ft.
Basement:	1,105 sq. ft.
Garage:	496 sq. ft.
Exterior Wall Framing:	2x6

Foundation options:
Daylight Basement (Plan H-952-1B).
Crawlspace (Plan H-952-1A).
(Foundation & framing conversion diagram available — see order form.)

Blueprint Price Code:	
H-952-1A:	B
H-952-1B:	D

TO ORDER THIS BLUEPRINT,
CALL TOLL-FREE 1-800-547-5570

Plans H-952-1A & -1B

PRICES AND DETAILS
ON PAGES 12-15

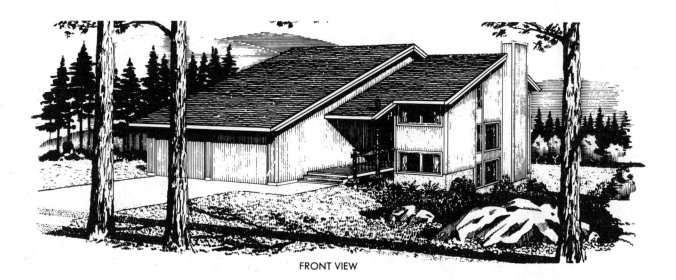

FRONT VIEW

Luxury on a Compact Foundation

Sky-lighted sloped ceilings, an intriguing stairway and overhead bridge and a carefully planned first floor arrangement combine to delight the senses as one explores this spacious 2737 sq. ft. home. A major element of the design is the luxurious master suite that is reached via the stairway and bridge. An abundance of closet space and an oversized bath are welcome features here.

Two bedrooms, generous bath facilities and a large family room provide lots of growing room for the younger members of the household.

All these features are available within a mere 36' width which allows the house to be built on a 50' wide lot — a real bonus these days.

Main floor:	1,044 sq. ft.
Upper level:	649 sq. ft.
Lower level:	1,044 sq. ft.
Total living area: (Not counting garage)	2,737 sq. ft.

(Exterior walls are 2x6 construction)

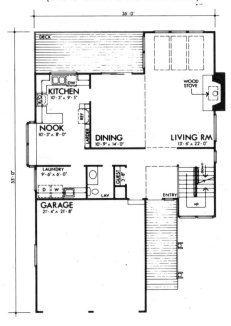

MAIN FLOOR
1044 SQUARE FEET

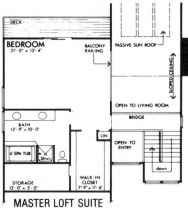

MASTER LOFT SUITE
649 SQUARE FEET

LOWER LEVEL
1044 SQUARE FEET

REAR VIEW

Blueprint Price Code D

Plan H-2110-1B

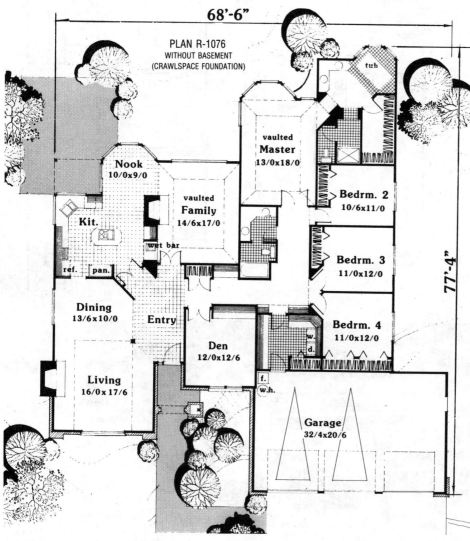

PLAN R-1076
WITHOUT BASEMENT
(CRAWLSPACE FOUNDATION)

68'-6"

77'-4"

Nook
10/0x9/0

vaulted
Master
13/0x18/0

tub

vaulted
Family
14/6x17/0

Bedrm. 2
10/6x11/0

Kit.

wet bar

ref.   pan.

Dining
13/6x10/0

Entry

Bedrm. 3
11/0x12/0

Bedrm. 4
11/0x12/0

w.
d.

Den
12/0x12/6

f.
w.h.

Living
16/0x17/6

Garage
32/4x20/6

Extraordinary Design

The gorgeous brick facade combined with the spacious three-car garage make this elegant four-bedroom home a most popular design within its size range.

The large island kitchen features a pantry, double corner sink and a view to the octagonal breakfast nook. Not to be overlooked is the large laundry room with closet, cabinets, and counter top.

The vaulted family room is equipped in style — with a fireplace and an adjacent wet bar. For secluded study and quiet times, there is a separate den.

The bedroom wing includes three bedrooms in addition to the spacious master suite. Each secondary bedroom has abundant wall-spanning closet space, and shares a common dual-vanity bath.

The vaulted master suite includes an octagonal projection that may be used as a sitting area for reading or study. The regal master bath is stunning. There is a raised, corner spa tub and a spacious walk-in wardrobe in addition to the dual vanity, oversized shower and toilet.

The home also features 2x6 exterior walls for energy efficiency.

Total living area: 2,796 sq. ft.
(Not counting garage)

Blueprint Price Code D
Plan R-1076

TO ORDER THIS BLUEPRINT,
188 **CALL TOLL-FREE 1-800-547-5570**

PRICES AND DETAILS
ON PAGES 12-15

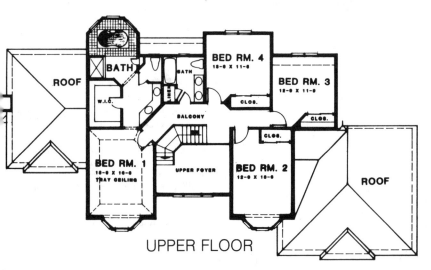

UPPER FLOOR

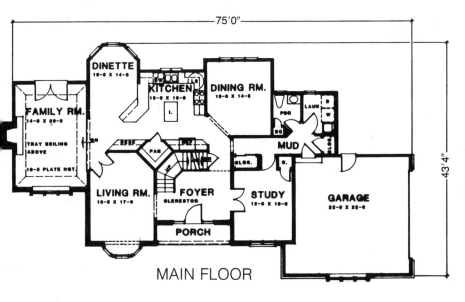

MAIN FLOOR

Meant to Impress

- This home was meant to impress, from inside and out. The exquisite detailing of the exterior is reminiscent of an English manor home. The interior features a floor plan that is designed for elegant entertaining as well as for comfortable family living.

- The kitchen is at the core of the design, between the dining nook and the formal dining room. A breakfast bar faces the bayed dinette for quick meals. An island work center provides extra space while directing traffic flow. A built-in desk, a deluxe walk-in pantry and a lazy Susan are other bonus features.

- The sunken family room is a natural extension of the kitchen and dining areas. A fireplace, a tray ceiling and French doors to the backyard make this room a family favorite.

- The stairway and vaulted foyer are illuminated by a clerestory window above the front door. The master bedroom suite offers a sumptuous spa bath. Three more bedrooms share another full bath.

Plan A-2210-DS

Bedrooms: 4-5	Baths: 2 ½
Space:	
Upper floor	1,208 sq. ft.
Main floor	1,634 sq. ft.
Total Living Area	**2,842 sq. ft.**
Basement	1,634 sq. ft.
Garage	484 sq. ft.
Exterior Wall Framing	2x6
Foundation options:	
Standard Basement	
(Foundation & framing conversion diagram available—see order form.)	
Blueprint Price Code	D

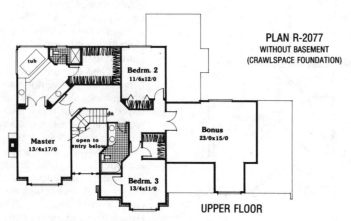

PLAN R-2077
WITHOUT BASEMENT
(CRAWLSPACE FOUNDATION)

tub

Bedrm. 2
11/6x12/0

Master
13/4x17/0

open to
entry below

dn

Bonus
23/0x15/0

Bedrm. 3
13/4x11/0

UPPER FLOOR

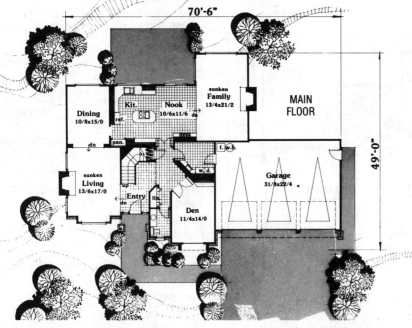

70'-6"

Dining
10/8x15/0

Kit.

ref.

Nook
10/6x11/6

sunken
Family
13/4x21/2

MAIN
FLOOR

49'-0"

pan.

dn

sunken
Living
13/6x17/0

up

Entry

dn

f. w. h.

w/d.

Garage
31/8x22/4

Den
11/4x14/0

Romantic Tudor Accents

Most buyers fall in love with this home before walking in the front door. With its romantic Tudor accents and handsome detailing, it possesses an ageless quality.

The sunken living room is warmed by a stately fireplace. Homeowners appreciate the illuminating effects of the many windows found throughout the home.

Included in the spacious kitchen is a pantry and an efficient center island with cooktop. The adjoining nook opens to the sunken family room one step below, creating an open, casual living area.

A secluded den is set apart from the rest of the household for a bit of quiet solitude. The adjacent utility room provides plenty of storage space and a convenient folding ironing board.

The vaulted entryway is connected to the three bedrooms upstairs by a curved stairway. Behind the double doors is a truly luxurious master suite opening off the balcony. Featured here is a relaxing spa tub, dual vanities, and an enormous walk-in closet. Located at the opposite end of the home is a large bonus room — great for parties and hobbies.

The home is constructed with 2x6 exterior walls for energy efficiency.

Main floor:	1,613 sq. ft.
Upper floor:	1,262 sq. ft.
Total living area: (Not counting garage)	2,875 sq. ft.
Bonus:	424 sq. ft.

Blueprint Price Code D
Plan R-2077

Angled Spaciousness

- This slope-to-the-front home looks impressive with the hip roof and generous windows.
- Upon entry, you may step up into the formal living room with fireplace, high ceiling and large window seats at each end, or into the dining room.
- The adjoining nook and kitchen have front sun deck and rear patio; the attached family room offers a corner wood stove and front bay window.
- A private bath and deck, walk-in closet and beautiful corner windows accentuate the master suite.
- An exciting game room and two additional bedrooms are found on the lower level.

Plan NW-507

Bedrooms: 3	Baths: 2½

Space:

Main floor:	1,963 sq. ft.
Lower floor:	917 sq. ft.
Total living area:	**2,880 sq. ft.**
Garage:	679 sq. ft.
Shop:	140 sq. ft.
Storage:	181 sq. ft.

Exterior Wall Framing:	2x6

Foundation options:
Daylight basement.
(Foundation & framing conversion diagram available — see order form.)

Blueprint Price Code:	D

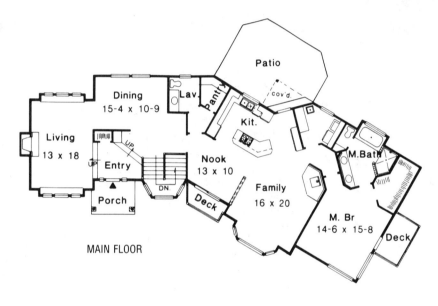

MAIN FLOOR

83' × 48'2"

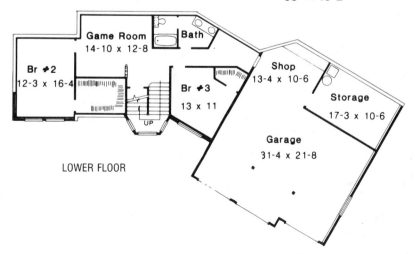

LOWER FLOOR

Nostalgic but New

- Triple dormers, a covered front porch and half-round windows lend a nostalgic country feel to this exciting two-story home.
- A dramatic two-story foyer makes an elegant introduction, leading into the vaulted living room with a fireplace, a window seat and round-top windows.
- The formal dining room, which features a tray ceiling, opens to the living room through an arch supported by stylish columns.
- The island kitchen has an open view into the breakfast nook and the family room with rear patio beyond.
- Upstairs, there are three bedrooms, plus a large bonus room that could be used as a fourth bedroom or as a playroom.
- The master suite dazzles with double doors, a sitting bay, a huge walk-in closet and an angled bath with a corner spa tub beneath windows.

Plan CDG-2031

Bedrooms: 3-5	Baths: 2½
Living Area:	
Upper floor	1,203 sq. ft.
Main floor	1,495 sq. ft.
Bonus room	238 sq. ft.
Total Living Area:	**2,936 sq. ft.**
Garage	811 sq. ft.
Exterior Wall Framing:	2x6

Foundation Options:

Crawlspace
(Typical foundation & framing conversion diagram available—see order form.)

BLUEPRINT PRICE CODE:	D

UPPER FLOOR

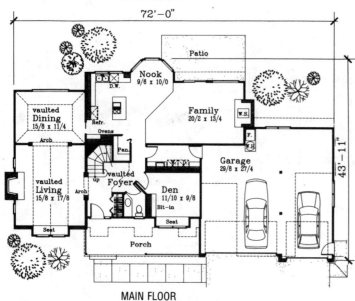

MAIN FLOOR

Balanced Beauty

- Symmetry and balance are the beauty of this design. The columned and gabled wings of the home set off the center portion, which features an arched transom window, a Palladian window and a half-round window.
- Ten-foot ceilings are the rule for the first floor, with the exception of the 12-ft. ceiling in the gigantic Great Room. This dazzling room is further expanded by a rear wall lined with French doors and topped by half-round windows.
- The stairway divides the Great Room from the sunny breakfast nook and the island kitchen. The formal dining room is convenient to both the kitchen and the Great Room.
- The first-floor master bedroom is a treat, with its corner garden tub and opposite shower, double vanity and walk-in closets. A bank of French doors and windows overlooks the backyard.
- The guest bedroom has its own bath. Another bath and two bedrooms are on the upper floor, which has 9-ft. ceilings.

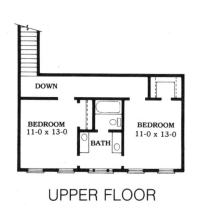

UPPER FLOOR

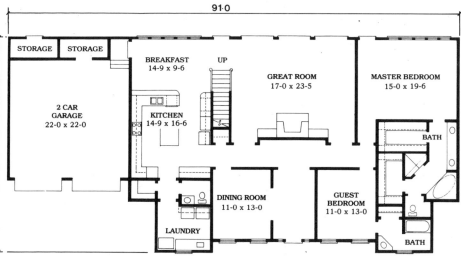

MAIN FLOOR

Plan V-2985

Bedrooms: 4	Baths: 3½
Space:	
Upper floor	591 sq. ft.
Main floor	2,394 sq. ft.
Total Living Area	**2,985 sq. ft.**
Garage	484 sq. ft.
Exterior Wall Framing	2x6

Foundation options:

Crawlspace
(Foundation & framing conversion diagram available—see order form.)

Blueprint Price Code	D

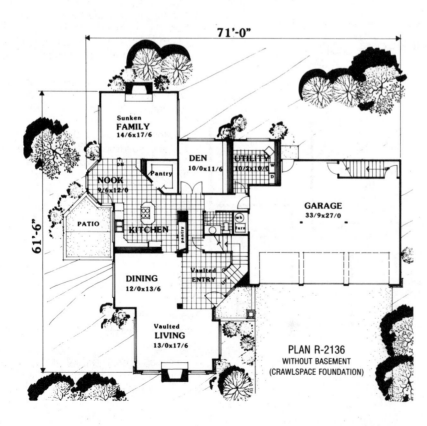

Sitting

MASTER
14/6x19/0

BDRM 2
11/0x12/0

linen

**STO /
OFFICE**
12/0x17/8

DN

Drssg/
bath

wardrobe

DN

BDRM 3
11/6x14/6

open to entry
below

71'-0"

Sunken
FAMILY
14/6x17/6

DEN
10/0x11/6

UTILITY
10/2x10/0

Pantry

NOOK
9/6x12/0

61'-6"

PATIO

KITCHEN

pantry

GARAGE
33/9x27/0

DINING
12/0x13/6

Vaulted
ENTRY

Vaulted
LIVING
13/0x17/6

PLAN R-2136
WITHOUT BASEMENT
(CRAWLSPACE FOUNDATION)

Broad, Sweeping Lines

The rich, warm, earth tones of brick accent the broad, sweeping lines of this lovely 3,073 sq. ft. home.

The vaulted entry provides easy access to all parts of the dwelling. Fireplaces grace both the living and family rooms. The former is vaulted while the latter is a step down from the kitchen/nook area.

In the spacious kitchen, note the island cooktop and wall pantry, in addition to the large walk-in pantry. The nook lends architectural appeal inside and out with its octagonal projection.

Elsewhere on the main floor is a den with library shelving across one entire wall. The laundry is much larger than the usual, offering a deep sink, extensive cabinets and a large countertop.

Classic hardwood styling with turned balusters and hand-carved newel accent the open stairway. On the second floor, the two secondary bedrooms share a corner bath, and both have their own walk-in closets as well as private vanities.

The master suite is masterful indeed, with its sitting bay and a bath that rivals five-star hotel accommodations. Also on this level is space for an office or additional storage above the garage.

The home is designed with 2x6 exterior walls for added insulation.

Main floor:	1,706 sq. ft.
Upper floor:	1,162 sq. ft.
Office/storage:	205 sq. ft.
Total living area: (Not counting garage)	3,073 sq. ft.

Blueprint Price Code E

Plan R-2136

PRICES AND DETAILS
ON PAGES 12-15

Traditional Elegance

- A stately traditional exterior is enhanced by brick with quoin corner details and a stunning two-story entry.
- The formal living and dining rooms flank the entry foyer at the front of the main floor.
- The informal living areas of the island kitchen, dinette bay, and sunken family room with fireplace face the rear yard.
- The main floor also includes a handy mud room with laundry and powder room accessible from a second entrance as well as a den/5th bedroom.
- The upper floor houses four spacious bedrooms and two full baths, including a lavish master bath with corner spa tub and separate shower.

Plan A-2230-DS

Bedrooms: 4-5	**Baths:** 2 ½

Space:

Upper floor	1,455 sq. ft.
Main floor	1,692 sq. ft.
Total Living Area	**3,147 sq. ft.**
Basement	1,692 sq. ft.
Garage	484 sq. ft.
Exterior Wall Framing	**2x6**

Foundation options:

Standard Basement

(Foundation & framing conversion diagram available—see order form.)

Blueprint Price Code	**E**

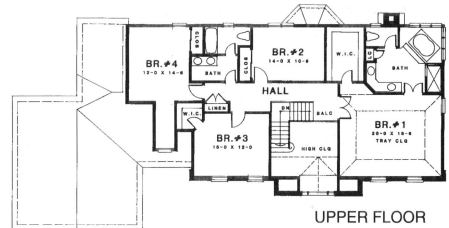

UPPER FLOOR

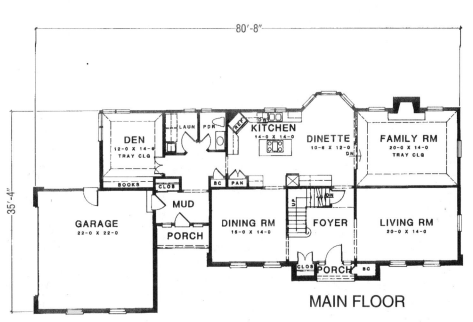

MAIN FLOOR

Traditional Design for Hillside Home

- Window walls and solarium glass capture the view and fill this home with light.
- Traditional exterior is at home in any neighborhood.
- Deluxe master bedroom suite opens onto private deck.
- Lower level features huge recreation room with abundant window space.
- Deck off kitchen/nook provides delightful outdoor dining area.

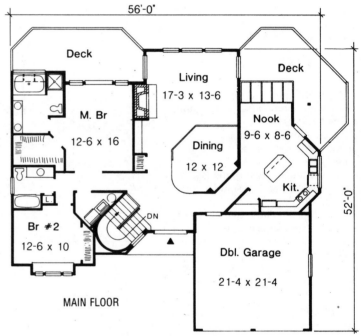

MAIN FLOOR

56'-0"
52'-0"

Deck
Deck
M. Br 12-6 x 16
Living 17-3 x 13-6
Nook 9-6 x 8-6
Dining 12 x 12
Kit.
Br #2 12-6 x 10
DN
Dbl. Garage 21-4 x 21-4

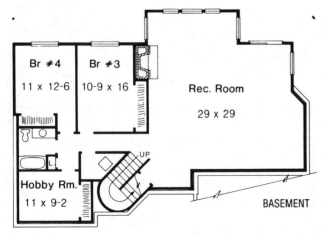

BASEMENT

Br #4 11 x 12-6
Br #3 10-9 x 16
Rec. Room 29 x 29
UP
Hobby Rm. 11 x 9-2

Plan NW-812

Bedrooms: 4		**Baths:** 3

Space:

Main floor:	1,685 sq. ft.
Lower floor:	1,611 sq. ft.
Total living area:	3,296 sq. ft.
Garage:	460 sq. ft.

Exterior Wall Framing:	2x6

Foundation options:
Daylight basement only.
(Foundation & framing conversion diagram available — see order form.)

Blueprint Price Code:	E

Open Living in a Modern Design

Spacious open living areas plus window-walls and wood decks are carefully combined in this contemporary home for both indoor and outdoor family activities and entertaining. Roof setbacks, skylights and windows over the high entry hall and strong fascia boards add interesting relief to the long slope of the gable roof.

In contrast, the rear wall of the home is obviously planned for enjoyment of a view, with a window-wall covering the five-sided, two-story extension of the Great Room. Sliding glass doors open onto the wide wood deck from the Great Room, dining room and master bedroom. Smaller viewing decks open off two second-floor rooms. The full-window treatment repeats in the daylight basement version of the plan.

All floors have open areas in this 2,089 sq. ft. home. The entry hall opens directly into the Great Room, including a free-standing fireplace, the dining area and the U-shaped kitchen. Adjoining this area are a three-quarters bathroom and the utility room. On the other side of the main floor is the master bedroom, including a walk-in wardrobe and a private bath with a window seat.

Open stairs lead off the entry hall to the 824 sq. ft. upper floor, which includes a large loft room overlooking the Great Room and warmed by a woodstove. A study, storage area, bathroom and two bedrooms are also included on the second floor.

The 1,210 sq. ft. daylight basement has a large recreation room with a wood stove, a fourth bedroom with walk-in closet, a full bath and an unfinished area that could become a workshop, crafts area or a guest room.

Exterior walls are 2x6 for energy efficiency.

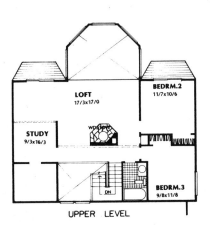

UPPER LEVEL

Main floor:	1,265 sq. ft.
Second floor:	824 sq. ft.
Total living area: (Not counting basement or garage)	2,089 sq. ft.
Daylight basement:	1,210 sq. ft.
Total with basement:	3,299 sq. ft.

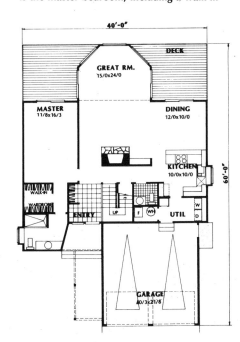

Blueprint Price Code E With Basement
Blueprint Price Code C Without Basement

Plans P-533-2A & -2D

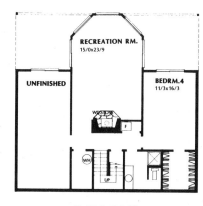

PLAN P-533-2D
WITH DAYLIGHT BASEMENT

PLAN P-533-2A
WITHOUT BASEMENT
(CRAWLSPACE FOUNDATION)

TO ORDER THIS BLUEPRINT,
CALL TOLL-FREE 1-800-547-5570

PRICES AND DETAILS
ON PAGES 12-15   **197**

Time-Tested Traditional Design

- The traditional exterior of this home encloses an up-to-date, interesting interior.
- The unique family room/nook/kitchen combination includes a fireplace and an island cooktop/snack bar.
- The sumptuous master bedroom suite features a deluxe bath and a huge walk-in closet.
- The bonus room above the garage offers plenty of space for a home office, a playroom or an extra bedroom.
- The entire main floor boasts 9-ft. ceilings, with standard 8-ft. ceilings on the upper floor.

Plan CDG-2012

Bedrooms: 4	Baths: 2 full, 2 half

Living Area:	
Upper floor	1,435 sq. ft.
Main floor	1,525 sq. ft.
Bonus room	348 sq. ft.

Total Living Area:	**3,308 sq. ft.**
Partial daylight basement	1,092 sq. ft.
Garage	620 sq. ft.

Exterior Wall Framing:	2x6

Foundation Options:
Partial daylight basement
Crawlspace
(Typical foundation & framing conversion diagram available—see order form.)

BLUEPRINT PRICE CODE: E

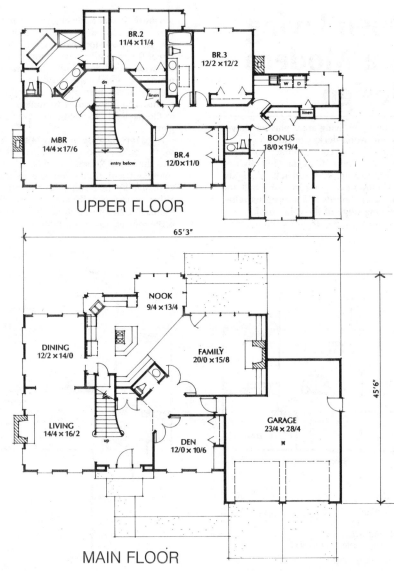

UPPER FLOOR

MAIN FLOOR

Curved Glass Class

- It is difficult to pigeonhole this unique design with its skillfully blended traditional and post-modern elements.
- Eye-catching floor to ceiling windows round the corner of the formal living room which includes built-in cabinetry and fireplace.
- You will discover more built-in cabinetry and shelves in the vaulted dining room and the study. Upstairs, built-in desk areas are located just outside the children's bedrooms.
- Dual staircases route traffic directly to the formal and informal living areas of the home.
- The kitchen includes a walk-in pantry, corner window sink, built-in desk, and large island counter with cooktop and eating bar.
- Skylights are skillfully incorporated into both the bathrooms upstairs and are also located over the back stairwell and upstairs hallway.
- A walk-in closet, spa tub, shower, and dual vanities are featured in the luxurious master bath off the cove-ceilinged master bedroom.

Plan CDG-2019

Bedrooms: 3-4	Baths: 2½

Space:

Upper floor:	1,426 sq. ft.
Main floor:	1,891 sq. ft.
Bonus area:	255 sq. ft.

Total living area:	3,572 sq. ft.
Garage:	676 sq. ft.

Exterior Wall Framing:	2x6

Ceiling Heights:

Upper floor:	8'
Main floor:	9'

Foundation options:
Crawlspace.
(Foundation & framing conversion diagram available — see order form.)

Blueprint Price Code:	F

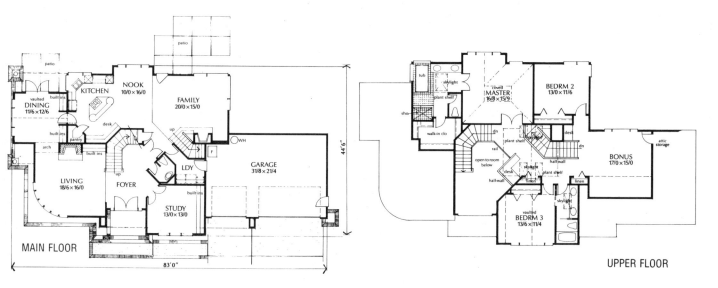

MAIN FLOOR

UPPER FLOOR

Handsome Hill-Hugging Haven

- Multiple octagonal rooms allow this dramatic home to take full advantage of surrounding views.
- A dazzling two-story entry greets guests from the three-car garage motor courtyard.
- Once inside the front door, a soaring dome ceiling catches the eye past the octagonal stairway.
- A sunken living and dining room

with cathedral and domed ceiling face out to the rear deck and views.
- The octagonal island kitchen and breakfast nook are sure to please.
- The main floor den features a second fireplace and front-facing window seat.
- The entire second floor houses the master bedroom suite with a sensational master bath.

UPPER FLOOR

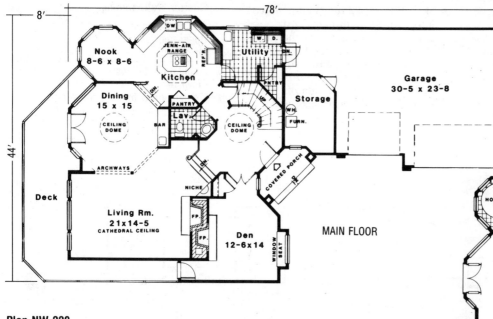

MAIN FLOOR

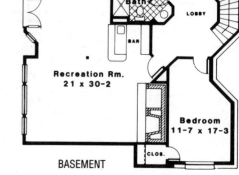

BASEMENT

Plan NW-229

Bedrooms: 2-4	Baths: 2½

Space:

Upper floor:	815 sq. ft.
Main floor:	1,446 sq. ft.
Daylight basement:	1,330 sq. ft.
Total living area:	**3,591 sq. ft.**

Exterior Wall Framing: 2x6

Foundation options:
Daylight basement.
(Foundation & framing conversion diagram available — see order form.)

Blueprint Price Code: F

A Secure Haven

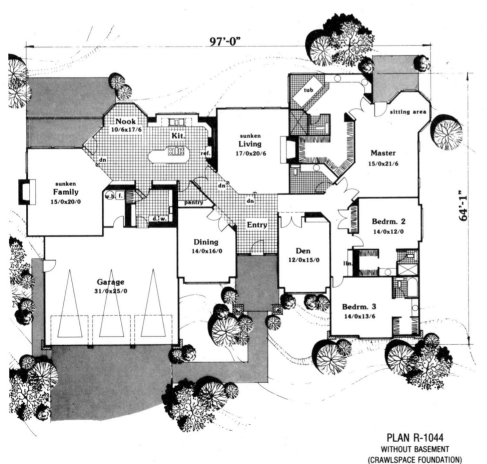

This stately home is highlighted by a dramatic roof line and rich brick facing. It evokes a feeling of quiet strength and provides a secure haven after a hectic day at the office.

Heightened ceilings throughout the home visually expand the interior and create an open and spacious feeling.

The kitchen is every homemaker's dream — with a large island, convenient walk-in pantry, and abundant windows to brighten the room. One step down from the nook, discover the family room, which is highlighted by a handsome fireplace to warm those cold winter nights. Space in the kitchen, nook, and family room easily flows from one area to another to create a very livable environment.

Note that each bedroom in this home includes its own private bath and walk-in closet. The master suite also features a cozy sitting area and spa tub for relaxation.

The blueprints call for energy-efficient 2x6 construction of exterior walls.

Total living area: 3,625 sq. ft.
(Not counting garage)

PLAN R-1044
WITHOUT BASEMENT
(CRAWLSPACE FOUNDATION)

Blueprint Price Code F
Plan R-1044

Private Master Bedroom Loft

- An exciting deck wraps around the formal living areas and kitchen of this spacious contemporary, perfect for a scenic site.
- Inside, an eye-catching curved staircase lies at the center of the open floor plan, which includes a sunken living room with fireplace, an updated island kitchen with pantry, nook and lovely corner window above the sink, and a private library.
- The upper loft is devoted entirely to the master suite; attractions include a private deck and study, fireplace, huge walk-in closet, and a bath with separate shower and luxury tub.
- The lower level provides space for two additional bedrooms, a rec room, full bar with wine storage and attached patio.

Plan NW-917

Bedrooms: 3-4	Baths: 3½
Space:	
Upper floor:	905 sq. ft.
Main floor:	1,587 sq. ft.
Lower floor:	1,289 sq. ft.
Total living area:	**3,781 sq. ft.**
Garage:	912 sq. ft.
Exterior Wall Framing:	2x6

Foundation options:
Daylight basement.
(Foundation & framing conversion diagram available — see order form.)

Blueprint Price Code:	F

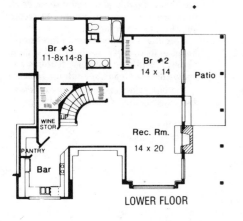

MAIN FLOOR

90'10" x 57'2"

LOWER FLOOR

UPPER FLOOR

Exciting Angles and Amenities

- The interior of this elegant stucco design oozes in luxury, with an exciting assortment of angles and glass.
- Beyond the 14-ft.-high foyer and gallery is a huge parlour with an angled stand-behind ale bar and an adjoining patio accessed through two sets of glass doors.
- The diamond-shaped kitchen offers a sit-down island, a spacious walk-in pantry and a pass-through window to a summer kitchen.
- Opposite the kitchen is an octagonal morning room surrounded in glass and a spacious, angled gathering room with a fireplace and a TV niche.
- The luxurious master suite features a glassed lounge area and a spectacular two-sided fireplace, and is separated from the three secondary bedroom suites. The stunning master bath boasts a central linen island and an assortment of amenities designed for two.
- The library could serve as a fifth bedroom or guest room; the bath across the hall could serve as a pool bath.
- An alternate brick elevation is included in the blueprints.

Plan EOF-59

Bedrooms: 4-5	**Baths:** 4

Living Area:

Main floor	4,021 sq. ft.
Total Living Area:	**4,021 sq. ft.**
Garage	737 sq. ft.
Exterior Wall Framing:	2x6

Foundation Options:

Slab

(Typical foundation & framing conversion diagram available—see order form.)

BLUEPRINT PRICE CODE: **G**

MAIN FLOOR

Ultimate Elegance

- The gracious foyer of this distinguished Southern home reveals a sweeping staircase and a direct view to the pool environment beyond.
- The grand parlour at center has a two-story ceiling, high-fixed glass, ale bar and fireplace.
- Open to the equally large gathering room is the gourmet island kitchen with menu desk, walk-in pantry and octagonal morning room which offers a second route to the upper level.
- Bright and luxurious, the master suite features a convenient morning kitchen, sunny octagonal sitting area that overlooks the covered veranda and optional pool, and a lavish bath.
- Three bedroom suites are located off the circular staircase and hall·bridge that overlooks the parlour; a sunset deck adjoins two of them.

Plan EOF-3

Bedrooms: 4-5	Baths: 5 ½
Space:	
Upper floor	1,150 sq. ft.
Main floor	3,045 sq. ft.
Total Living Area	**4,195 sq. ft.**
Garage	814 sq. ft.
Exterior Wall Framing	2x6

Foundation options:

Slab

(Foundation & framing conversion diagram available—see order form.)

Blueprint Price Code	**G**

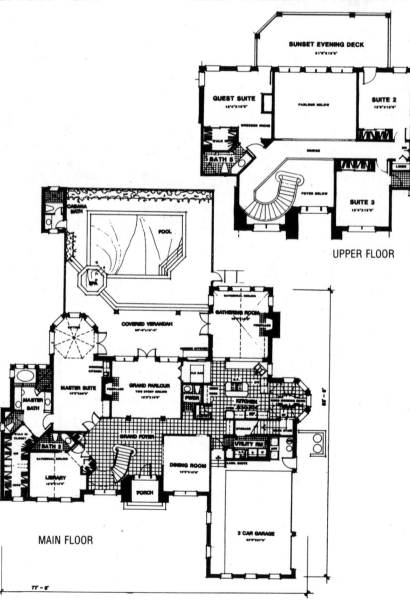

UPPER FLOOR

MAIN FLOOR

Design Leaves out Nothing

- This design has it all, from the elegant detailing of the exterior to the exciting, luxurious spaces of the interior.
- High ceilings, large, open rooms and lots of glass are found throughout the home. Nearly all of the main living areas, as well as the master suite, overlook the veranda.
- Unusual features include a built-in ale bar in the formal dining room, an art niche in the Grand Room and a TV niche in the Gathering Room. The Gathering Room also features a fireplace framed by window seats, a wall of windows facing the backyard and a half-wall open to the morning room. The island kitchen is open to all of the main living areas.
- The delicious master suite includes a raised lounge, a three-sided fireplace and French doors that open to the veranda. The spiral stairs nearby lead to the "evening deck" above. The master bath boasts two walk-in closets, a sunken shower and a Roman tub.
- The upper floor hosts two complete suites and a loft, plus a vaulted bonus room reached via a separate stairway.

Plan EOF-61

Bedrooms: 3-5	Baths: 4½
Living Area:	
Upper floor	877 sq. ft.
Main floor	3,094 sq. ft.
Bonus room	280 sq. ft.
Total Living Area:	**4,251 sq. ft.**
Garage	774 sq. ft.
Exterior Wall Framing:	2x6

Foundation Options:

Slab

(Typical foundation & framing conversion diagram available—see order form.)

BLUEPRINT PRICE CODE:	**G**

UPPER FLOOR

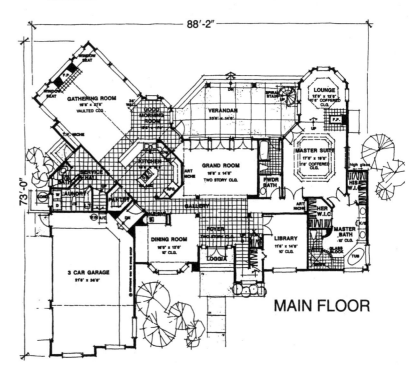

MAIN FLOOR

Plan DD-4300-B

Bedrooms: 4	Baths: 4½

Space:

Upper floor	868 sq. ft.
Main floor	3,416 sq. ft.

Total Living Area	**4,284 sq. ft.**

Basement	3,416 sq. ft.
Garage	633 sq. ft.
Storage	approx. 50 sq. ft.

Exterior Wall Framing	2x4 or 2x6

Ceiling Heights:

Upper floor	9'
Main floor	10'

Foundation options:

Standard Basement
Crawlspace
Slab
(Foundation & framing conversion diagram available—see order form.)

Blueprint Price Code	**G**

Colonial Recall

- The symmetry, massing, materials, and colonnaded entry porch all recall the best of colonial design on this estate home.
- The formal dining and parlor rooms, each with high glass windows, flank the entry's graceful curved staircase.
- The informal living spaces are oriented to the rear greenspaces. They include a two-story volumed family room with fireplace, transom windows and an adjoining library room, as well as a large island kitchen with breakfast eating area.
- The main-floor master suite presses all the right buttons with its fireplace wall, his and her walk-in closets, and private bath with platform tub, separate shower, compartmented tub and double vanities.
- The three additional bedrooms each boast full private baths.

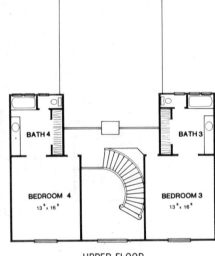

UPPER FLOOR

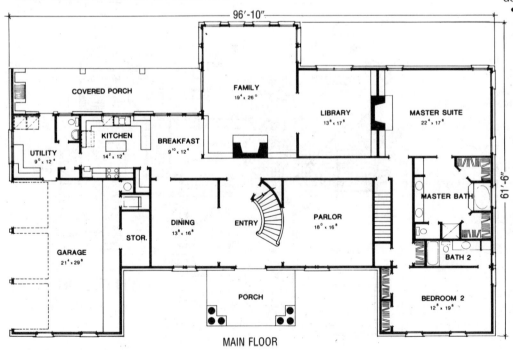

MAIN FLOOR

Plan DD-4300-B

PRICES AND DETAILS ON PAGES 12-15

UPPER FLOOR

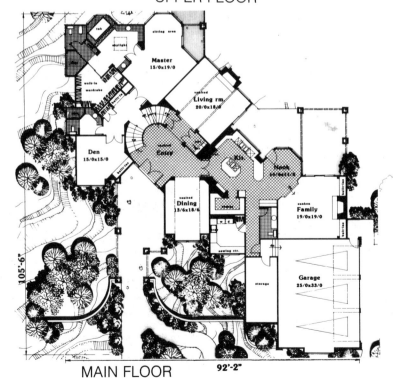

MAIN FLOOR

92'-2"

Elegance at Every Turn

- For a home that is truly outstanding in both beauty and space, this design is hard to beat!
- Elegance is found in every corner, from the spectacular curved stairways in the foyer to the luxurious master suite.
- The huge central living room features a vaulted ceiling, decorative entry columns and a dramatic fireplace.
- The gourmet kitchen and breakfast nook are hidden behind double doors. The kitchen has a cooktop island, a walk-in pantry and a snack counter. The octagon-shaped nook opens to the backyard and adjoins a large sunken family room.
- Up one flight of stairs is the master suite and a quiet den with built-in bookshelves. The master bedroom is entered through elegant double doors and offers a sunny sitting area and a skylighted private bath with an exciting garden tub, a separate shower and a toilet room with a bidet.
- A second stairway accesses two more bedrooms, each with a private bath.

Plan R-4029

Bedrooms: 3	Baths: 4½
Living Area:	
Upper floor	972 sq. ft.
Main floor	3,346 sq. ft.
Partial basement	233 sq. ft.
Total Living Area:	**4,551 sq. ft.**
Garage	825 sq. ft.
Exterior Wall Framing:	2x6
Foundation Options:	
Partial basement (Typical foundation & framing conversion diagram available—see order form.)	
BLUEPRINT PRICE CODE:	**G**

REAR VIEW

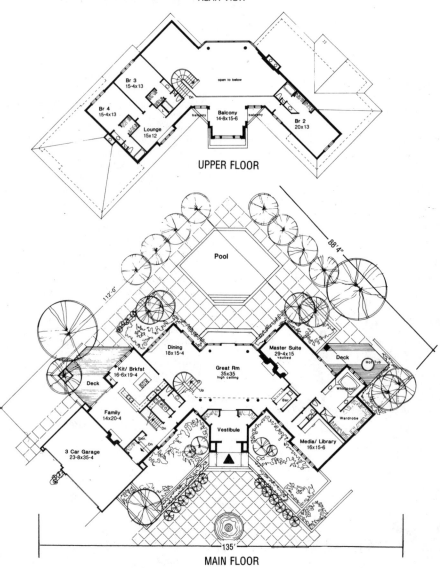

UPPER FLOOR

Br 3
15-4x13

Br 4
15-4x13

Lounge
15x12

open to below

Balcony
14-8x15-6

Br 2
20x13

MAIN FLOOR

Pool

Dining
18x15-4

Kit/ Brkfst
16-6x19-4

Deck

Great Rm
35x35
high ceiling

Master Suite
29-4x15
vaulted

Deck

Hot Tub

Whirlpool

Family
14x20-4

3 Car Garage
23-8x35-4

Vestibule

Media/ Library
16x15-6

Wardrobe

Bar

88-4'

112-0'

135'

Ornate Estate

- This lavish, sprawling plan is luxuriously outfitted in the latest details for the most discriminating homebuyers.
- The entry is appropriately ornate, and lends an air of luxury and importance so necessary in this size range.
- The vestibule serves as an entry focus for the grand rear two-story window wall of the Great Room.
- Adjacent dining room under curved staircase, wet bar, and fireplace all add to the area for important social gatherings.
- The plan hasn't forgotten the family, with an informal wing off the island kitchen with breakfast room adjoining the family room with fireplace and rear deck.
- The master suite is a page out of the magazines with its vaulted ceiling, fireplace, sitting area overlooking a private deck with hot tub, an indoor whirlpool and bedroom-size walk-in closet.

Plan B-05-85

Bedrooms: 4 +		Baths: 4 + 2
Space:		
Upper floor:		1,720 sq. ft.
Main floor:		3,900 sq. ft.
Total living area:		5,620 sq. ft.
Basement:		3,900 sq. ft.
Garage:		836 sq. ft.
Exterior Wall Framing:		2x6

Foundation options:
Standard basement.
(Foundation & framing conversion diagram available — see order form.)

Blueprint Price Code:	G

Sunlit Elegance

- This elegant contemporary design offers just about all the amenities today's families expect in a home.
- The formal dining room is large enough for a good-sized dinner party.
- The living room is sunken and vaulted and includes a handsome fireplace.
- The spacious kitchen includes a large island and a pantry, and is open to the vaulted family room.
- Upstairs, the master bedroom is impressive, with a private master bath, large closets and easy access to a private deck. (If the greenhouse is built, stairs go from the master bath down to the hot tub.)
- The second floor also includes a roomy library and a bonus room or extra bedroom.
- The plan also offers an optional solar greenhouse, which may contain a hot tub or simply offer a great space for green plants and sunbathing.

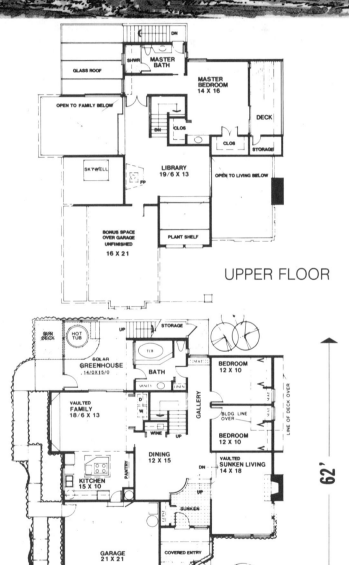

UPPER FLOOR

MAIN FLOOR

62'

50'-6"

Plan S-8217

Bedrooms: 3-4	Baths: 2
Living Area:	
Upper floor	789 sq. ft.
Main floor	1,709 sq. ft.
Bonus room	336 sq. ft.
Total Living Area:	**2,834 sq. ft.**
Partial basement	1,242 sq. ft.
Garage	441 sq. ft.
Exterior Wall Framing:	2x6

Foundation Options:

Partial basement
Crawlspace
Slab
(Typical foundation & framing conversion diagram available—see order form.)

BLUEPRINT PRICE CODE:	D

Sprawling, Substantial Ranch

- Here's another design that proves it pays to keep it simple.
- Clean lines and a straightforward floor plan make for solid, economical construction and easy-living comfort.
- A welcoming porch with columns and planters opens to a functional, attractive entryway, leading ahead to a magnificent family room or to a formal living/dining area at the right.
- The huge family room features a vaulted, beamed ceiling, impressive fireplace and hearth with a built-in wood box, plus built-in bookshelves and desk.
- The large, beautiful kitchen is between the formal dining room and informal eating area, and next to a convenient and spacious utility area, half-bath and garage entry.
- The majestic master suite includes a sumptuous private bath and huge walk-in closet.
- Three secondary bedrooms likewise have large closets, and share a second full bath.

Plan E-2700

Bedrooms: 4	Baths: 2½	Exterior Wall Framing:	2x6

Space:

		Foundation options:
Total living area:	2,719 sq. ft.	Crawlspace.
Garage:	533 sq. ft.	Slab.
Storage:	50 sq. ft.	(Foundation & framing conversion
Porches:	350 sq. ft.	diagram available — see order form.)

Blueprint Price Code:	D

Dramatic Western Contemporary

- Dramatic and functional building features contribute to the comfort and desire of this family home.
- Master suite offers a spacious private bath and luxurious hydro spa.
- Open, efficient kitchen accommodates modern appliances, a large pantry, and a snack bar.
- Skylights shed light on the entryway, open staircase, and balcony.
- Upper level balcony area has private covered deck, and may be used as a guest room or den.

REAR VIEW

UPPER FLOOR

MAIN FLOOR

Plans H-3708-1 & -1A

Bedrooms: 4	Baths: 2½

Space:	
Upper floor:	893 sq. ft.
Main floor:	2,006 sq. ft.

Total living area:	2,899 sq. ft.
Basement:	approx. 2,006 sq. ft.
Garage:	512 sq. ft.

Exterior Wall Framing:	2x6

Foundation options:
Daylight basement (Plan H-3708-1).
Crawlspace (Plan H-3708-1A).
(Foundation & framing conversion diagram available — see order form.)

Blueprint Price Code:	D

Photo courtesy of Breland and Farmer Designers, Inc.

Verandas Add Extra Charm

- Porches, columns and dormers give this home a charming facade.
- The interior is equally appealing, with its beautiful two-story foyer and practical room arrangement.
- The central living room has a fireplace and access to a covered porch.
- A great island kitchen is conveniently situated between the two dining areas.
- A multipurpose room and an office are perfect for hobbies and projects.
- The secluded master suite offers a private study with a sloped ceiling. The master bath is large and symmetrical.
- Three bedrooms upstairs share a compartmentalized bath.

Plan E-2900

Bedrooms: 4	Baths: 2½
Living Area:	
Upper floor	903 sq. ft.
Main floor	2,029 sq. ft.
Total Living Area:	**2,932 sq. ft.**
Standard basement	2,029 sq. ft.
Garage and storage	470 sq. ft.
Exterior Wall Framing:	2x6

Foundation Options:
Standard basement
Crawlspace
Slab
(Typical foundation & framing conversion diagram available—see order form.)

BLUEPRINT PRICE CODE:	D

NOTE: The above photographed home may have been modified by the homeowner. Please refer to floor plan and/or drawn elevation shown for actual blueprint details.

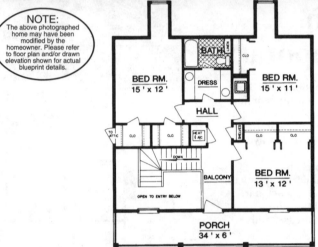

UPPER FLOOR

MAIN FLOOR

TO ORDER THIS BLUEPRINT,
CALL TOLL-FREE 1-800-547-5570

Plan E-2900

PRICES AND DETAILS
ON PAGES 12-15

REAR VIEW

Solar Flair

- Full window walls and a sun room with glass roof act as passive energy collectors in this popular floor plan.
- Expansive living room features wood stove and vaulted ceilings.
- Dining room shares a breakfast counter with the merging kitchen.
- Convenient laundry room is positioned near kitchen and garage entrance.
- Second level is devoted entirely to the private master suite, featuring vaulted ceiling and a balcony view to the living room below.

Plans H-877-5A & -5B

Bedrooms: 3-4	Baths: 2-3

Space:

Upper floor:	382 sq. ft.
Main floor:	1,200 sq. ft.
Sun room:	162 sq. ft.

Total living area:	1,744 sq. ft.
Basement:	approx. 1,200 sq. ft.
Garage:	457 sq. ft.

Exterior Wall Framing:	2x6

Foundation options:
Daylight basement (Plan H-877-5B).
Crawlspace (Plan H-877-5A).
(Foundation & framing conversion diagram available — see order form.)

Blueprint Price Code:

Without basement:	B
With basement:	D

UPPER FLOOR

MAIN FLOOR

PLAN H-877-5B
WITH BASEMENT

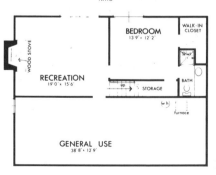

BASEMENT

FRONT VIEW

Photo by Gil Ford

Spacious and Stately

- Covered porches front and rear.
- Downstairs master suite with spectacular bath.
- Family/living/dining areas combine for entertaining large groups.
- Classic Creole/plantation exterior.

Plan E-3000

Bedrooms: 4	Baths: 3½

Space:

Upper floor:	1,027 sq. ft.
Main floor:	2,008 sq. ft.
Total living area:	**3,035 sq. ft.**
Porches:	429 sq. ft.
Basement:	2,008 sq. ft.
Garage:	484 sq. ft.
Storage:	96 sq. ft.

Exterior Wall Framing:	2x6

Typical Ceiling Heights:

Upper floor:	8'
Main floor:	9'

Foundation options:
Standard basement.
Crawlspace.
Slab.
(Foundation & framing conversion diagram available — see order form.)

Blueprint Price Code:	E

**NOTE: The above photographed home may have been modified by the homeowner. Please refer to floor plan and/or drawn elevation shown for actual blueprint details.

UPPER FLOOR

CLO. CLO. LIN LIN
BATH
VANITY
BED RM. 16' x 12'
CLO.
HEAT B/A/C WH
HALL
ATTIC
ATTIC
BED RM. 14' x 12'
BED RM. 14' x 12'
CLO. CLO. CLO. CLO.

STOR 8' x 6'
GARAGE 22' x 22'
STOR 8' x 6'
ATTIC STAIRS
DECK
WOOD RAILING
BREEZEWAY 22' x 8'
PORCH 24' x 6'
WH WASH DRY
ENTRY
UTILITY
SINK
LIN FREEZ
BATH
STOR
CLO.
PANT. OVEN
KITCHEN 18' x 16'
COOK TOP
BAR
PANT. REF. D.W. SINK
BATH
CLO.
SHV'S
SKYLIGHT
SLOPE CEILING
VANITY
SHOWER
SEAT
SHV'S
MASTER SUITE 18' x 16'
HEAT & A/C
FAMILY RM 25' x 15'
SINK
SITTING
LIVING 15' x 14'
ENTRY
DINING 15' x 14'
EATING
PORCH 34' x 8'
WOOD RAILING

MAIN FLOOR

66'

74'

Tudor-Inspired Hillside Design

- The vaulted entry opens to a stunning living room with a high ceiling and massive fireplace.
- The dining room, five steps higher, overlooks the living room for a dramatic effect.
- Double doors lead into the informal family area, which consists of a beautifully integrated kitchen, nook and family room.
- The magnificent master suite, isolated downstairs, includes a sumptuous bath, enormous wardrobe and double-door entry.
- The upstairs consists of three more bedrooms, a bath and balcony hallway open to the entry below.
- Three-car garage is tucked under the family room/dining room area.

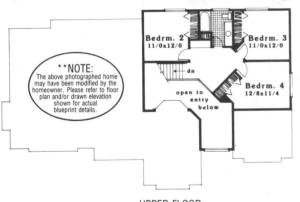

**NOTE:
The above photographed home may have been modified by the homeowner. Please refer to floor plan and/or drawn elevation shown for actual blueprint details.

Bedrm. 2
11/0x12/0

Bedrm. 3
11/0x12/0

dn

open to entry below

Bedrm. 4
12/8x11/4

UPPER FLOOR

68'-6"

43'-0"

PATIO

sewing

Nook
10/0x10/0

Kit.

bar

wardrobe

tub

dressing

Family
20/2x18/0

Dining
12/0x13/0

up

dn

Entry

Master
13/10x16/6

Living
13/4x17/6

MAIN FLOOR

Plan R-4001

Bedrooms: 4	Baths: 2½

Living Area:	
Upper floor	709 sq. ft.
Main floor	2,388 sq. ft.
Total Living Area:	**3,097 sq. ft.**
Garage	906 sq. ft.
Exterior Wall Framing:	2x6

Foundation Options:

Crawlspace
(Typical foundation & framing conversion diagram available—see order form.)

BLUEPRINT PRICE CODE: E

Garage
32/0x28/4

Proven Plan Features Passive Sun Room

- A passive-solar sun room, an energy-efficient woodstove and a panorama of windows make this design really shine.
- The open living/dining room features a vaulted ceiling, walls filled with glass and access to the dramatic decking. A balcony above gives the huge living/dining area definition while offering spectacular views.
- The streamlined kitchen has a convenient serving bar that connects it to the living/dining area.
- The main-floor bedroom features dual closets and easy access to a full bath. The laundry room, located just off the garage, doubles as a mudroom and includes a handy coat closet.
- The balcony hallway upstairs is bathed in natural light. The two nice-sized bedrooms are separated by a second full bath.

Plans H-855-3A & -3B

Bedrooms: 3	Baths: 2-3
Living Area:	
Upper floor	586 sq. ft.
Main floor	1,192 sq. ft.
Sun room	132 sq. ft.
Daylight basement	1,192 sq. ft.
Total Living Area:	**1,910/3,102 sq. ft.**
Garage	520 sq. ft.
Exterior Wall Framing:	2x6
Foundation Options:	**Plan #**
Daylight basement	H-855-3B
Crawlspace	H-855-3A
BLUEPRINT PRICE CODE:	**B/E**

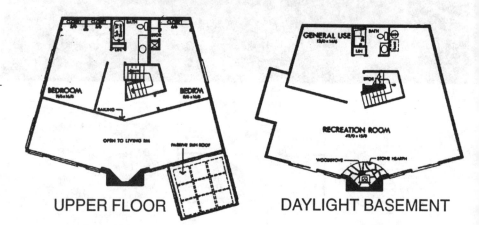

UPPER FLOOR   DAYLIGHT BASEMENT

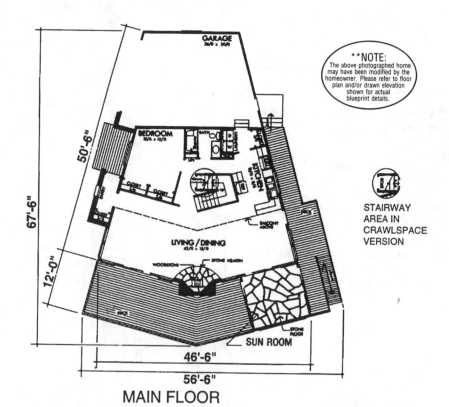

NOTE:
The above photographed home may have been modified by the homeowner. Please refer to floor plan and/or drawn elevation shown for actual blueprint details.

STAIRWAY AREA IN CRAWLSPACE VERSION

MAIN FLOOR

Plans H-855-3A & -3B

PRICES AND DETAILS ON PAGES 12-15

Wrap-around Porch Accents Victorian Farmhouse

- Fish-scale shingles and horizontal siding team with the detailed front porch to create this look of yesterday. The sides and rear are brick.
- The main level features a center section

of informal family room and formal living and dining rooms. They can all be connected via French doors.

- A separate workshop is located on the main level and connected to the main house by a covered breezeway.
- The master bath ceiling is sloped and has built-in skylights. The kitchen and eating area have high sloped ceilings also. Typical ceiling heights are 8' on the basement and upper level and 10' on the main level.
- This home is energy efficient.
- This home is designed on a full daylight basement. The two-car garage is located under the workshop.

MAIN LEVEL

UPPER LEVEL
PLAN E-3103
WITH DAYLIGHT BASEMENT

Exterior walls are 2x6 construction.

Heated area:	3,153 sq. ft.
Unheated area	2,066 sq. ft.
Total area: (Not counting basement)	5,219 sq. ft.

Blueprint Price Code E
Plan E-3103

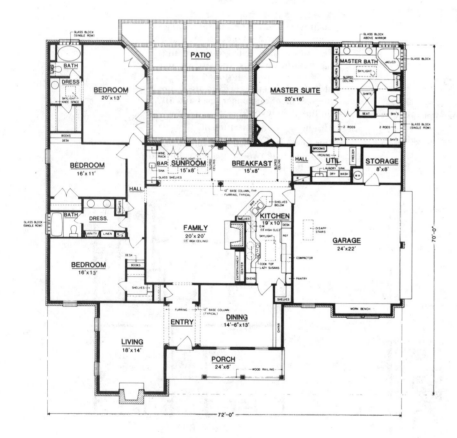

PLAN E-3102
WITHOUT BASEMENT

Exterior walls are 2x6 construction.
Specify crawlspace or slab foundation.

Ranch-Style Designed for Entertaining

- This all-brick home offers both formal living and dining rooms.

- The family room is large scale with 13' ceilings, formal fireplace and an entertainment center. An adjoining sun room reveals a tucked away wet bar.

- The master suite has private patio access and its own fireplace. An adjoining bath offers abundant closet and linen storage, a separate shower and garden tub with glass block walls.

- The home contains three additional bedrooms and two baths. Each bath has glass block above the tubs and separate dressing rooms.

- The master bedroom ceiling is sloped to 14' high. Both the sun room and the breakfast room have sloped ceilings with skylights. Typical ceiling heights are 9'.

- The home is energy efficient.

Heated area:	3,158 sq. ft.
Unheated area:	767 sq. ft.
Total area:	3,925 sq. ft.

Blueprint Price Code E
Plan E-3102

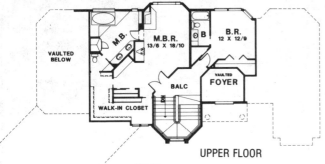

UPPER FLOOR

**NOTE:
The above photographed home may have been modified by the homeowner. Please refer to floor plan and/or drawn elevation shown for actual blueprint details.

89'-9"

MAIN FLOOR

Designed with Elegance in Mind

- This expansive home boasts 3,220 sq. ft. of living space designed with elegance in mind.
- The front of the home is finished in stucco, with the rest in lap siding for economy.
- The vaulted foyer leads directly into an impressive sunken and vaulted living room, guarded by columns that echo the exterior treatment.
- The formal dining room is visually joined to the living room to make an impressive space for entertaining.
- An unusually fine kitchen opens to a large family room, which boasts a vaulted ceiling, a corner fireplace and access to a sizable rear deck.
- In the front, the extra-wide staircase is a primary attraction, with its dramatic feature window.
- A terrific master suite includes a splendid master bath with double sinks and a huge walk-through closet.
- A second upstairs bedroom also includes a private bath.

Plan LRD-11388

Bedrooms: 3-4	Baths: 3
Living Area:	
Upper floor:	1,095 sq. ft.
Main floor	2,125 sq. ft.
Total Living Area:	**3,220 sq. ft.**
Standard basement	2,125 sq. ft.
Garage	802 sq. ft.

Exterior Wall Framing:	2x6
Foundation Options:	

Standard basement
Crawlspace
Slab
(Typical foundation & framing conversion diagram available—see order form.)

BLUEPRINT PRICE CODE: E

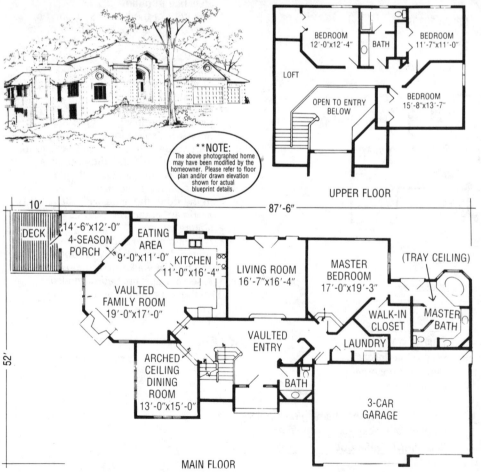

**NOTE:
The above photographed home may have been modified by the homeowner. Please refer to floor plan and/or drawn elevation shown for actual blueprint details.

UPPER FLOOR

- BEDROOM 12'-0"x12'-4"
- BATH
- BEDROOM 11'-7"x11'-0"
- LOFT
- OPEN TO ENTRY BELOW
- BEDROOM 15'-8"x13'-7"

MAIN FLOOR

- 10'
- 87'-6"
- 52'
- DECK
- 14'-6"x12'-0" 4-SEASON PORCH
- EATING AREA 9'-0"x11'-0"
- KITCHEN 11'-0"x16'-4"
- LIVING ROOM 16'-7"x16'-4"
- MASTER BEDROOM 17'-0"x19'-3"
- (TRAY CEILING)
- VAULTED FAMILY ROOM 19'-0"x17'-0"
- VAULTED ENTRY
- WALK-IN CLOSET
- MASTER BATH
- LAUNDRY
- ARCHED CEILING DINING ROOM 13'-0"x15'-0"
- BATH
- 3-CAR GARAGE

Dream Home Loaded with Amenities

- Unique family room with vaulted ceiling.
- Large vaulted entry.
- Luxurious master suite.
- Large island kitchen.
- Striking design inside and out.

Plan AH-3230

Bedrooms: 4	Baths: 2½
Space:	
Upper floor:	890 sq. ft.
Main floor:	2,340 sq. ft.
Total living area:	3,230 sq. ft.
Basement:	2,214 sq. ft.
Garage:	693 sq. ft.
Exterior Wall Framing:	2x6
Ceiling Heights:	
Upper floor:	8'
Main floor:	9'
Foundation options:	
Basement only.	
(Foundation & framing conversion diagram available — see order form.)	
Blueprint Price Code:	E

Spectacular Sweeping Views

- The elegant brick facade of this exciting home conceals a highly contemporary interior.
- The foyer opens to a huge Grand Room that further opens to a delightful rear porch, also accessed through the morning room, pool bath and master suite.
- Completely surrounded in windows and high fixed glass is a spacious gathering room, also featuring a three-sided fireplace and built-in entertainment center.
- The spectacular master suite is secluded to the rear of the home, but wrapped in windows and offering its own fantastic bath with luxury tub and bidet.
- Two additional sleeping suites found at the other end of the home share a bath with private vanities.

Plan EOF-8

Bedrooms: 3-4	**Baths:** 3 ½
Space:	
Main floor	3,392 sq. ft.
Total Living Area	**3,392 sq. ft.**
Garage	871 sq. ft.
Exterior Wall Framing	2x6
Foundation options:	
Slab	
(Foundation & framing conversion diagram available—see order form.)	
Blueprint Price Code	**E**

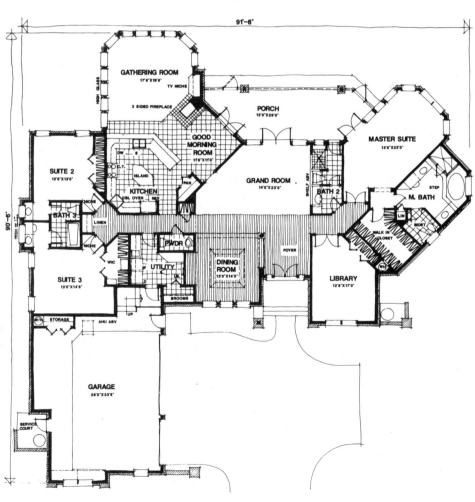

PLAN H-2114-1B REAR VIEW

Designed for Outdoor Living

- Dining room, living room, and spa are oriented toward the full-width deck extending across the rear of the home.
- Floor-to-ceiling windows, vaulted ceilings, and a fireplace are featured in the living room.
- Spa room has tile floor, operable skylights, and private access through connecting master suite.
- Upper level offers two bedrooms, spacious bathroom, and a balcony view of the living room and scenery beyond.

MAIN FLOOR

PLAN H-2114-1A
WITHOUT BASEMENT

PLAN H-2114-1B
WITH DAYLIGHT BASEMENT

UPPER FLOOR

Plans H-2114-1A & -1B

Bedrooms: 3-4	Baths: 2½-3½

Space:

Upper floor:	732 sq. ft.
Main floor:	1,682 sq. ft.
Spa room:	147 sq. ft.

Total living area:	2,561 sq. ft.
Basement:	approx. 1,386 sq. ft.
Garage:	547 sq. ft.

Exterior Wall Framing:	2x6

Foundation options:
Daylight basement (Plan H-2114-1B).
Crawlspace (Plan H-2114-1A).
(Foundation & framing conversion diagram available — see order form.)

Blueprint Price Code:

Without basement:	D
With basement:	F

Plans H-2114-1A & -1B

PRICES AND DETAILS ON PAGES 12-15

All in the Family

- With increasing demands outside the home, many of today's families have very little time to spend together. This design allows family members to carry out their activities inside the home, whether they be leisure or work activities.

- A round window and louvered vent draws attention to the striking entry outlined in brick. Columns and a trellised roof usher guests through the swinging café-style gates and up to the inviting front porch.

- The square grids of the exterior are designed to accommodate future siding materials, such as plastic or fiberglass squares or window modules, that can be changed as tastes and styles change.

- The sunken "Us" room is the center of attention, with its vaulted ceiling and two-story fireplace. The room is surrounded by the family living areas, such as the adjacent kitchen and dining room, the unique activity room and the loft above.

- A curved glass-block stairway leads to the loft, which features a roomy exercise area, a kid's study and a home office. Skylights and built-in desks typify the luxurious yet highly functional features found throughout the home.

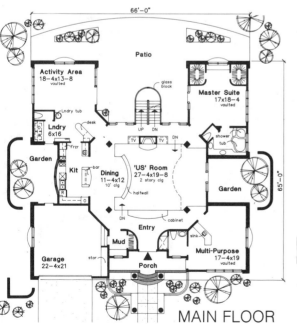

MAIN FLOOR

NOTE:
The above photographed home may have been modified by the homeowner. Please refer to floor plan and/or drawn elevation shown for actual blueprint details.

UPPER FLOOR

Plan B-91010

Bedrooms: 3-4	Baths: 4½
Space:	
Upper floor	1,452 sq. ft.
Main floor	2,768 sq. ft.
Total Living Area	**4,220 sq. ft.**
Basement	2,768 sq. ft.
Garage	469 sq. ft.
Exterior Wall Framing	2x6

Foundation options:

Standard Basement
(Foundation & framing conversion diagram available—see order form.)

Blueprint Price Code	**G**

Photo by Mark Englund/HomeStyles

Living in Symmetry

- This symmetrical Plantation-style home offers tremendous room for relaxation.
- Large formal areas that overlook the dramatic columned porch flank the big foyer.
- At the center of the home is a spacious Great Room with an inviting fireplace and lots of space for family gatherings.
- Nestled between the Great Room and the Keeping Room, which also offers a fireplace, is a wet bar. The adjoining

kitchen features a modern island worktop.
- The spectacular master suite has his 'n hers baths, two walk-in closets and a spiral staircase access to the study on the upper level.
- A versatile sitting room rests at the center of the upper floor, surrounded by three bedrooms, two baths and a study or optional fifth bedroom. Generous closet space is found throughout.

Plan V-4566

Bedrooms: 4-5	**Baths:** 4½

Space:

Upper floor	1,847 sq. ft.
Main floor	2,719 sq. ft.
Total Living Area	**4,566 sq. ft.**
Exterior Wall Framing	2x6

Foundation options:

Crawlspace
(Foundation & framing conversion diagram available—see order form.)

Blueprint Price Code	**G**

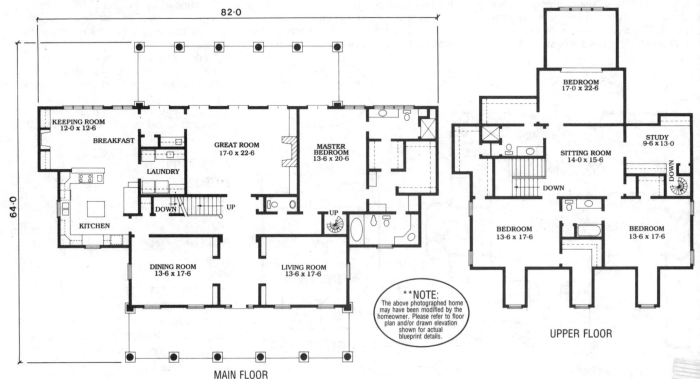

**NOTE:
The above photographed home may have been modified by the homeowner. Please refer to floor plan and/or drawn elevation shown for actual blueprint details.

MAIN FLOOR

UPPER FLOOR